Bhagavad Gītā

The Beloved Lord's Secret Love Song

Graham M. Schweig

HarperSanFrancisco
A Division of HarperCollins*Publishers*

HarperCollins books may be purchased for educational, business, or sales promotional use. For information please write: Special Markets Department, HarperCollins Publishers, 10 East 53rd Street, New York, NY 10022.

HarperCollins Web site: http://www.harpercollins.com
HarperCollins®, ®, and HarperSanFrancisco™ are
trademarks of HarperCollins Publishers.

FIRST EDITION
Designed by Joseph Rutt

Library of Congress Cataloging-in-Publication Data

Bhagavadgita. English & Sanskrit.
Bhagavad Gītā : the beloved Lord's secret love song / Graham M. Schweig.
p. cm.
In English and Sanskrit (romanized); includes translation from Sanskrit.
Includes bibliographical references and index.
ISBN: 978-0-06-075425-9
ISBN-10: 0-06-075425-7
I. Schweig, Graham M. II. Title.
BL1138.62.E5 2006
294.5′92404521—dc22 2006041312

07 08 09 10 11 RRD (H) 10 9 8 7 6 5 4 3 2 1

Contents

Introduction

The Meaning of the Bhagavad Gītā

The Bhagavad Gītā comes to us from sacred India. Its verses of ancient wisdom on the mysteries of human existence speak to us today as if they had just been spoken. The Bhagavad Gītā is one of the most loved works among the collections of scriptural texts found within the Hindu traditions. It also stands out among the holy books of the major world religions, for its flowing Sanskrit verses present a uniquely vivid portrait of the intimacy between humanity and divinity. Indeed, this divine intimacy is revealed in the form of a dialogue that takes the soul on an inward journey culminating in the ultimate state of yoga, in which souls unite with the heart of God.

The Bhagavad Gītā, often called simply "the Gītā,"[1] is essentially a book on yoga.[2] This profound teaching is the book on yoga par excellence because it presents yoga in the most comprehensive sense of the term and in all its depth. As discussed in "Textual Illuminations," yoga covers a broad range of practices and visions, significantly more than what we encounter in the West, or for that matter more than what a reading of famous treatises on yoga, such as the Yoga Sūtra of Patanjali, may yield. In the Gītā, the concept of the sacred connection of humanity with divinity is gradually introduced and developed, then fully disclosed as the "supreme secret of yoga."[3]

Bhagavad Gītā may be translated as "the song of the Beloved Lord," which conveys a divine yearning. The word *Bhagavad*[4] means "the Beloved Lord," referring to Krishna, whose voice is prominent

---

1 Throughout this discussion, the title Bhagavad Gītā is shortened to "the Gītā." In footnotes and verse references the title is abbreviated as BG. When specific verses are referenced, the chapter number appears first, followed by the verse number.

2 The word *yoga* is found 78 times in the BG, appearing in every chapter except three (chapters 1, 15, and 17). The word *yoga* and related words, such as *yogi* (found 28 times) and *yukta* (found 49 times), appear 155 times. This means that in over 20 percent of the Gītā's verses the word *yoga* or its related forms appear.

3 This phrase is found in the words *guhyaṁ paraṁ yogam* in BG 18.75. The "supreme secret" is discussed at length in the "Textual Illuminations."

4 The *g* in *Bhagavad* is pronounced as in *go;* the *a* is pronounced as in *about.* See "Pronunciation of Sanskrit." The word *Bhagavad,* translated as "the Beloved Lord," is a modified form of *bhagavat,* according to the Sanskrit rules of euphonic combination, *sandhi.* The word often appears in other works as *bhagavān,* the word's inflected form in the nominative case.

throughout the work. In the Bhagavad Gītā, Krishna, perhaps the most loved of all manifestations of divinity in India, is identified as the ultimate and supreme Lord, from whom all other divine manifestations emanate. *Gītā*[5] means "song," in this case one coming from Krishna or God. Clearly the text is a philosophical poem and not a song in the literal sense. At a deeper level, however, it is a song issuing forth from the heart of God. It is the secret call of the divinity for all souls to love him, to take the journey to him, to be blissfully united with him.

The Bhagavad Gītā in Context

Although India is the birthplace of a variety of religious traditions, including Buddhism, Jainism, and Sikhism, it is Hinduism that is the dominant religion in India today. Hinduism is composed of several primary and numerous less familiar traditions, all theologically distinctive, yet each acknowledging the revelational authority of a common ancient scriptural source. Possibly the oldest sacred text in the world, dating as far back as 2500 to 1500 BCE, the collection of Sanskrit hymns known as the Vedas are foundational for the myriad traditions that come under the umbrella of Hinduism. These traditions make up the largest constituency of religious practitioners in South Asia. Among these, the traditions that focus upon the supreme divinity of Krishna or his cosmic manifestation of Vishnu are known as Vaishnava, and they constitute the dominant form of religion. The Bhagavad Gītā comes to us from this Vaishnava tradition, which is present throughout India and, in the second half of the twentieth century, around the globe.[6]

This beloved book of India is often called the "bible of Hinduism" in the West. As the Bible is for Christians and the Qur'an

---

5 Pronounced "geet-ah."

6 A. C. Bhaktivedanta Swami Prabhupāda (1896–1977), as an elderly monk, along with his disciples, established the orthodox practice of the Chaitanya school of Vaishnavism (as the modern Krishna movement) in many major cities around the world, beginning with the United States in 1965. His translation and traditional commentary on the Gītā, *Bhagavad-gītā As It Is* (New York: Macmillan Publishing Co., 1972; Los Angeles: Bhaktivedanta Book Trust, 1983, 1989), is by far the most widely read and distributed in the world.

for Muslims, so it could be said that the Bhagavad Gītā is for Hindus, for it is the single most influential philosophical sacred text coming from South Asia. Though it is, since the seventh century, the most widely read and commented on holy text in all of India, it comes from a tradition that reveres many sacred texts, unlike Western religious traditions, which focus on one sacred book of revelation. Moreover, though the Bhagavad Gītā is usually read alone, it is a small section of a substantially larger text, perhaps the largest epic poem in the world, the Mahābhārata. The philosophical verses of the Gītā stand gracefully as an autonomous text with a beginning, middle, and end, despite their original placement within the continuum of this greater epic poem. The Mahābhārata, containing approximately 100,000 verses, is thought by Western scholars to have appeared in its final form sometime between 500 BCE and 200 CE, though traditional dating of events in the text places them in the third millennium BCE. The eighteen chapters of the Gītā appear as chapters 23 through 40 in the Book of Bhīshma, the sixth of the Mahābhārata's eighteen books.

Historically, we first come to know of the divinity of Krishna in the Bhagavad Gītā text. Although his identity as "the divine lover" is not revealed in the Gītā, Krishna is traditionally appreciated as the divinity who sends out a love call to all souls. His call is intended for those who relate to him in loving intimacy, not for those who regard him with reverential awe, worshipping primarily his attributes of cosmic power and majesty. As the supreme divinity, Krishna plays multiple roles, adopts a variety of personae, and displays numerous grand and cosmic manifestations, yet he is also delightfully playful and personal. The various roles that Krishna assumes in his more intimate acts, particularly as a youthful cowherd, are considered the most exquisite, revealing endearing and beautiful visions of the supreme.

Most enchanting and charming, Krishna is loved and worshipped by Hindus in a variety of forms: as a sweet but mischievous child, as the closest friend, or even as the ultimate lover. In these intimate relationships with the divinity, Krishna, famous for his divine love call, sends forth his call by producing captivating music on his flute. He is best known for alluring the lovely cowherd maidens of the paradisal village of Vraja out of their homes, one serene autumn evening. Upon hearing his irresistibly sweet flute music, the maidens abruptly abandon their families and household duties to join him in the moonlit forest. On this sanctified night, the maidens and Krishna enact the famous Rāsa Līlā, which I have broadly translated as the "dance of divine love."[7]

In the Bhagavad Gītā, Krishna's call to love, the expression of his divine longing, is a more hidden feature of the text, though it carries the Gītā's most powerful message: the heart of God passionately desires to connect with the hearts of humans. Here, Krishna's love call is directed to Arjuna, his dearest friend, who already knows Krishna's love but finds himself in a devastating worldly crisis that distracts him from the heart of God. In the dialogue that ensues between Krishna and Arjuna, Krishna gently and compassionately brings Arjuna's heart back to his divine heart, even in the midst of the most trying of circumstances—war. As might be expected, the outer conflict that distracts Arjuna from his relationship with Krishna is accompanied by intense inner conflict. This personal crisis, however, serves to reunite Arjuna with the divinity, enabling him to return to the overwhelming challenges of the outer world with renewed strength and resolve.

Outer and Inner Conflict

When turning to the first verse, the reader steps into a greater story that is already taking place. The opening words are spoken by a king, which we discover from his epithetical name, Dhritarāshtra, meaning "powerful ruler." From the background story that surrounds the Gītā event we learn that this king, significantly, was born blind. The sons of the king are prepared to lead his army into battle against the sons of his deceased younger brother,

---

7 This celebrated passage is found in the Bhāgavata Purāṇa, tenth book, chapters 29–33. See my *Dance of Divine Love: India's Classic Sacred Love Story: The Rāsa Līlā of Krishna* (Princeton, NJ: Princeton University Press, 2005) for a translation and comprehensive treatment of this sacred text, with an introduction.

Pāndu, who inherited the throne from their renowned ancestor, the great King Bharata, due to the older son's blindness. Unfortunately, when the noble and righteous Pāndu passed away, his five sons (the Pāndavas) were too young to assume the throne. Their envious uncle, in his blindness, thus took over the kingdom and ruled for many years, with devastating results. The Pāndavas, led by Pāndu's grown son, the general and archer Arjuna—the mightiest warrior of his time—fervently desire to take charge of the kingdom to restore peace. Their uncle and his sons, however, led by the eldest son, Duryodhana, have refused to surrender the throne. Consequently, a battle is inevitable.

This great classic of some seven hundred Sanskrit verses opens with the tension of imminent battle, as each army, lined up like pieces on a chessboard, looks over the other, setting the stage for the dialogue of the Bhagavad Gītā. The first half of the first chapter can be understood as the narration of Arjuna's outer conflict (BG I.1–I.27) and the second half as the expression of his inner conflict (BG I.28–I.47). The full impact of the looming confrontation weighs on Arjuna as he prepares to lead his men against an enemy army composed of many of his teachers, friends, and even relatives. Anticipating that he will have to fight and slay those whom he loves and reveres, Arjuna is overcome by grief and hurled into debilitating despair:

> My limbs are sinking down
>   and my mouth has
>   become very dry.
> Also, my body trembles
>   and the hairs of
>   my limbs stand on end.
>
> My bow, Gāndīva,
>   falls from my hand
>   and even my skin is burning.
> I also am unable
>   to stand steadily and
>   my mind seems to be reeling.
>
> (BG I.29–I.30)

While experiencing such agonizing symptoms of dread, Arjuna is unable to respond in accordance with his nature as a warrior to the outer conflict he faces.

The Gītā begins, then, by introducing a seemingly irresolvable ethical challenge: should the virtuous Arjuna protect the innocent by fighting an enemy army composed of loved ones and gurus? The ethical codes of ancient India command him to carry out his duty as the leading warrior of his time, to protect the innocent from ruthless forces; yet these same codes forbid a warrior to kill family, friends, and especially a teacher or beloved guru. Indeed, the Gītā informs us that there always will be ethical conflict in the outer world. Consequently, the text does not attempt to resolve the dilemma that befalls Arjuna, at least not directly. Instead it points to something deeper.

This work of Indian spirituality not only raises the question of the appropriate action for Arjuna to adopt, it also defines the existential challenge facing every human being. As struggling souls we ultimately attempt to transform our precarious painful world into a meaningful one. In the first half of the opening verse, spoken by the blind king Dhritarāshtra, the Gītā presents such an existential tension:

> On the field of dharma,
> on the field of Kuru,
> assembled together
> desiring to fight,
> Were my armies
> and indeed those
> of the sons of Pāndu—
> how did they act, O Sanjaya?
>
> (BG I.I)

The first two lines, *dharma-kshetre,* "on the field of dharma" and *kuru-kshetre,* "on the field of Kuru," set the stage for this tension. The field of Kuru, the holy place known as Kurukshetra, is presented here as a place of "dharma." Named after the pious King Kuru, the common ancestor of Dhritarāshtra and Pāndu, Kurukshetra is, ironically, the site where the civil war between the sons of these two brothers, along with their respective armies, is about to take place. The reader learns that in the world of human interaction, we have an opportunity to live a life of dharma—a godly life promoting true happiness in relation to our worldly responsibilities and ultimate spiritual goals—or an ungodly life, in which forces destructive to dharma constantly prevail. The armies of the Pāndavas, the sons of Pāndu, represent the life of dharma; Dhritarāshtra's armies, the Kauravas, are destroyers of dharma.

Like Arjuna, we humans often are caught between Pāndava– and Kaurava–like forces, vacillating between thoughts and activities that elevate the spirit, helping us to rise above the destructive forces surrounding us, and those that degrade the spirit and further embroil us in the perils of worldly existence. The Gītā speaks deeply to each of us, for at some point, doesn't every soul, like Arjuna, face a unique battlefield in the outer world as well as within? Throughout, Krishna proffers not only *that* we must act, but also *how* we must act to fight our individual battles. The axial core of the Gītā is this perpetual existential tension that we encounter—but not without purpose, the Gītā propounds.

The foundational theme for the entire Gītā is dramatically established in the opening verse through the king's inquiry, "How did they act, O Sanjaya?" This question reveals the major theme of action, around which the teaching of the Bhagavad Gītā revolves: what action is, why and how we must act, our relation to action and nonaction, when action is right or wrong, and how we should understand action in all circumstances. The blessings that surround us in this world, symbolized by the holy place of Kurukshetra as a place of dharma; the struggles that we face in the world, represented by the desire to fight; and the dilemma of how to act in light of the tension between the two, expressed by the king's question, combine to make this opening verse of the Gītā the "seed" verse of the whole text.[8]

The Gītā's ultimate teaching—its response to the question of how souls should act in this world—is that souls should at all

8 The practice of implanting the essential idea or "seed," around which the whole text revolves, in an opening passage or verse, often occurs in great Sanskrit works.

times and in every circumstance *act out of love.* By hearing Krishna's call to love, Arjuna discovers a more elevated state of consciousness, then an inner state of transcendence, and finally, a state of eternal freedom in which his heart can fully love God and, consequently, all beings. From this newfound fortitude and love, Arjuna is prepared to act with full-heartedness.[9]

The opening question concerning action is posed by the troubled King Dhritarāshtra. He approaches his minister Sanjaya, who functions as a sage. This forms the outer dialogue of the text. As we have seen, the king is an illegitimate ruler, misguided and selfish. Thus he is emblematic of our human condition, for we all can be, in a sense, blinded by myopic vision, by self-centeredness. We are blind kings ruling over our false kingdoms, misguided and selfish in our individual existences. Our false kingdoms are the very fleeting worlds to which we impute eternal significance, as if our impermanent lives were going to last forever. The king's troubled state leads him to inquire from his minister, who is granted exceptional vision. The Gītā also encourages us in our "blindness" to seek out someone of broad spiritual insight for divine guidance:

> Learn this
> by humble submission,
> by thorough inquiry,
> and by serving.
> They will impart
> this knowledge to you,
> for they are knowers
> and seers of the truth.
>
> (BG 4.34)

Sanjaya, who has a vision of the truth, through his outer dialogue with the king, becomes the narrator of the private inner dialogue between Krishna and Arjuna. This conversation is then meant to be contemplated deeply within the heart and lived by in our challenging worlds.

---

9 Full-heartedness refers to the state of *bhakti* in which the heart is brimming over with love for the divinity and therefore, for all beings in whose hearts the divinity resides.

Literary Dimensions

The journey of the soul to the divinity and the ways in which the divinity embraces the soul are described in the Bhagavad Gītā in narrative, conversational, philosophical, and didactic verse. The Gītā presents a variety of paths leading the soul to the divine, along with various manifestations of divinity. The majority of its verses focus on three concepts: (1) a philosophical vision of the human self and the nature of the precarious "outer world"; (2) the various paths and practices that lead the self to the "inner world" of transcendence and personal presence of the divine; and (3) the "innermost world" of the heart, where divinity is encountered directly in a dialogue between the soul and God, as represented by the heartfelt exchange between Arjuna and Krishna.

In effect, then, the Gītā takes us, along with Arjuna, on an internal journey to the innermost region of the heart. The hardships of the outer world often distract the soul from the inner world, hurling the soul into despondency. The Gītā demonstrates how souls can reconnect with the divine in their hearts, thereby attaining a state of full-heartedness. From this position of inner strength and fulfillment, the soul is able to return to the battlefield of the outer world with courage, fully prepared to act. The inner dialogue between Arjuna and Krishna is private; no one on the battlefield is close enough to hear or directly observe it. This intimate conversation is a deeply loving exchange that discloses the secret love song of the divinity, relieving Arjuna of his insurmountable grief and awarding him a full heart.

The voices of Krishna and Arjuna are heard throughout the Gītā, along with an occasional supporting narrative by Sanjaya. Of these, it is Krishna's voice that is heard the most.[10] Although his voice appears only once in the first chapter, it dominates the other seventeen. Arjuna's voice is prominent in the first and eleventh chapters, and is heard in only twenty-eight verses in twelve other chapters.[11] Sanjaya's voice is heard most frequently in the first chapter and is found in three others. The text concludes with five

---

10 Krishna speaks in 575 verses, roughly 82 percent of the text.

11 Arjuna speaks in 83 verses, roughly 12 percent of the text.

effusive verses spoken by Sanjaya to Dhritarāshtra, thus resuming the outer dialogue, which expresses the bliss the soul derives from recalling the words spoken between Krishna and Arjuna.

For one encountering the work for the first time, it is important to note that Krishna and Arjuna are given numerous epithets in the text. Arjuna is given at least twenty other names and Krishna at least thirty-three. One encounters such names as: Govinda (one who tends the cows), Supreme Person, and Slayer of Madhu for Krishna; and Pārtha (son of Prithā), Mighty-Armed, and Bhārata (descendant of King Bharata) for Arjuna. The devotee of Krishna experiences endless delight in affectionately calling the beloved Lord by any number of these names. Indeed, another section of the Mahābhārata text, known as *Vishnu Sahasra Nāma,* "The Thousand Names of Vishnu," bespeaks this practice.[12] Therefore, it should not surprise the reader to find such variety of nomenclature in the Gītā. (The complete list of epithets for Arjuna and Krishna appears in the "Dramatis Personae.")

The Bhagavad Gītā is reminiscent of other sacred texts, in particular the Vedas and the Upanishads, which contribute to the work's synthetic character. As stated above, Vaishnava traditions, along with other Hindu traditions, revere these scriptural works for their foundational revelations. Beginning with the Vedas, a significant part is dedicated to devotional Sanskrit hymns. To compare, in the following passage Arjuna marvels at the magnificence and divinity of Krishna:[13]

> You are the indestructible,
> the supreme object of knowledge.
> You are the supreme
> resting place of all.
> You are the everpresent
> protector of lasting dharma.
> You are the eternal Person—
> so it is understood by me.
>
> (BG 11.18)

---

12 Found in Anuśāsan Parvan of the Mahābhārata and in the Padma Purāna.
13 See BG 10.12–18; 11.15–31.

Here one is reminded of the Vedic worshipper whose voice extols the greatness of the divine in its myriad forms.

The Gītā is also reminiscent of the dialogues between student and teacher found in the Upanishads, the other source mirrored in the text. The following verses of the Gītā remind one of the Upanishads:

Arjuna said:

What is the description
 of one established
 in profound knowledge,
 who is established
 in perfect meditation,
 O Keshava?
How would
 one established
 in thought speak?
 How would one sit?
 How would one move about?

The Beloved Lord said:

When a person gives up
 all selfish desires
 arising from the mind,
 O Pārtha,
Satisfied within the self
 by the self alone,
 then that person
 is said to be established
 in profound knowledge.
(BG 2.54–2.55)

The dominant literary structure of the Bhagavad Gītā text is a dialogue, comprised of both inner and outer dialogues. The voice of the master is by far the most prominent within the inner dialogue and reflects an important dimension of Krishna's relationship with Arjuna, that of the compassionate teacher with the submissive student. Arjuna asks several questions in the text, and Krishna responds with didactic words. Arjuna submits to Krishna as his humble student in the following words: "I am your student—instruct me, for I have offered myself unto you" (BG 2.7). This paradigm of the student inquiring from the spiritual guide, characteristic of the Upanishads, is present early on and throughout the Gītā. It is no wonder that the Gītā is sometimes called Gitopanishad, expressing its close relationship to the Upanishads.

I have presented briefly some key literary and philosophical aspects of the Bhagavad Gītā to facilitate the reader's encounter with this great dialogue. The "Textual Illuminations" provides a more elaborate discussion of the complex theology of the work, as well as an exploration of various dimensions of the "secret love song" of the divinity. Because the Bhagavad Gītā engages many traditions of spiritual practice and philosophy and is framed within a complex epic, it is challenging for any reader to penetrate its essential message. Indeed, traditional schools of India often have taken minor practices or philosophies engaged in the text to be the whole intent of the text's message. And Western readers typically have grasped only that part which reflects something familiar from the Abrahamic traditions, thereby ignoring essential themes of the Gītā.

My purpose, therefore, is to offer the reader an overall vision derived directly from the text that allows one to appreciate every aspect of the work. This vision is one of love, beginning with God's heart yearning for the love of souls. For now, I invite the reader to encounter the ideas and messages of this complex text with an open heart. As you consider the predicament of the soft-hearted Arjuna, take the journey along with him into your own heart, where you will begin to experience an authentic ancient voice of spiritual wisdom that for millennia has moved the hearts of countless millions the world over.

Bhagavad Gītā

Dramatis Personae

(in order of appearance)

Dhritarāshtra

Speaker of the first verse; the king to whom the whole text is narrated, for whose throne the war is being fought

Sanjaya

Narrator; the king's minister, who has been given special power to hear and see events on the battlefield and the great dialogue between Arjuna and Krishna

Duryodhana

A leading general of the Kauravas; cousin of Arjuna; eldest son of Dhritarāshtra; the prime instigator of the fratricidal conflict

Arjuna

A leading general of the Pāndavas; cousin of Duryodhana; son of Pāndu (the younger brother of Dhritarāshtra), who speaks with Krishna throughout the text (see Epithets below)

The Beloved Lord

Krishna, Arjuna's chariot driver, who imparts teachings and engages in personal dialogue with Arjuna for the greater part of the text (see Epithets below)

The Setting

Geographic location: the holy site of Kurukshetra ("the field of Kuru"), a rural area located in central northern India about one hundred miles north of Delhi.

The scene on the Kurukshetra battlefield: The massive opposing armies, composed of the righteous army of the sons of Pāndu, the Pāndavas, led by Arjuna, and the unrighteous army of the sons of Dhritarāshtra, the Kurus, led by Duryodhana, the eldest son. On his chariot, Krishna drives Arjuna into the middle of the battlefield, between the armies, to survey the warriors and battle scene.

Epithets

Arjuna

Pāndava
Dhananjaya
Gudākesha
Pārtha
Son of Kuntī
Scorcher of the Enemy
Bhārata
Best Among Men
Mighty-Armed
Kaunteya
Descendant of Kuru
Conqueror of Wealth
Blameless One
Leader of the Bharatas
Subduer of the Enemy
Best of the Kurus
Son of Pāndu
Son of Kuru
Best of the Bharatas
Best of the Embodied
Destroyer of the Enemy
Hero of the Kurus
Masterful Archer
Fighter of the Enemy
Tiger Among Men
Holder of the Bow

The Beloved Lord, Krishna

Mādhava
Hrishīkesha
Achyuta
Keshava
Govinda
Madhusūdhana
Janārdana
Descendant of Vrishni
Slayer of the Enemy
Vārshneya
Ultimate Person
Supreme Person
Source of Beings
Divinity of Divinities
Master of the Universe
Yogi
One with Lotus-like Eyes
Highest Supreme Lord
Ultimate Person
Supreme Lord of Yoga
Lord
Hari
Divinity
All-Pervasive Supreme Lord
Mighty Self
Mighty-Armed
Lord of Divinities
Vishnu
Best of Divinities
Extraordinary Self
Unlimited Lord
One of Unlimited Form
Everything
Yādava
Friend
Unfathomable One
One of Incomparable Being
Thousand-Armed One
Universal Form
Vāsudeva
Majestic One
Slayer of Keshi

Translation

I

Arjuna's Conflict and Despair

Dhritarāshtra said:

On the field of dharma,
on the field of Kuru,
assembled together
desiring to fight,
Were my armies
and indeed those
of the sons of Pāndu—
how did they act, O Sanjaya?[1] I

1 Dhritarāshtra: The hard-hearted king of the Kurus, blind from birth, while sitting in his palace, desires to know what is occurring on the battlefield, where a civil war between his sons and nephews, the heroic sons of his brother Pāndu, is about to begin.

On the field of dharma: Translates *dharma-kṣetre.* This phrase tells the reader that the field of Kuru, or Kurukshetra, is a holy place, a place of dharma (see meaning of *dharma* below).

On the field of Kuru: Translates *kuru-kṣetre,* the name of the holy place Kurukshetra, about 100 miles north of Delhi, India's modern capital city.

Dharma: A state of righteousness, a personal calling to goodness, cosmic harmony, sound ethical law, or justice. The very first word in the opening Sanskrit verse.

Kuru: Name of a common ancestral king for the leaders of both armies, the sons of Dhritarāshtra and the sons of his brother, Pāndu.

The sons of Pāndu: Also known as the Pāndavas, the five sons of King Pāndu, whose names are presented in verses 15 and 16 below; also, the name of the army led by Arjuna.

Pāndu: The younger brother of Dhritarāshtra, who was king before his untimely death.

How did they act: The word *act* translates an active form of the verbal root *kṛ,* which means "to act." The noun form, *karma,* meaning "action," is a major theme of the BG. All words that derive from this verbal root are here translated with some form of the word *act.*

Sanjaya: The king's minister, endowed by Vyāsa with the power to see what is transpiring on the battlefield at every moment, recounts these events to the king.

Sanjaya said:

Now seeing the armies
of the Pāndavas arrayed
in battle formation,
King Duryodhana,
approaching his teacher,
spoke these words:[2] 2

[Duryodhana said:]

Behold these mighty warriors
of the sons of Pāndu,
O Revered Teacher,
Arrayed in
battle formation
by the son of Drupada,
your own skillful student.[3] 3

Here are their heroes,
powerful archers equal
to Bhīma and Arjuna in battle:
Yuyudhāna and Virāta,
and King Drupada,
the great chariot warrior;[4] 4

---

2 Pāndavas: The sons of the Pāndus and the army led by Arjuna. Beginning with this verse, Duryodhana reviews the powerful warriors on the opposing side.

King Duryodhana: The oldest son of King Dhritarāshtra and the leading general of the Kuru warriors who oppose the righteous Pāndavas. The name Duryodhana means "dirty fighter." This is the first of nine consecutive verses spoken by Duryodhana (BG 1.3–11).

His teacher: Refers to Dronacharya, the great teacher of warfare for both Arjuna and Duryodhana.

3 In verses 3 through 6, Duryodhana, the leader of the unrighteous Kurus, observes the powerful warriors in the opposing army, led by Arjuna, his cousin. In verses 7 through 11, he then speaks about the superior power of his own men.

The son of Drupada: Dhristadyumna, the leading commander of the Pāndavas.

4 Bhima: One of five Pāndava brothers known to be a great warrior.

Arjuna: One of five Pāndava brothers who lead the Pāndava army; the loving friend of Krishna to whom the teachings of the BG are spoken.

Yuyudhāna and the other men named in this verse, as well as in the following two verses, are all well-known and powerful warriors in the Pāndava army.

Dhrishtaketu, Chetikāna,
and the heroic king of Kāshi;
Purojit and Kuntibhoja,
and Shaibya, leader among men; 5

And the courageous
Yudhāmanyu, also
the valorous Uttamaujas;
The son of Subhadrā
and the sons of Draupadi—
all certainly great chariot warriors.[5] 6

However, our own men,
the most distinguished—
learn about them,
O Best of the Twice-Born.
To inform you,
I will tell you the names
of those who are
the leaders of my forces.[6] 7

They are yourself and Bhīshma,
also Karna and Kripa,
victorious in battle;
Also Ashwatthāma
and Vikarna, and indeed,
the son of Somadatta;[7] 8

---

5 Son of Subhadrā: Refers to Abhimanyu; Subhadrā is Krishna's sister.

Sons of Draupadi: Draupadi is the wife of each of the five Pāndavas, each with whom she has a son.

6 O Best of the Twice-born: Translates *dvijottama,* addressing Duryodhana's teacher, Drona, as the best of the Brahmins.

7 Bhīshma: The most venerated of the Kaurava warriors, who is the grand uncle of the Pāndavas.

Karna: A half-brother and chief rival of Arjuna and a highly skilled bowman.

Kripa and the other warriors mentioned here are all prominent in the opposing Kaurava army.

And many other heroes
who are willing to relinquish
their lives for my sake—
Wielding various weapons,
all are highly skilled in battle. 9

Unlimited are our forces
protected by Bhīshma,
Whereas limited are their forces
protected by Bhīma.[8] 10

Thus in all maneuvers
from your respective positions,
You must certainly guard Bhīshma—
indeed, every one of you.[9] 11

[Sanjaya continued:]

Giving him [Duryodhana] a thrill,
the revered elder
of the Kurus [Bhīshma]
Cried out the roar
of a lion and blew
his conch with great vigor. 12

Then conches and kettledrums,
cymbals, drums, and trumpets
Were all sounded at once—
the vibration became tumultuous. 13

---

8 Unlimited: Translates the word *aparyāptam,* also meaning paradoxically, "inadequate." Similarly, "limited," in the second half of the verse, translates *paryāptam,* the positive form of this word, which also means "adequate." This double meaning expresses how Duryodhana's overconfidence compensates for his insecurity regarding the outcome of the battle.

9 Duryodhana, after directing his words to his teacher, now turns to his men to instruct them.

Thereupon, standing
in a magnificent chariot
yoked with white horses,
Mādhava [Krishna]
and the Pāndava [Arjuna]
sounded their divine conch shells.[10] 14

Hrishīkesha [Krishna]
blew the conch Panchajanya;
Dhananjaya [Arjuna]
blew the conch Devadatta;
And Bhīma,
the voracious eater
who is terrifying in action,
blew the great conch Paundra.[11] 15

King Yudhishthira,
the son of Kuntī,
blew his conch Anantavijaya;
While Nakula and Sahadeva
blew their conches,
Sughosha and Manipushpaka.[12] 16

---

10 Mādhava: Name of Krishna meaning "a descendant of Madhu" (of the Yadu dynasty). This name indicates Krishna's distant family relationship with Arjuna, whose ancestry goes back to Puru. Yadu and Puru were sons of the great king Yayāti. This name is also associated with Krishna as the husband of the Great Goddess, Lakshmī Devī, the embodiment of all auspiciousness, success, prosperity, and happiness. This is the first verse in which Krishna is introduced.

11 Hrishīkesha: Name of Krishna meaning "the lord of the senses."

Dhananjaya: Name of Arjuna throughout the BG, meaning "conqueror of wealth."

Bhīma: One of the five Pāndavas and brother of Arjuna. The other three brothers are named in the next verse.

12 Yudhishthira: The eldest of the Pāndava brothers.

Nakula and Sahadeva: Two Pāndava brothers.

Also, the king of Kāshi,
  an expert archer,
  and Shikhandī,
  a great chariot warrior;
Dhrishtadhyumna and Virāta,
  along with Sātyaki,
  the unconquerable; 17

Drupada and the sons
  of Draupadī,
  grouped together,
  O Lord of the Earth;
And the mighty-armed
  son of Subhadrā—
  all of them blew
  their conches one by one.[13] 18

That sound shattered the hearts
  of the sons of Dhritarāshtra,
And indeed, the tumult caused
  the heavens and earth to resound.[14] 19

---

13 The son of Subhadrā: Abhimanyu, the son of Arjuna's second wife.

O Lord of the Earth: An epithet for Dhritarāshtra, the king to whom Sanjaya narrates this text.

14 The sons of Dhritarāshtra: Sanjaya identifies Dhritarāshtra's sons using a slightly altered Sanskrit form of the king's name while narrating the events occurring far from the king. Thus Sanjaya is not ignoring the fact that the king sits before him by speaking of him in the third person. Rather, in Sanskrit, offspring are identified by a slightly altered form of the father's name, here as Dhārtarāshtra.

Thus observing
the sons of Dhritarāshtra
lined up in battle formation,
The Pāndava [Arjuna],
his chariot displaying
the banner of the monkey,
lifted his bow as weapons
began to clash.[15] 20

Then, O Lord of the Earth,
to Hrishīkesha,
he spoke these words:
Between the two armies
place my chariot,
O Achyuta [Krishna],[16] 21

So that I may look upon those
who are standing here
desiring battle—
With whom
must I battle while
engaging in this war? 22

I look upon those
about to engage in battle,
who are assembled here
Desiring to please
the evil-minded son
of Dhritarāshtra in battle.[17] 23

15 The Pāndava: A son of King Pāndu, referring to Arjuna.

The banner of the monkey: The particular monkey referred to here is Hanumān, the great monkey servant of Rāma, a manifestation of Vishnu.

16 O Lord of the Earth: This epithet refers to Dhritarāshtra.

17 The evil-minded son of Dhritarāshtra: Duryodhana, who leads the Kuru army.

[Sanjaya continued:]

Hrishīkesha, thus addressed
by Gudākesha [Arjuna],
O Bhārata [Dhritarāshtra],
Placed his magnificent chariot
between the two armies.[18] 24

Facing Bhīshma, Drona,
and all the kings
of the earth,
He [Krishna] said,
"O Pārtha [Arjuna],
behold these Kurus
assembled here!" 25

Pārtha saw,
standing there—
fathers, then grandfathers,
Teachers, maternal uncles,
brothers, sons, grandsons,
as well as companions; 26

Fathers-in-law,
and even dear friends,
present in both battalions.
The Son of Kuntī [Arjuna],
observing all of them,
his kinsmen arrayed for battle; 27

---

18 O Bhārata: Son of Bharata, here referring to Dhritarāshtra. Gudākesha: "The full-haired one."

Filled with deep compassion
and falling into despair,
spoke the following:
Seeing my own relations,
O Krishna, standing
nearby ready to fight,[19] 28

My limbs are sinking down
and my mouth has
become very dry.
Also, my body trembles
and the hairs of
my limbs stand on end. 29

My bow, Gāndīva,
falls from my hand
and even my skin is burning.
I also am unable
to stand steadily and
my mind seems to be reeling. 30

And I perceive signs of chaos,
terrible reversals,
O Keshava [Krishna],
And I foresee
no benefit in slaying
my own relations in battle.[20] 31

19 With deep compassion: Translates *kṛpayā parayā*.
Falling into despair: Translates *viṣīdan*.

20 Keshava: Name of Krishna meaning "the one with beautiful hair."

I do not desire victory,
O Krishna,
nor a kingdom,
nor happiness.
What use is a kingdom to us,
O Govinda [Krishna]?
What is the use of pleasures
or purpose in living?[21] 32

Those persons for
whose sake we desire
such kingdom, pleasures,
and happiness—
They stand here arrayed
in battle readiness,
relinquishing
their lives and wealth: 33

Our teachers,
fathers, and sons;
also grandfathers,
Maternal uncles,
fathers-in-law,
grandsons,
brothers-in-law,
and other kinsmen. 34

21 Govinda: Name of Krishna meaning "the one who herds the cows." Considered to be an especially endearing and intimate name for Krishna.

I do not wish to slay them,
even those who are
about to slay,
O Madhusūdana [Krishna],
Even for the rule
of the three worlds—
how much less, then,
for the rule of the earth?[22] 35

What joy would there be for us,
O Janārdana [Krishna],
in slaying the sons
of Dhritarāshtra?
Certainly misfortune
would fall upon us
having slain them
whose bows are drawn.[23] 36

Therefore, we are not entitled
to slay the sons of
Dhritarāshtra,
our kinsmen.
Indeed, in slaying
our own relations,
how could we realize
happiness, O Mādhava?[24] 37

---

22 Madhusūdana: "Slayer of the demon Madhu," a well-known name for Krishna. Arjuna's use of this name suggests, "You slay demons, but even you don't slay persons whom you love and revere!"

23 Janārdana: Name of Krishna meaning "one who inspires human beings."

Misfortune: Translates *pāpa,* often rendered as "sin," which carries too much of the narrower Christian sense. I have chosen to translate as "misfortune" or "trouble," indicating both the unfortunate things that can befall a person as well as something unfortunate that a person has caused. The word *pāpa* means anything disturbing that creates conflict internally and externally, an impediment in one's spiritual evolution causing effects that impede one's progress. The word *sin* has a much narrower application that carries a particular Christian sense not present in the Sanskrit word *pāpa*.

24 Happiness: Translates *sukhinaḥ*.

Even if, with their thoughts
overcome by greed,
they do not perceive
The harm caused by acts
that destroy the family,
nor the crime in
harming a friend;[25] 38

Still, how can we not know
to turn away from
this wrongdoing,
With our understanding of
the harm caused by acts
that destroy the family,
O Janārdana?[26] 39

In destroying the family,
the eternal dharma
of the family is lost.
When dharma is lost,
whatever opposes dharma
also overcomes the entire family.[27] 40

Because of the prevalence
of that which opposes dharma,
the women of the family
become degraded.
When the women are degraded,
O Descendant of Vrishni [Krishna],
disorder between classes of society arises.[28] 41

---

25 Greed: Translates *lobha*.
Destroy the family: Translates *kula-kṣaya*.
Crime in harming a friend: Translates *mitra-droha*.

26 Wrongdoing: Translates *pāpa*.
Harm: Translates *doṣa*.

27 Dharma of the family: Translates *kula-dharma*.
Whatever opposes dharma: Translates *adharma,* meaning lawlessness, chaos, or evil.

28 Disorder between classes of society: Translates *varṇa-saṁkaraḥ*. Sometimes taken as "confusion of caste."

This disorder certainly leads
to a place of torment
for destroyers of the family
and the family itself.
Indeed, the spirits of
their ancestors fall,
deprived of their ritual
offerings of rice and water. 42

By these wrongdoings of
the destroyers of the family,
which produce disorder
between the classes of society,
The dharmas of
lineages are ruined,
along with the eternal
dharma of the family.[29] 43

When the family dharma
of human beings
has been ruined,
O Janārdana,
Dwelling in a place of torment
certainly becomes their fate—
so we have heard
from sacred sources. 44

Ah yes!
what great misfortune
we are resolved to enact,
For which, out of greed
for the happiness of royalty,
we are prepared to slay
our own people. 45

---

29 The dharmas of lineages: Translates *jāti-dharmāḥ,* meaning the "dharmas of the castes." The BG focuses, however, mostly on varṇa, or the four major classes of society.

If without my acting
in opposition
and without any
weapons for myself,
The sons of Dhritarāshtra,
with weapons in their hands,
should slay me in battle—
that would be
a greater peace for me! 46

Thus speaking
in the midst of conflict,
Arjuna sat upon
the seat of the chariot.
Casting aside
his bow and arrow,
his mind was
tormented by sorrow. 47

2

The Way of Discernment

Sanjaya said:

To him who was thus
overwhelmed by compassion,
whose troubled eyes were
full of tears,
Who was deeply depressed,
Madhusūdana
spoke these words. 1

The Beloved Lord said:

From where
does your weakness
come at this time of crisis?
It is not befitting
the noble-minded,
nor does it lead
to celestial realms—
it causes disgrace, O Arjuna.[1] 2

---

1 The Beloved Lord: Translates *bhagavān* or *bhagavat,* the same word as in the title—an epithet that refers to Krishna, which introduces Krishna's words throughout the text. This is the first verse in which the words of Krishna are introduced.

Do not yield to
this weakness, O Pārtha;
it is inappropriate for you.
Relinquishing this poor
faint-heartedness,
stand up,
O Scorcher of the Enemy! 3

Arjuna said:

How shall I,
in battle against
Bhīshma and Drona,
O Madhusūdana,
Fight back with arrows
against those who
are worthy of respect,
O Slayer of the Enemy? 4

Indeed, rather than slaying
greatly revered gurus,
It would be better
to subsist in this world
by begging for alms.
For slaying such gurus,
though they desire
selfish gain in this world,
Surely would taint
with their blood
any pleasures I might enjoy.[2] 5

---

2 Desire: Translates the word *kāma*. This word, simply, means "desire," but most often carries the negative sense of "selfish" or "worldly" desire throughout the BG.

And we know not
which of the two is better:
Whether we should conquer them
or they should conquer us.
For having slain them
we should not wish to live—
They who are standing here before us,
the sons of Dhritarāshtra.[3] 6

My very being
is afflicted by a piteous
weakness of spirit.
My thoughts on dharma
are completely bewildered.
I ask you, tell me what
is definitely better for me!
I am your student—
instruct me, for I have
offered myself unto you. 7

Indeed, I cannot foresee
what would dispel
This grief that is
drying up my senses,
Even if achieving an unrivaled
flourishing kingdom on earth,
Or the sovereignty
of celestial beings.[4] 8

---

3 Up until this verse, Arjuna has been speaking in the first person singular; here Arjuna speaks in the first person plural, "we," referring to himself and the leading generals of his army.

4 Celestial beings: Translates the plural form of *sura*.

Sanjaya said:

Thus having spoken
to Hrishīkesha,
Gudākesha,
the subduer of the enemy,
Said to Govinda,
"I shall not fight!"
Having spoken thus,
he fell silent. 9

Hrishīkesha,
as if about to laugh,
O Bhārata [Dhritarāshtra],
In the midst of the two armies,
spoke these words to him
who was feeling despondent. 10

The Beloved Lord said:

You have grieved for that
which is not worthy of grief,
and yet you speak words
of profound knowledge.
The learned grieve
neither for those
who have passed on,
nor for those
who have not departed.[5] 11

---

5 Krishna's teachings commence with this verse. Profound knowledge: Translates *prajñā,* often rendered as "wisdom."

Never, truly,
have I ever not existed—
nor you, nor these kings
who protect the people,
And never
shall any of us
ever cease to be,
now or forevermore. 12

Just as the embodied
while in this body
passes through childhood,
youth, and old age,
So also the embodied
attains another body—
the wise person
is not bewildered by this. 13

Certainly, contact
of the senses with matter,
O Kaunteya [Arjuna],
which results in cold, heat,
happiness, and suffering,
Comes and goes,
and is impermanent—
you must strive
to tolerate this,
O Bhārata [Arjuna]. 14

Indeed, the person whom
these do not trouble,
O Best Among Men,
The wise one for whom
suffering and happiness
are the same—
that one is prepared
for immortality. 15

Of the impermanent
one finds no being;
one finds no nonbeing
of the permanent.
Indeed, the certainty
of both of these
has been perceived
by seers of the truth. 16

Now, know that
to be indestructible
by which all this
is pervaded.
No one is able
to bring about
the destruction
of the everpresent. 17

These bodies,
said to have an end,
belong to the embodied,
which is eternal,
Indestructible,
and immeasurable—
therefore fight,
O Bhārata! 18

One who considers
it [the self] a slayer,
and one who thinks
it is slain,
Both of these
fail to understand—
it does not slay,
nor is it slain. 19

It does not take birth,
nor does it ever die.
Such a being has never
come into being,
nor shall it ever
come to be.
It is unborn, eternal,
everlasting,
and primeval.
It is not slain
when the body is slain.[6] 20

One who knows this [self]
to be indestructible,
eternal, unborn,
and everpresent—
How and whom does
that person slay, O Pārtha?
And whom does
that one cause to slay? 21

As a person abandoning
worn-out garments
acquires other new ones,
So the embodied,
abandoning worn-out bodies,
enters other new ones. 22

---

6 This verse continues the chapter's theme on the self's eternal presence of being. The self has not come into existence at any time in the past nor does it have any end in the future (BG 2.12). If the self were not to exist at any time, then it would have no true being; and of the self's being there can be no nonexistence (BG 2.16). In the first quarter of this verse, the self does not take birth nor does it die. In the second quarter, it is a being (*bhūya*) that is eternally present, which has never come into being (*bhūtvā*) and shall never come into being (*bhavitā*). Although the noun "being," referring to the self (*bhūya*), can be taken as a verb or an adverb, the most compelling translation as a noun is dictated by its philosophical context found in the two previous aforementioned verses. Most other translations render this verse philosophically inconsistent with these preceding verses.

Weapons do not pierce it,
fire does not burn it,
And water does not moisten it;
nor does wind wither it. 23

It cannot be pierced;
it cannot be burned,
moistened, or
even withered;
Eternal,
present everywhere,
stationary, immovable—
it is everlasting.[7] 24

This [self] is unmanifest,
it is inconceivable,
it is spoken of
as unchangeable.
Therefore,
knowing this to be so,
you should not grieve. 25

Further, if you think
of this [self] as
always being born
or always dying—
Even then,
O Mighty-Armed,
you should not
grieve for this. 26

---

7 Present everywhere: Translates *sarva-gataḥ*. This phrase can mean that the self is present everywhere in the body, or that selves permeate the whole universe. It can also refer to the Self, namely the divinity, who is present everywhere in the universe. Thus the BG's idea of self can indicate either the individual or the supreme self. The Sanskrit word *ātman* is translated as "self" to indicate the self of the living being, or "Self" to indicate the supreme divinity present within the very self of every living being (as first seen in BG 4.6). Many verses can be taken as speaking about both simultaneously.

Indeed, for one who is born
death is certain,
and for one who has died
birth is certain.
Therefore, since this
process is inevitable,
you ought not to grieve. 27

Unmanifest are the beginnings
of beings; manifest are
their interims, O Bhārata;
Then again, unmanifest
are their endings—
what is lamentable about this? 28

Rarely, someone
perceives this [self];
Rarely, another
also speaks of it.
And rarely, indeed,
another hears about it;
Even having heard about it,
no one truly knows it. 29

The embodied,
eternally indestructible,
dwells within the body
of everyone, O Bhārata.
Therefore you
should not grieve
for any living being. 30

Moreover, considering
your own dharma,
you should not waver.
Truly, for a warrior,
nothing better exists
than a battle fought
according to dharma. 31

And if by good fortune
what is gained
is an opened door
to the celestial world,
Happy are the warriors,
O Pārtha,
who obtain such a fight. 32

Now, if you should not
undertake this battle,
which is in accordance
with dharma,
Then, abandoning
your own dharma
and reputation,
you shall meet
with misfortune. 33

Also, people certainly will speak
of your undying infamy.
And for one who has been honored,
such infamy is worse than death. 34

The great chariot warriors
will believe you have retreated
from battle out of fear.
And among those who once
held you in high esteem,
you shall come to be taken lightly. 35

And many unspeakable words
your enemies
will speak of you,
Deriding your ability—
now what could be
greater misery than this? 36

Either having been slain
you shall reach the celestial world,
or conquering
you shall enjoy the earth.
Therefore, rise up,
O Kaunteya,
acting with firm
resolve for battle. 37

Acting the same in
happiness and suffering,
gain and loss,
victory and defeat,
Then prepare for battle—
thus you shall not
suffer misfortune. 38

This discernment
has been explained to you
in [the philosophy of] Sānkhya;
now hear about this
in [the practice of] yoga.
Be absorbed in yoga
with discernment, O Pārtha,
by which you shall throw off
the bondage of action.[8] 39

Here there is no loss of effort,
nor is any diminution found.
Even a little of this dharma
delivers one from great danger. 40

Discernment that is resolute in nature
is singular in this world,
O Descendant of Kuru [Arjuna],
For many-branched and endless
is the discernment
of those who are irresolute. 41

---

8 Discernment: Translates *buddhi,* an important word that appears fifty-three times in the text. The word can have the meanings of "intelligence," "wisdom," "insight," or "understanding." *Discernment* is used here because it gives the active sense engaged in the BG.

Sānkhya: This term refers to the theistic system of Sānkhya, which shares much of its philosophy with the nontheistic Sānkhya school, focusing on the ultimate elements and objects of this world. It is one of six primary philosophical systems, including Yoga, Mīmāmsā, Vedānta, Nyāya, and Vaisheshika.

Yoga: Refers to the process that connects the individual self to the supreme Self. It is a complex term that can either refer to any one of the various means for achieving union with the divine or any one of the various perfectional states achievable in union with the divine. This is the first appearance of this word in the BG. It appears seventy-eight times in its noun form.

Absorbed in yoga: Translates *yukta,* the verbal form of the well-known word *yoga,* which has the essential meaning of "connection" or "union," referring to the connection of the self to the Supreme. This word appears thirty-six times in the BG. I have translated as "absorbed in yoga."

Those who lack understanding
speak this flowery language,
Delighted by the words
of the Vedas, O Pārtha,
declaring, "There is nothing else."[9] 42

For the self full of desire,
whose intent is on
the celestial world,
[this flowery language]
bestows another birth
as the fruit of action.
Preoccupied with
various ritualistic acts,
[this self] is directed
toward the goal of worldly
pleasure and power. 43

For those attached to
worldly pleasure and power,
whose thoughts are stolen
away by this [flowery language],
Discernment that
is resolute in nature
is not discovered
in perfect meditation.[10] 44

9 The Vedas: The original sacred writings of India, consisting of numerous Sanskrit hymns that were originally transmitted orally by priestly families, and then later preserved in written form.

10 Perfect meditation: Translates *samādhi,* the attainment of total absorption in which the meditator becomes self-forgetful and is only aware of the object of meditation. This perfect meditative state in yoga is the eighth "limb" in the Ashtānga Yoga system as described by Patanjali.

The domain of the Vedas
is the three essential 'qualities';
be free of these three
'qualities', O Arjuna,
Beyond duality,
always established
in pure existence, beyond
acquisitions and security,
in possession of one's self.[11] 45

As much value
as there is in a well
when all about it
waters flow abundantly,
Such is the value
of all the Vedas
for a Brahmin who
has realized knowledge.[12] 46

It is in action alone
that you have a claim,
never at any time to
the fruits of such action.
Never let the fruits of action
be your motive;
never let your attachment
be to inaction. 47

---

11 Three 'qualities': Translates *traiguṇya.* The word *guṇa,* or 'quality', can also mean "strand" or "string" or "rope," expressing how these primary qualities arising from primordial nature bind one like a rope. It is a technical term used in Sānkhya philosophy that is a recurring theme in the BG.

12 Brahmin: The priestly or learned class of society, one of four *varṇas* that make the social order whole and complete. Note that this word is not to be confused with Brahman, meaning the ultimate reality or supreme spirit.

Established in yoga,
perform actions,
having relinquished attachment,
O Conqueror of Wealth [Arjuna],
While remaining the same
in success and in no success—
such sameness is said to be yoga. 48

Still, action is by far inferior
to the yoga of discernment,
O Conqueror of Wealth.
Seek shelter in discernment—
miserly are those
who are motivated
by the fruits [of action]. 49

One absorbed in
the yoga of discernment
casts off in this world
both good and bad acts.
Therefore,
be absorbed in yoga,
for yoga is skillfulness
in action. 50

Indeed, those wise ones
who are absorbed
in the yoga of discernment,
relinquishing the fruits
born of action,
Who are freed
from the bondage
of repeated births,
go to a place beyond suffering. 51

When your discernment
crosses beyond the jungle
of bewilderment,
Then you shall become
completely indifferent
to that which is to be heard
and that which has been heard.[13] 52

When this [discernment]
is no longer perplexed
by the heard scriptures,
when it shall remain
without change,
When discernment
is unchanging within
perfect meditation—
then you shall attain yoga. 53

Arjuna said:

What is the description
of one established
in profound knowledge,
who is established
in perfect meditation,
O Keshava?
How would
one established
in thought speak?
How would one sit?
How would one move about? 54

13 That which has been heard: Refers to *śrūti,* the Vedas. Another term for the Vedas found in the BG is *śabda-brahma,* "the sound of Brahman." The Vedas offer worldly results, but superficial reading of this text is discouraged in the BG; Krishna encourages a more esoteric reading that reveals himself: "And by all the Vedas only I am to be known" (BG 15.15).

The Beloved Lord said:

When a person gives up
all selfish desires
arising from the mind,
O Pārtha,
Satisfied within the self
by the self alone,
then that person
is said to be established
in profound knowledge. 55

One whose mind is
undisturbed in suffering,
who is free from desire
in all kinds of happiness,
Whose passion, fear,
and anger have departed—
such a person,
established in thought,
is said to be a sage. 56

One who, everywhere,
is without sentimentality
upon encountering this or that,
things pleasant or unpleasant,
Who neither rejoices nor despises—
the profound knowledge
of such a person
is firmly established. 57

And when one withdraws
completely,
as a tortoise
all of its limbs,
The senses from
their sense objects—
the profound knowledge
of such a person
is firmly established. 58

Sense objects fade away
for the embodied who
does not partake of them,
Except for the taste—
for one who has
seen the Supreme,
even this taste fades. 59

Indeed, even for one
who is striving,
O Kaunteya,
for the person
of discrimination,
The impetuous senses
forcibly carry away
the mind. 60

Restraining all these [senses],
one should be seated
while absorbed in yoga,
wholly intent on me.
For one whose senses
are under control—
for that one,
profound knowledge
is firmly established.[14] 61

For a person dwelling
on the objects of the senses,
attachment to them develops;
From attachment,
selfish desire develops;
from desire, anger develops. 62

---

14 This is the first verse in which Krishna introduces the practice of meditation on him, with the words *mat-paraḥ,* "wholly intent on me."

From anger comes
bewilderment;
from bewilderment,
disturbed memory;
From disturbed memory,
loss of discernment;
from loss of discernment
one becomes lost. 63

Without being absorbed
in attraction and repulsion
as the senses are moving
toward their objects—
With self-restraint,
the self that
can be governed
attains calmness. 64

In calmness,
the cessation of all
one's suffering occurs.
Indeed, for one whose
thought has been calmed,
discernment is quickly established. 65

There is no discernment for one
who is not absorbed in yoga;
and for one not absorbed in yoga,
there is no meditative state;
And for one who has
no meditative state,
there is no peace—
for one who is not peaceful,
from where is happiness to come? 66

Indeed, when the mind
is being pulled
by the roaming senses,
Then just one of them
can carry away one's
profound knowledge,
as wind does a ship at sea. 67

Therefore,
O Mighty-Armed,
whosoever has
completely withdrawn
The senses from
the objects of the senses—
the profound knowledge of
such a person is firmly established. 68

During that which is night
for all beings,
the deeply meditative
person is awake.
During that time in which
beings are awake,
that is night for
the insightful sage.[15] 69

15 The deeply meditative person: Translates the word *saṁyamī,* meaning a person absorbed in the yoga processes of *saṁyama*. The term *saṁyama* refers to the final three "limbs of yoga" in the Patanjali Yoga Sūtra: *dhāraṇa* ("concentration"), *dhyāna* ("meditation"), and *samādhi* ("total absorption in perfect meditation"). See Yoga Sūtra 3.4.

Continually being filled,
the ocean remains unmoved
and stands still, though
waters enter into it.
That person into whom
all desires enter
in this same way
attains peace—
not one who is desirous
to fulfill such desires. 70

Abandoning all selfish desires,
a person moves through life
free from worldly longings,
Without the sense of 'mine',
without the notion
of 'I am acting'—
that one attains peace.[16] 71

16 Without the sense of 'mine': Translates *nirmama,* meaning literally, "without mine." This term conveys a state of being that is without the false sense of possessiveness. Because of the temporary nature of things in this world, no one actually possesses anything permanently, yet one holds on to such a conception.

Without the notion of 'I am acting': Translates *nirahaṁkāra,* meaning literally, "without I am acting." The phrase "I am acting" connotes egocenteredness; an essential message of the BG is the need for the self to develop a vision of theocenteredness, one centered upon the divinity, implied by the phrase "without the notion of 'I am acting'." The term "I am acting" (*ahaṁkāra*) conveys the idea that a person falsely thinks oneself to be acting independently of the various physical, cosmic, and spiritual aspects of "action," explained in later verses. It conveys the false confidence of mistaken identity, wherein one feels oneself to be in complete control, falsely identified with the body and the impermanent roles one assumes in this world. In a realized state, a person "without the notion of 'I am acting' " (*nirahaṁkāra*) no longer identifies with anything temporary, including one's body, gender, family, country, race, etc., nor does one claim ownership or possession of anything (*nirmama*).

The added single quotation marks for "mine" and for "I am acting" are meant to distinguish this type of translated word or phrase from those containing double quotation marks, assigned because they are indicated in the text itself.

This is the state of
the feminine energy
of Brahman, O Pārtha,
having attained which
one is not bewildered.
Being established in this,
even if only at
the end of one's life,
one reaches
the Nirvāna of Brahman.[17] 72

17 The feminine energy of Brahman: Translates the word *brāhmī.* Quite literally, it is the *śakti,* or "female energy," of Brahman. This word is most often taken as a neutered adjective in this verse, meaning simply a Brahman-like state. However, this latter approach ignores the strong feminine presence in the verse, expressed by three feminine gendered words: a pronoun (*eṣā*), and two nouns (*brāhmī* and *sthiti*), all found in the first quarter line. Note that the key word of this chapter, namely *buddhi,* "discernment," is also feminine gendered. Thus this chapter concludes that the state of Brahman's feminine energy supports the nature of the self's discernment.

Nirvāna: Literally, "blown out," meaning "the extinguishing of any worldly existence or experience whatsoever," a spiritual state found within the Brahman that entails a complete calming of the senses, often described as a state of serenity and peacefulness.

Brahman: Supreme spiritual existence, the eternal ultimate reality or the whole of reality. This word is to be distinguished from the words Brahmin and Brahmā. A Brahmin is a person of the priestly or educator class belonging to traditional Indian society, and its first instance is in BG 2.46. Brahmā is the cosmic deity of creation (see BG 8.16), whose counterpart is Shiva, the deity of cosmic transformation or dissolution.

3

The Way of Action

Arjuna said:

If you consider discernment
to be better than action,
O Janārdana,
Then why do you engage me
in dreadful action,
O Keshava? I

With very confusing words,
you seem to bewilder
my intellect.
Therefore, speak definitely
of that one thing by which
I may attain the greater good. 2

The Beloved Lord said:

In this world
the established path is twofold,
as stated previously by me,
O Blameless One:
The yoga of knowledge
for the followers of Sānkhya,
and the yoga of action
for the yogis.[1] 3

1 Yogis: Plural of *yogi,* meaning a practitioner of yoga. The word appears twenty-eight times in the BG, and is also in the English lexicon.

Not by avoiding actions
  does a person gain
  freedom from action,
And not by renunciation
  alone does a person
  attain perfection. 4

Certainly no one,
  not even for a moment,
  ever lives without
  performing action.
Indeed, against one's will,
  everyone is forced
  to perform action
  by the 'qualities' born
  of primordial nature.[2] 5

Having controlled
  the senses of action,
  one who continues
  with the mind to dwell
On the objects of the senses—
  that one,
  whose self is bewildered,
  is called one with false behavior. 6

---

2 The 'qualities': Translates the plural form of *guṇa,* which is translated by this word throughout this translation. The plural of *guṇa* refers to the three primary qualities of nature, *sattva, rajas,* and *tamas,* which are first presented in BG 7.12. In general, these fundamental distinctions describe degrees of self-centeredness and conditions of the heart: self-giving, selfish, self-destructive; or capacities of the soul to illumine the worldly condition: transparency, translucency, opacity; or level s of consciousness: conscious, subconscious, unconscious. The Gītā's teachings on the essential qualities encourage the soul to attain its original state beyond these qualities, a state of pure *sattva,* to establish a relationship with transcendence and the divine in a state of selflessness, pure transparency, or super-consciousness, respectively.

Primordial nature: Translates the word *prakṛti,* referring to the original source of the physical world or the world of matter, from which the essential qualities arise. The word can mean more generally the original nature of something, and is also applied in some verses below to the divinity himself. The word in Sanskrit is of feminine gender, and the BG presents *prakṛti* as part of the divine feminine energy that complements the ultimate *puruṣa,* or the supreme masculine divinity, Krishna.

But one who,
with the mind
controlling the senses,
O Arjuna, engages in
The yoga of action
with the senses of action,
remaining unattached—
that person is superior. 7

Perform your prescribed actions,
for action is certainly better
than inaction.
And even the subsistence
of one's body cannot be
accomplished without action. 8

Other than action
that has sacrifice
as its purpose,
action is bondage
in this world.
Perform action
for this purpose,
O Kaunteya,
free from attachment. 9

Having previously sent forth
created beings
along with sacrifice,
the Lord of Created Beings said:
May you flourish
by this [sacrifice]!
Let this be the sacred cow
that fulfills your desires.[3] 10

3 The sacred cow that fulfills your desires: Translates *iṣṭa-kāmadhuk*. See the word *kāmadhuk*, "sacred cow," in verse 10.28.

With this [sacrifice] give
pleasure to the divinities;
may those divinities
please you.
By pleasing one another,
you shall attain
the greatest good.[4] 11

Indeed, the divinities,
satisfied by sacrifice,
will give you desired pleasures.
Without giving back to them,
one who enjoys these gifts
is only a thief. 12

Virtuous persons
who eat the remnants
of sacrifice are
freed from all faults,
Whereas wretched persons
only ingest suffering
when they cook
for their selfish motives. 13

4 Divinities: Translates the plural of *deva*. Divinities are not beings with eternal functions, as is the supreme Divinity. Rather, they are superior beings, functioning under the supreme Divinity, Krishna. They are beings who preside over the natural elements, divine only in the sense that they function on behalf of the divine.

From foodstuffs
beings come into being;
from rain
foodstuffs manifest;
From sacrifice
rain comes into being;
sacrifice arises
from action. 14

Understand that action arises
from Brahman, the Vedas;
this Brahman arises originally
from the Imperishable.
Therefore eternal Brahman,
which pervades everything,
is established in sacrifice.[5] 15

Thus the [sacrificial] cycle
has been set into motion;
one who does not
keep it turning in this world,
Whose life is impure,
who delights in the senses—
such a person lives in vain,
O Pārtha. 16

However, the human being
who delights
only in the self,
who is self-satisfied
And finds full contentment
in the self alone—
for that person
there is nothing to be enacted. 17

---

5 The Imperishable: Translates *akṣara,* which can also mean the sacred syllable "OM," the most prominent utterance in mantras.

Surely, such a person
has no [selfish] motives,
either in acting
or in not acting
in this world.
And nor has such a person,
in relation to all beings,
any need whatsoever
for [selfish] motives. 18

Therefore, without attachment,
perform action
that is to be enacted.
Indeed, by performing action
without attachment,
a person attains the Supreme. 19

For by action alone,
King Janaka and others
attained full perfection.
Even if only considering
the welfare of the world,
you are obliged to act.[6] 20

Whatever the greatest one does,
that very thing
other persons will do.
Whatever standard
the greatest one enacts,
that the world follows. 21

6 King Janaka: Known to have attained perfection by his actions as a king. He is the father of Sītā, the queen consort of the divine manifestation of Vishnu as Rāma.

For me, O Pārtha,
there is nothing
whatsoever to be enacted
in the three worlds,
Nor is there anything
not attained that is
to be attained—
even so, I engage in action. 22

Indeed, if ever I should not
engage in action untiringly,
Human beings everywhere
would follow my path, O Pārtha. 23

These worlds would perish
if I should not perform action,
And I would be the cause of chaos—
I would destroy these procreated beings. 24

As the ignorant act,
attached to action,
O Bhārata,
So the wise should act
without attachment,
desiring to act for
the welfare of the world. 25

One should not cause
confusion in the discernment
of those attached to action,
who are without knowledge.
One should leave them
to pursue all actions—
one who is thus wise,
performing all actions
while fully absorbed in yoga. 26

Actions are being carried out
in every instance
by the 'qualities'
of primordial nature.
The self, bewildered by
the notion of 'I am acting',
thinks, "the creator of action am I."[7] 27

However, O Mighty-Armed,
one who knows the truth
about the distribution
of the 'qualities'
and their actions,
Being mindful that
"the 'qualities'
are operating on
those very 'qualities' "—
that one is not attached.[8] 28

---

7 The creator of action: Translates *kartā,* which can mean "the doer," "the agent of action," or literally, "the one who acts." The word can also refer to cosmogenesis: "the creator of the universe." The sense here is that the soul depends upon much beyond itself, such as the workings of the essential qualities of nature, in order to act in the world, and ego-centeredness prevents the soul from knowing this, giving it a false sense of power.

8 Distribution of . . . actions: Refers to the types of social obligations in the *varṇas.*

Distribution of the essential qualities: As they are found in numerous permutations and combinations, and the ways they affect souls in determining their *varṇas.*

See BG 4.13, which also contains the phrase *guṇa-karma-vibhāgaśaḥ.*

Those deluded
by the 'qualities'
of primordial nature
are attached to the actions
of those 'qualities'.
One whose knowledge
is complete should not
disturb those who are dull,
whose knowledge is incomplete. 29

Renouncing all actions in me,
with one's thought on
the 'principle of self',
Without longings,
without a sense of 'mine'—
fight, with grief cast off.[9] 30

Those persons who
constantly follow
my teaching,
Who are full of faith
and envy no one,
also are freed from
[the effects of] action. 31

However, those who are
envious of my teaching,
who do not follow it,
Bewildered by all knowledge—
know them to be lost
and thoughtless. 32

---

9 Following BG 2.61, this is the next instance that introduces the ultimate message of the BG, with the words "renouncing all actions in me." These two verses anticipate the beginning of chapter 4, in which Krishna boldly declares his secret of divine love and his identity as the Divinity.

The 'principle of self': Translates *adhyātmā,* which is introduced more thoroughly beginning in BG 7.29.

One acts according
to one's own nature,
even a person of knowledge,
For beings
follow their nature—
what shall repression accomplish? 33

For any one of the senses,
upon the object of that sense,
both attraction and
aversion are placed.
One should not come
under the control
of either of these, for
indeed they block one's path. 34

Better is one's own dharma
even if imperfect
than another's dharma
followed perfectly.
Better is death in following
one's own dharma,
for another's dharma
brings danger.[10] 35

Arjuna said:

By what, then,
is a person compelled
to do wrong
Even against one's will,
O Vārshneya [Krishna],
as if driven by force? 36

10 Better is one's own dharma . . . : The first half of this verse is repeated as the first half of BG 18.47.

Dharma: The word is used here more generally, carrying over the sense of "path" from the last word of the previous verse.

The Beloved Lord said:

It is selfish desire,
it is anger, arising from
the 'quality' of *rajas*.
All-consuming and
greatly calamitous,
know it to be
the enemy in this world. 37

As fire is covered by smoke
and a mirror by dust,
As an embryo is covered by a womb,
so this world is covered by this. 38

The knowledge of the knower
is obscured by
this constant enemy
In the form of selfish desire,
O Kaunteya,
a fire that indeed
is impossible to satisfy. 39

The senses, the mind,
and the faculty of
discernment
are said to be
the resting place
of this [enemy];
Through these
it bewilders
the embodied,
obscuring knowledge. 40

Therefore, first having
controlled the senses,
O Leader of the Bharatas,
You must strike down this vice
that destroys knowledge
and realized knowledge. 41

The senses are beyond
[matter], they say;
beyond the senses
is the mind;
Still beyond the mind is
the faculty of discernment—
yet that which is beyond all else,
above the faculty of discernment,
is indeed this [self]. 42

Thus having discerned what
is higher than the faculty
of discernment,
sustaining the self
by the self,
Destroy the enemy,
O Mighty-Armed,
in the form
of selfish desire,
so difficult to overcome. 43

4

The Way of Knowledge

The Beloved Lord said:

Unto Vivisvān
I have spoken this yoga,
which is everlasting.
Vivisvān spoke it to Manu,
and Manu imparted it
to Ikshvāku.[1] 1

Thus received through
a line of succession,
the royal seers
understood it.
By the powerful effect
of time, this yoga was lost
[to this lineage] in the world,
O Subduer of the Enemy. 2

---

1 Vivisvān: The presiding deity of the sun.
Manu: The name means "man," referring to the first progenitor of humankind; the son of Vivisvān.
Ikshvāku: The name of an ancient king of eastern India; son of Manu.

This same ancient yoga
is now spoken
by me to you:
"Having offered your love,
you have also
become my friend"—
truly, this is the ultimate secret.[2] 3

Arjuna said:

Your birth
came later,
Vivisvān's birth earlier.
How then should I
understand this—
that you, in the beginning,
"have spoken"?[3] 4

The Beloved Lord said:

Through many births
have I passed,
as have you, O Arjuna.
I know all of them—
you know them not,
O Subduer of the Enemy. 5

---

2 Having offered your love: Translates *bhakta*: "devoted," "lovingly devoted," or simply "one who is devoted [to the Lord]," or "a devotee." The word can also mean "one who is loved [by the Lord]." Thus it is a verb that can also act as a noun. This is the first of fifteen instances. The first appearance of the noun form *bhakti* is found in BG 7.17 and it appears fourteen times in the text.

Friend: Translates the word *sakhā*. Krishna states that Arjuna has offered his heart to him, and that he also loves Arjuna as a friend.

3 "Have spoken": Arjuna is quoting Krishna's precise words from verse 1 of this chapter: "Unto Vivisvān I *have spoken* . . ."

As the one without birth,
the everpresent Self,
as the supreme
Lord of beings
Presiding over
my own nature,
I become fully
manifest by Māyā,
the very power of my Self.[4] 6

Indeed, whenever there is
a decline of dharma,
O Bhārata,
And an emerging
of what opposes dharma—
at that time I send forth my Self. 7

For protection of the virtuous
and for destruction of evil acts,
For the purpose of establishing dharma,
I become fully manifest age after age.[5] 8

One who thus truly knows
the birth and acts
of my divine being,
Upon relinquishing the body,
does not come to another birth—
such a person comes to me, O Arjuna. 9

4 Māyā, the very power of my Self: Translates *ātmā-māyā*. Māyā is the supreme feminine power of Krishna by which he reveals himself to souls, as expressed in this verse, or conceals himself from souls who are not yet ready to know him (see BG 7.14–15). Māyā is Krishna's divine illusive power, which either bewilders souls to facilitate their forgetfulness of divinity or facilitates the revelation of the intimate form of divinity. In BG 18.61, Māyā is the force that facilitates the movement of all beings while in their bodies.

My own nature: Translates *prakṛtiṁ svām*. Here, *prakṛti* refers to the nature of divinity, which is feminine, and in this instance, could include primordial nature as well.

5 Age: Translates the word *yuga*. A *yuga* is a vast period of time, stretching over part of the cosmic cycle.

Freed from passion,
fear, and anger;
immersed in me,
taking full refuge in me,
Many, purified by
the austerity of knowledge,
have come to my
loving state of being. 10

In the way they offer
themselves to me,
in just that way
I offer my love
to them reciprocally.
Human beings
follow my path
universally,
O Pārtha. 11

Desiring success
from their actions,
persons here on earth
offer sacrifice to deities.
For in the world of humans,
quickly comes success
that is born of
[sacrificial] action.[6] 12

---

6 Deities: Translates the plural form of *devatā,* meaning "deity," while *deva* is translated throughout as "divinity." Krishna is *the* divinity in the singular, and when the plural of the word is used, it refers to those Vedic deities or divinities, superior entities, who preside over the natural phenomena of this world. This word appears in the plural in two other places, BG 7.20 and BG 9.23.

The four social orders
are sent forth by me,
with divisions based on
'qualities' and actions.
Of this know me
as the creator, yet
also as the non-creator,
who is everpresent. 13

Actions do not taint me,
nor do I aspire
to the fruit of actions.
One who understands me
in this way is never
bound by actions. 14

Having known this,
the ancient seekers
of liberation also
performed action.
Indeed, perform action
as the ancient ones
enacted previously,
in ancient times. 15

"What is action?
What is inaction?"—
even the wise are
perplexed by this subject.
I shall describe
action to you,
knowing which
you shall be freed
from misfortune. 16

Indeed, the nature of action
is to be discerned;
the nature of unfit action
is to be discerned;
And the nature of inaction
is to be discerned—
the ways of action
are profound. 17

One who can perceive
inaction within action,
and action within inaction—
That one among human beings
possesses discernment,
is absorbed in yoga,
and performs all action. 18

One whose every
endeavor is without
the intention of
selfish desire,
Whose actions
have been consumed
by the fire of knowledge—
those of discernment
call that person learned. 19

Relinquishing attachment
to the fruits of action,
always satisfied and
without dependence
Even while
engaged in action—
indeed, one does not
enact anything whatsoever. 20

Without desire, with self
and thought restrained,
having relinquished
all possessiveness;
Acting only for maintaining
the activities of the body,
one incurs no fault. 21

Satisfied with gain
that comes spontaneously,
crossing beyond duality,
free from envy,
The same in success and
in the absence of success—
even though acting,
such a person is not bound. 22

Freed from attachment,
liberated, with thought
established in knowledge,
Acting for the sake of sacrifice—
for such a person,
action is completely dissolved. 23

Brahman is the ritual instrument;
Brahman is the offering,
which is poured by Brahman
into the fire of Brahman.
Brahman alone
is to be attained by one
who is in perfect meditation
on the actions of Brahman.[7] 24

Indeed, some yogis
worship the divinities
through sacrifice.
Into the fire of Brahman,
through sacrifice itself,
others make sacrificial offerings. 25

Others offer the senses,
those of hearing and the rest,
into the fires of perfect discipline.
While others offer
the objects of the senses,
sound and so forth,
into the fires of the senses.[8] 26

Still others offer the actions
of all the senses and
actions of the life-breath
Into the fire of yoga,
the perfect discipline of self
kindled by knowledge. 27

---

7 Five components of the Vedic sacrifice are presented here: the ritual instrument or ladle, the butter offering, the pouring, the fire, and perfect meditation. These components represent essential elements of religious principles and are found in the next nine verses, through BG 4.33. To understand these principles, Krishna states that one should consult a seer of the truth (BG 4.34).

Perfect meditation: Translates *samādhi*. The state of one who is "completely absorbed" in the object of meditation; sometimes translated simply as "trance." The eighth and last limb of Patanjali's "eight limbs" of yoga in the Yoga Sūtra (2.29).

8 Perfect discipline: Translates the word *saṁyama*. This word first appears in BG 2.69, translated as "the deeply meditative person."

Those whose sacrifice
    is of material possessions,
    those whose sacrifice
    is of austerity,
    also those whose sacrifice
    is of yoga,
And those whose sacrifice
    is of knowledge in
    the study of scripture—
    such persons are
    striving ascetics who
    observe strict vows. 28

Still others offer
    the incoming breath
    into the outgoing breath,
    likewise, the outgoing breath
    into the incoming breath.
Having restrained
    the movements of incoming
    and outgoing breaths,
    they are wholly focused upon
    control of the life-breath. 29

And others,
    who have restricted
    their intake of food,
    offer the life-breath
    into the life-breath.
Indeed, all of these
    are knowers of sacrifice,
    cleansed of their impurities
    through sacrifice. 30

Those who enjoy
the immortal nature
of the remnants of sacrifice
go to the eternal Brahman.
Even this world is not meant
for one without sacrifice—
how then the next,
O Best of the Kurus? 31

Thus, sacrifices of many types
have been prepared for
the mouth of Brahman.
Know them all
to be born of action—
understanding this,
you shall be liberated.[9] 32

Better than the sacrifice
of material objects
is the sacrifice of knowledge,
O Chastiser of the Enemy.
All [sacrificial] actions,
without exception,
O Son of Prithā,
culminate in knowledge. 33

Learn this
by humble submission,
by thorough inquiry,
and by serving.
They will impart
this knowledge to you,
for they are knowers
and seers of the truth.[10] 34

---

9 The mouth of Brahman: Refers to the central arena of the Vedic fire sacrifice.

10 Knowledge: Refers to the knowledge of the Vedas and derivative scriptures.

Knowing which,
you shall thus never
again fall into illusion,
O Pāndava.
By this you shall see,
without exception,
all beings within the Self,
then within me. 35

Even if, among troubled persons,
you are one who performs
the most troubling acts—
By the boat of knowledge,
you shall indeed
cross over all affliction. 36

As firewood is
transformed into ashes
by a blazing fire, O Arjuna,
So all actions are
transformed into ashes
by the fire of knowledge. 37

There is no means of purification
found in this world
that is equal to knowledge.
In time, one perfected
in yoga personally finds
that [knowledge] within the self. 38

One who is full of faith
obtains knowledge,
being devoted to that
with the senses
perfectly controlled.
Obtaining this knowledge,
one achieves
supreme peace
without delay. 39

Not knowing,
and lacking faith,
the self who is full
of doubt is destroyed.
Neither this world,
nor the higher one,
nor happiness exists
for the doubting self. 40

For one who has fully
renounced action in yoga,
whose doubt is completely
severed by knowledge,
Who is in possession
of one's self—
action does not bind,
O Conqueror of Wealth. 41

Therefore, that doubt
which is produced from
the absence of knowledge
and resides within the heart—
Having severed this
with the sword of knowledge
belonging to the self,
rise in yoga!
Rise up, O Bhārata! 42

5

The Way of Renunciation

Arjuna said:

You commend renunciation
of actions, O Krishna,
and also yoga.
Tell me which one
of these two
is definitely better. 1

The Beloved Lord said:

Renunciation
and the yoga of action
both lead to ultimate happiness.
Of the two, however,
the yoga of action is superior
to the renunciation of action. 2

One is to be known
as a steadfast renouncer
who neither hates
nor desires.
Indeed, such a person,
who is without duality,
O Mighty-Armed,
is easily freed
from bondage [of action]. 3

Sānkhya and yoga are
completely separate paths,
so the childish declare,
though not the learned.
For perfectly following
even one [of these],
one achieves the fruit of both. 4

That stance attained by
the followers of Sānkhya
is also reached by
the followers of yoga.
Sānkhya and yoga
are thus one—
one who sees this,
that one truly sees. 5

However, renunciation,
O Mighty-Armed,
is difficult to attain
without yoga.
The sage
absorbed in yoga
reaches Brahman
without delay. 6

One absorbed in yoga
through yoga practice,
with the self purified;
whose self is controlled
with senses conquered;
Whose self becomes
connected to
the self in all beings—
that one is not tainted
even while acting.[1] 7

"Never do I act alone"—
one absorbed in yoga,
who knows reality,
is thus mindful.
While seeing,
hearing, touching,
smelling, eating, walking,
sleeping, breathing; 8

While talking, eliminating,
grasping, even opening
and closing one's eyes,
One is convinced that,
"The senses are engaged
by their sense objects." 9

---

1 Whose self becomes connected to the self of all beings: Consistent with the teachings of the BG as a whole, the self "becomes" (*bhūta*) the self of others empathetically, not ontologically. This statement expresses the BG's version of the "golden rule."

Offering one's actions
to Brahman,
having relinquished
attachment—
For one who thus acts,
misfortune does not cling,
as water does not cling
to the leaf of a lotus. 10

With the body, with the mind,
with one's discernment,
even with the senses alone—
Yogis enact [all] action,
relinquishing attachment
for purity of the self. 11

One who is absorbed in yoga,
having relinquished
the fruit of action,
attains lasting peace.
One who is not absorbed in yoga,
who is attached to the fruit,
is bound by action arising
from selfish desire. 12

Renouncing all actions
within the mind,
the master sits happily
As the embodied
in the city of nine gates,
neither acting nor causing to act.[2] 13

---

2 The city: Refers to the body.

Nine gates: The nine "gates" consist of the nine bodily passages of generation and evacuation, passages of seeing (the eyes), passages of hearing (the ears), passages of breathing (the nostrils), and the passage of ingestion and speaking (the mouth).

Neither the means of action
nor the actions of
those in the world
does the master create,
Nor the conjunction
of actions with their fruits;
rather, one's state of being
is set forth into motion.[3] 14

The Omnipresent
certainly does not
assume anyone's misdeeds
or virtuous deeds.
Knowledge is covered by
the absence of knowledge,
by which living beings
are bewildered. 15

But for those in whom
this absence of knowledge
of the self is destroyed
by knowledge—
For them, knowledge,
like the sun,
causes illumination,
as does the Supreme. 16

3 The master: Translates the subject noun *prabhu*, which refers to the self within the "city of nine gates," or to the supreme "master." In the following verse, translating the related word *vibhu* (note the verbal stem *bhū* in *prabhu* and *vibhu*, taken here to mean "present"), the subject noun is "the Omnipresent." Here, too, it could be the soul who is "omnipresent" in the body, or it could refer to the supreme Lord, who is omnipresent in all bodies and in everything.

Those whose discernment
is focused on that [Supreme],
whose self is absorbed in that,
whose foundation is that,
wholly devoted to that—
Such persons proceed
to that from which
there is no return,
their misdeeds shaken off
by knowledge.[4] 17

In a Brahmin endowed with
learning and gentle conduct,
in a cow, in an elephant,
Even in a dog and
in one who cooks dog—
wise ones see the same [Supreme]. 18

Even here in this world,
creation has been conquered
by those whose minds
are established in sameness.
Indeed, Brahman is flawless
and [forever] the same;
therefore they are
established in Brahman.[5] 19

4 That from which there is no return: This is considered to be a positive statement. When one has reached the very highest heaven, where there is no birth and death, one does not have to return to the lower regions of birth and death, such as this world.

5 Creation: Translates *sarga*. The part of creation that is overcome includes birth and death.

Such a person would neither
rejoice upon attaining
what is pleasing,
nor be shaken upon
attaining what is not pleasing.
With steady discernment,
without being bewildered,
the knower of Brahman
is established in Brahman. 20

The self who is not attached
to external contacts,
who finds happiness
within the self—
That one, whose self
is absorbed in the yoga
of Brahman through yoga,
attains imperishable happiness. 21

Certainly, pleasures born
of [sense] contact
are only sources
of suffering;
As they have a beginning
and end, O Kaunteya,
a wise person does
not delight in them. 22

One who, in this very life,
before giving up the body,
is able to endure
Agitation arising from
desire and anger—
that one is absorbed in yoga;
happy is that person. 23

One whose happiness is within,
whose pleasure is within,
and likewise, whose light
comes only from within—
Such a yogi, being
united with Brahman,
attains the Nirvāna of Brahman. 24

The Nirvāna of Brahman
is attained by those seers
whose misdeeds
have been destroyed,
Whose conflict
has been severed,
whose self is disciplined,
who delight in
the welfare of all beings. 25

Among those seekers
who are separated
from desire and anger,
whose thought is controlled,
The Nirvāna of Brahman
exists close at hand—
for such knowers of the self. 26

Keeping the action of
the outer sensations outside,
and one's vision inside,
just between the eyebrows;
Making the action of incoming
and outgoing breaths the same
as they move through the nostrils; 27

The sage with senses, mind,
and discernment controlled,
whose highest goal
is liberation,
From whom desire, fear,
and anger have departed—
one who is always so,
that one indeed is liberated. 28

As the beloved recipient
of sacrifices and austerities,
as the exalted supreme
Lord of all the worlds,
As the innermost heart
of all beings—
thus knowing me
one attains peace.[6] 29

6 Innermost heart: Translates *suhṛdam,* so as to provide a more literal and theological meaning of the word, which contains two parts, *su-* (innermost) and *hṛd* (heart). The word is most often translated as "friend," and perhaps could receive a protracted but more dedicated translation as "most kind-hearted [friend]." It is interesting to note that the BG uses another word for friend, *bandhu,* in verses 5, 6, and 9 in the following chapter (also, see its use in BG 1.27). My etymological translation expresses how Krishna is a friend to beings, the closest companion of all creatures: he is intimately present in the hearts of all living beings as "the innermost heart"—the supreme Self within the self. This is one of the most important manifestations of divinity described in the BG.

6

The Way of Meditation

The Beloved Lord said:

One who, without depending
on the fruits of action,
enacts that action which
is a prescribed act—
That person is
a renouncer and a yogi,
not one who makes no sacred fire
nor one who performs no ritual acts. 1

What they call "renunciation,"
know that as yoga,
O Son of Pāndu;
For without having
renounced selfish motive,
no one becomes a yogi. 2

For the sage who desires
to ascend to yoga,
action is said
to be the means.
Only for that one who
has ascended to yoga
is calmness said
to be the means. 3

When one is not attached
to the objects of the senses
nor to actions,
Renouncing
all selfish motives,
then one is said
to have ascended to yoga. 4

One should raise
the self by the self;
one should not
degrade the self.
Indeed, the self alone
is the self's friend;
the self alone
is the self's enemy.[1] 5

The self is the friend
of that self
by whose self
the very self is conquered.
But for one who is not
truly one's self—
in enmity, that very self
would remain like an enemy.[2] 6

---

1 Self: The self that either ascends, that becomes elevated, or the self that becomes lost in the temporary world; the self that turns toward or away from the true nature of the self. The usage here highlights the free will of the self to ascend to yoga or to "degrade" to selfishness, indicating the dual nature of the self, comprised of a higher and lower self. The higher self can also be taken as the supreme Self or can include the supreme Self.

2 One who is not truly one's self: Translates *anātman,* one who has lost oneself; as commentators state, losing oneself to extensions of the self, such as things of the world and relatives.

Enemy: The enemy here is found in the self and not so much on the battlefield.

For one whose self is conquered,
who is peaceful—
that one is fully absorbed
in the higher self
While in cold and heat,
happiness and suffering,
likewise, honor and dishonor.[3] 7

One whose self is
content in knowledge
and in realized knowledge,
who is focused on the highest
with senses conquered—
That one,
"absorbed in yoga,"
is said to be a yogi
for whom earth, stones,
and gold are the same. 8

While among intimates, friends,
enemies, the disinterested,
mediators, the hateful,
and family members;
Even among saintly
and troubled persons—
one whose discernment
remains the same is preeminent. 9

---

3 Fully absorbed in the higher self: Translates *paramātmā,* meaning "wholly absorbed (*parama-*) in the self (*-ātmā*)." The word can mean "the higher self" or "the supreme Self," the latter referring to the divinity dwelling within the individual self.

The yogi should absorb
the self constantly in yoga,
remaining in secrecy,
Alone, with thought
and self subdued,
without cravings and
free from all possessiveness. 10

In a clean place,
one should establish
for oneself a firm seat,
Neither too high nor too low,
made of kusha grass, then
covered with a deerskin and cloth.[4] 11

There, having the mind actively
focused upon a single point,
with thought and
sense activity controlled,
Sitting on a seat,
one should practice yoga
for purification of the self. 12

With an aligned body,
head, and neck—
keeping these steady,
without movement;
Focusing the vision toward
the tip of one's nose
without looking about
in any direction; 13

---

4 Kusha grass: A type of grass that is considered sacred, utilized in religious ceremonies.

With the self quieted,
with fear dissipated,
established in
a vow of chastity;
Controlling the mind
with thought
focused upon me—
one should be seated
while absorbed in yoga,
holding me as the highest. 14

Thus always absorbing
one's self in yoga,
the yogi, whose
mind is subdued,
Achieves peace
that culminates in
the highest state of Nirvāna,
which rests in me.[5] 15

However, for one who
eats too much
there is no yoga,
nor for one who
does not eat at all,
Nor for one who
sleeps too much,
nor for one who
is ever awake, O Arjuna. 16

---

5 This instance of Nirvāna is the last time it appears, after first appearing in BG 2.72 and then in BG 5.24–26. Note that here Nirvāna is associated with Krishna, in its highest form.

For one who is thus absorbed
in yoga while eating
and in recreation,
who is absorbed
in the ways of yoga
while performing actions,
And who is absorbed in yoga
while sleeping
and in wakefulness—
for such a person,
yoga becomes
the destroyer of suffering. 17

When, with thought
fully subdued,
one abides
in the self alone,
Without longings
for any selfish desires,
then that one is said to be
"absorbed in yoga." 18

As a lamp standing
in a windless place
does not flicker,
the analogy is recalled
Of the yogi
with subdued thought,
who is absorbed
in practicing the yoga
of the self. 19

That place where
thought comes to rest,
held steady by
the practice of yoga;
And where,
seeing the Self
by the very self,
one becomes satisfied
within the self; 20

That boundless happiness
beyond the senses,
which is grasped
through discernment;
That place where
one knows this,
indeed, is established in it
and does not swerve from the truth; 21

And which having obtained,
one is mindful that
no other gain
is greater than this;
Situated in which
one is not shaken
even by heavy suffering— 22

Let this be understood
as the disjunction
from one's conjunction
with suffering—
this is called yoga.
One is to be absorbed
in yoga with determination,
such yoga being without
discouraging thought.[6] 23

Relinquishing,
without exception,
all desires that arise
from selfish intentions;
Completely controlling
the collective senses
with the mind alone; 24

Little by little,
one should become
quieted by discernment
that is firmly held.
Actively establishing
the mind in the self,
one should not
think of anything else. 25

6 Disjunction: Translates *viyoga,* which can also mean "disunion."
Conjunction: Translates *saṁyoga,* which also means "communion," "perfect union," or "complete union."

Wherever
  the flickering
  unsteady mind strays,
Pulling it back
  from here and there,
  one should bring it
  under control
  within the very self. 26

For such a yogi,
  whose mind is peaceful,
  ultimate happiness
  is attained.
One whose
  passion is calmed,
  who is without impurity,
  becomes united with Brahman. 27

Thus, with the self
  always absorbed in yoga,
  the yogi who is completely
  free from impurity,
Happily enjoys,
  due to contact
  with Brahman,
  boundless happiness. 28

One who sees the Self
present in all beings
and all beings present
within the Self—
Such a person,
whose self
is absorbed in yoga,
sees the same everywhere. 29

One who sees me everywhere
and sees all things in me,
To such a person I am never lost
nor is such a person ever lost to me. 30

One who,
abiding in oneness,
offers love to me
as the One who abides
in all beings,
In whatever way one
appears to be living—
that one is a yogi
who lives in me. 31

One who sees,
by comparison to one's self,
the same in all [beings],
O Arjuna,
Whether it be happiness
or suffering—
that yogi is considered
to be the highest.[7] 32

Arjuna said:

This yoga,
which has been described
as a state of sameness,
O Madhusūdana—
I do not see the permanent
establishment of this,
due to unsteadiness. 33

For the mind
is unsteady, O Krishna,
impetuous, powerful,
and unyielding.
I believe that
controlling it
is as difficult as
controlling the wind. 34

7 The yogi is one who exercises a high degree of sympathy, experiencing others' selfhood in comparison to one's own. If one sees one's own higher self in happiness and suffering, then one can see that same higher self in others.

The Beloved Lord said:

Without doubt,
O Mighty-Armed,
the mind is unsteady
and difficult to control.
But with practice,
O Kaunteya,
and with dispassion,
it can be controlled. 35

"For one whose self
is not striving fully,
yoga is difficult
to achieve"—
this is my opinion.
But for one whose
self is controlled,
with striving it is
possible to achieve
by the proper approach. 36

Arjuna said:

One who does not strive
yet possesses faith,
whose mind has
deviated from yoga
Without achieving
full perfection in yoga—
to what destiny does
that one go, O Krishna? 37

Having fallen from both,
does that one not perish
like a dissipated cloud,
Having no foundation,
O Mighty-Armed,
bewildered on
the path of Brahman? 38

This doubt of mine,
O Krishna,
you are able
to dissipate fully.
Other than you,
truly there is no
forthcoming dissipator
of this doubt. 39

The Beloved Lord said:

O Pārtha, indeed,
neither in this world
nor in the next
is the destruction of such
a person to be found.
For no one who acts
in virtuous ways
ever goes to
an unfortunate
destiny, my dear friend. 40

Reaching the worlds of
those who have performed
virtuous acts, dwelling
there for countless years,
Then into the home
of those who are pure,
who are prosperous—
one who has fallen
from yoga is born again. 41

Or one is born into
a family of true yogis
endowed with wisdom.
That is even more difficult
to attain in the world,
a birth such as this. 42

There, one attains
a full connection with
that discernment from
the previous body,
And from there
one strives again
for complete perfection,
O Son of Kuru. 43

By that same previous practice,
one is indeed carried forward
even without one's effort.
Even one who only
desires to know of yoga
transcends the sound of Brahman.[8] 44

However, due to striving
with great effort,
completely cleansed
of all impurities,
The yogi,
fully perfected
after many births,
then goes to
the supreme destination. 45

8 The sound of Brahman: Translates *śabda-brahman,* the Vedas, referring to the sacrificial rituals of the Vedas, for achieving everything the temporary world has to offer. This phrase implies the recitation of mantras in the Vedic sacrifice, an attempt to achieve one's self-interest through ritualistic actions; the Vedas as they are associated with the three essential qualities of nature, as expressed in BG 2.45.

The yogi is superior to ascetics
and considered superior
even to those who
cultivate knowledge;
And the yogi
is superior to those
who perform sacred acts—
therefore be a yogi, O Arjuna![9] 46

Even among all yogis,
one whose inner self
has come to me,
Who is full of faith,
who offers love to me—
that one is considered by me
to be the most deeply
absorbed in yoga. 47

---

9 Ascetics: Translates *tapasvī,* "one who performs *tapas* or rigorous austerity."

Those who cultivate knowledge: Translates the plural of *jñāni*.

Those who perform sacred acts: Translates *karmī*.

7

The Way of Realized Knowledge

The Beloved Lord said:

With mind deeply attached to me,
O Pārtha, practicing yoga
with dependence on me,
You shall know me
completely,
beyond all doubt—
hear about how this is so. 1

I shall explain this knowledge
to you, along with
realized knowledge,
with nothing left unsaid;
Knowing which,
nothing further
in this world
is left to be known. 2

Among thousands
of human beings,
perhaps one may
strive for perfection.
Even among those
who strive for
and achieve perfection,
perhaps one may truly know me. 3

"Earth, water, fire,
air, space, mind,
the faculty of
discernment,
And indeed the notion
of 'I am acting'"—
this is my
primordial nature,
which is divided eightfold.[1] 4

This is not the higher [nature],
for there is another
nature of mine—
know it as higher.
It consists of living beings,
O Mighty-Armed,
by whom this universe
becomes animated. 5

This is the cosmic womb
for beings, for all of them—
try to understand this.
I am, of the entire universe,
the coming forth
into being as well as
the going forth into
cosmic absorption.[2] 6

---

1 Faculty of discernment: Translates *buddhi*. Before this, *buddhi* has been presented as an attribute of self, so I have translated as "discernment." As an element of nature, however, *buddhi* is translated as "faculty of discernment."

2 Cosmic womb: Translates the plural of *yoni,* literally "womb." Here, the word is a neuter plural form of what is almost always a feminine word, *yonī*. Its neuter gender indicates the cosmic status of this womb. This cosmic sense of the word as source is found in BG 14.3 and 14.4, in relation to the *mahatattva*.

The coming forth into being: Translates *prabhava,* often translated as "source" or "origin." My translation here attempts to express the rich etymological sense of the word, which conveys *purāṇic* cosmology: *pra-* ("forth") and *–bhava* ("the coming . . . into being"). See other instances of the word in BG 9.18, 10.2, 10.8, and 18.41.

The going forth into cosmic absorption: Translates *pralaya,* often given the general and somewhat misleading meaning of "dissolution." In puranic cosmology, the universe is not dissolved; it is absorbed into a dormant cosmic state until it comes forth into being (*prabhava*) once again.

There is nothing else
superior to me,
O Conqueror of Wealth.
On me all this
[universe] is strung
like pearls on a thread. 7

I am the taste in water,
O Kaunteya;
I am the radiance
of the moon and the sun,
The sacred utterance
in all the Vedas,
the sound in space,
the prowess in men.[3] 8

The pure fragrance in earth
and the brilliance
in fire am I.
The life in all beings
and the austerity
in austere persons am I. 9

As the seed of all beings,
know me to be
the eternal,
O Pārtha.
Among the discerning,
I am discernment;
of the splendid,
I am splendor. 10

3 Sacred utterance: Translates *praṇavaḥ*, and refers to the sacred syllable OM.

And among the powerful,
I am power devoid
of desire and passion.
In beings, I am desire
that does not
conflict with dharma,
O Best of the Bharatas. 11

And those very states
of being that are
of the nature of
sattva, rajas, and *tamas,*
Know that they
are from me alone,
yet I am not in them—
they are in me. 12

By these three states of being,
composed of
the three 'qualities',
this entire world,
Bewildered,
does not recognize me—
I am beyond these
as the everpresent. 13

For that which consists
of the 'qualities'
is my illusive power, Māyā,
so difficult to cross beyond.
Only those who
offer themselves to me
cross over this
illusive power of Māyā. 14

Maleficent persons are
those who are bewildered,
those who do not
offer themselves to me,
the lowest of humankind,
Those whose knowledge
has been stolen by
the illusive power of Māyā,
and those who have taken shelter
of an ungodly existence. 15

Of beneficent persons,
four types offer
their love to me,
O Arjuna:
One who is distressed,
one desiring knowledge,
one seeking personal gain,
and one possessing knowledge,
O Best of the Bharatas. 16

Among these,
the person of knowledge,
who is constantly absorbed
in yoga that is solely
an offering of love,
is exceptional.
For I am so dearly loved
by the person of knowledge,
and that person
is dearly loved by me.[4] 17

4 Offering of love: Translates *bhakti,* a word that appears fourteen times in the BG. This is the first instance in which this noun appears. Its verbal form, *bhakta,* "offered love," first appears in BG 4.3.

Certainly all of these are exalted,
but one who has knowledge
is my very self;
this is my opinion.
For one whose self
is absorbed in yoga
abides only in me,
the incomparable goal. 18

At the end of many births,
one who has knowledge
offers oneself to me, realizing,
"Vāsudeva is everything!"—
such an exalted self
is very rarely found.[5] 19

Persons whose knowledge
has been carried away
by desires for this or that
offer themselves
to different deities.
Following
this or that rule,
they are ruled
by their own worldly nature.[6] 20

---

5 Vāsudeva: A name of Krishna. The name means "the son of Vasudeva." The word *vāsu* means "the Soul of the universe," and *deva* means "divinity" or "sport" or "play." Thus this name for Krishna can mean "the divine play of the Soul of the universe." It also means "completely pure existence," and is an abbreviation for a person who is beyond primordial nature (*prakṛti*) and the primary 'qualities' of nature (*guṇas*) arising from it.

"Vāsudeva is everything!": Krishna explains here that it is a very rare soul who can exclaim how the divinity is wonderfully omnipresent. See BG 11.40, where Arjuna addresses Krishna as "Everything" and expresses how Krishna is "everything" and pervades "everything."

6 Different deities: Translates *anya-devatāḥ*. The word *sarvam* ("everything") in the previous verse contrasts with the word *anya* ("different") in this verse.

Whoever, with faith,
has offered love
to whatever form that
person desires to worship—
Upon every such person,
I bestow this
immovable faith. 21

Such a person,
absorbed in
yoga with faith,
longs to worship that [form]
And obtains one's
desires from that,
though they are
bestowed by me alone. 22

But the fruit
that comes to those
of little intelligence
is temporary.
Those who sacrifice
to the divinities
go to the divinities;
those who offer
their love to me,
surely they come to me. 23

The undiscerning
consider me to be
an unmanifest existence
that has become
visibly manifest,
Not knowing
my highest being,
which is everpresent
and incomparable.[7] 24

I am not revealed to everyone,
being concealed by
the divine power of yoga,
Yoga-Māyā.
This bewildered world
does not recognize me
as the unborn and everpresent.[8] 25

I know those beings
who have passed on,
those who are living,
O Arjuna,
And those who
have yet to come—
but none of them know me. 26

---

7 Unmanifest existence: Translates *avyaktam,* which carries the sense of "indistinct and formless," that is, the impersonal manifestation of the divine.

Visibly manifest: Translates *vyaktim,* which carries the sense of "distinct form and personality"; that is, "manifest being" refers to the personal being of the divinity.

Highest being: Translates *paraṁ bhāvam,* which could be translated as Krishna's "supreme being" or "supreme heart."

8 Yoga-Māyā: Essentially the word Māyā presented in earlier verses, translated here as "the divine power of yoga." This divine power (Māyā) uses "yoga" either to "connect" souls with the bewildering energy of this world to conceal such souls from the divinity, or to "connect" souls with the blissful energy of Krishna to reveal the divinity to such souls.

With the rising up
of desire and hatred,
with the bewilderment
of duality, O Bhārata,
All beings go to a state
of complete bewilderment
at the time of their birth,
O Scorcher of the Enemy. 27

Now those whose misdeeds
have come to an end,
whose actions are virtuous—
Such persons, freed from
the bewilderment of duality,
offer their love to me
with intense devotion.[9] 28

Striving for release
from aging and death,
those who have
taken shelter of me
Know Brahman completely
and action entirely,
and the 'principle of self'.[10] 29

---

9 Misdeeds: Translates *pāpam.*
Virtuous: Translates *punyam.*
Intense devotion: Translates *dṛdha-vratāḥ.*

10 The 'principle of self': Translates *adhyātmā,* introduced again in BG 8.1. The principles of 'becoming', 'divinity', and 'sacrifice' are to follow. As principles, these terms refer to all things pertaining to these essential subject matters for understanding reality.

Those who know me as
the 'principle of becoming',
along with the 'principle of divinity'
and the 'principle of sacrifice',
Even at the time of passing on—
they know me,
for their thought
is absorbed in yoga.[11] 30

11 The 'principle of becoming': Translates the term *adhibhūta*.

The 'principle of divinity': Translates the term *adhidaiva*. The word *daiva* means "divine" and can also mean "destiny" or "fate," and most relevantly, carries the sense of the aggregate of the various divine beings within the cosmic government that comprise the ultimate Person, the *puruṣa*. The word is translated here in the most general sense as "divinity," but it pertains to the multiple cosmic divinities. A slight variation of this term appears as *adhidaivatā* in BG 8.4.

The 'principle of sacrifice': Translates the term *adhiyajña*.

8

The Transcendent Brahman

Arjuna said:

What is that Brahman?
What is the 'principle of self'?
What is action,
O Ultimate Person?
And the 'principle of becoming',
what is said about it?
The 'principle of divinity',
what is it declared to be? 1

What is the 'principle of sacrifice',
and how is it present
here within this body,
O Madhusūdana?
And how, at the time
of passing on,
are you to be known by
those who are self-disciplined? 2

The Beloved Lord said:

Brahman is
the supreme indestructible;
the 'principle of self'
is described as one's
state of intrinsic being.
The activity of beings
that brings about their
emerging states of being
is the creative force
known as action.[1] 3

The 'principle of becoming'
is the transitory state of being,
and the 'principle of divinity'
is the Person.
Indeed, I am
the 'principle of sacrifice'
here in the body,
O Best of the Embodied.[2] 4

And at the time of one's end,
remembering me alone
while giving up the body—
One who thus goes forth,
goes to my state of being;
about this there is no doubt. 5

---

1 Emerging states of being: Translates the phrase *bhāvodbhava,* referring here to the successive life-states occurring in reincarnation.

Creative force: Translates *visarga,* referring to the epiphenomenal creative or active process, the actions that create things within this creation.

2 The Person: Translates *puruṣa,* referring to the *virāṭ puruṣa* found in the Vedas, the macrocosmic Person.

Furthermore,
whatever state of being
one remembers upon
giving up the body
at the end [of life],
To that very state
one always goes,
O Kaunteya,
being conditioned
by that state of being. 6

Therefore, at all times
remember me
and fight!
With your mind and
discernment offered to me,
certainly you shall come to me—
of this there is no doubt. 7

By absorption in yoga
through the practice of yoga,
with thought not wandering
to anything else,
One approaches
the supreme divine Person,
O Pārtha, continuously
focusing one's thought [on him]. 8

One should continuously
remember [him]
As the wise one,
the most ancient one,
the perpetual governor,
the one who is smaller
than the atom;
As the arranger
of everything,
whose form
is inconceivable;
As the one who is
luminous like the sun,
beyond all darkness. 9

At the time
of passing on,
with undisturbed mind,
Absorbed in yoga
by offering one's love
and by the very power of yoga;
Intently focusing
the vital life-breath
between the eyebrows—
One reaches that
supreme divine Person. 10

The imperishable, which
knowers of the Vedas describe,
Into which enter the ascetics
who are free from passion,
Desiring which those persons
lead a life of chastity—
That place I shall
briefly explain to you. 11

Controlling all
the [bodily] gates
and stopping the mind
from within the heart,
Placing the self's
vital life-breath at
the top of the head,
one is established
in yoga concentration.[3] 12

"OM"— thus sounding
Brahman as a single syllable,
continuously remembering me,
One who passes away,
relinquishing the body—
such a person passes on
to the supreme destination. 13

3 The [bodily] gates: Refers to the nine passages of the body spoken of in BG 5.13 as the "city of nine gates."

One whose thought
 is never on anything else,
 who remembers me
 continuously—
For that one, O Pārtha,
 I am easily attained,
 for the yogi who is
 constantly absorbed in yoga. 14

Once having come to me,
 they do not come
 to repeated birth,
 to that impermanent
 place of suffering;
For those whose selves
 are extraordinary
 have gone to
 the supreme perfection. 15

From the earth up to
 the realm of Brahmā,
 the worlds undergo
 repeated cycles, O Arjuna.
Having come to me,
 however, O Kaunteya,
 one does not find
 repeated birth.[4] 16

---

4 The realm: Translates *bhuvana,* the highest station of this universe.

Brahmā: The cosmic deity who presides over creation within the great cycle of creation and dissolution (the latter presided over by the deity Shiva) in the physical universe. Note that this name is different from Brahman, the ultimate reality, the supreme spirit.

Those who know of Brahmā's day,
having the duration of
a thousand ages,
And of his night,
ending after a thousand ages,
are persons who know
what is day and what is night. 17

All manifestations arise
from the unmanifest
with the coming of
the day [of Brahmā].
With the coming of
the night [of Brahmā],
they are absorbed,
then and there, in that
which is called the unmanifest. 18

This very same totality of beings,
repeatedly coming into being,
is reabsorbed helplessly
With the coming of the night,
O Pārtha;
it [again] comes forth
with the coming of the day. 19

Beyond this, however,
there is another,
unmanifest state of being
that is eternal,
Which, when all beings
perish, itself does
not ever perish. 20

The unmanifest is called
"the indestructible";
they declare it to be
the supreme destination,
Achieving which,
they do not return—
that is my supreme domain. 21

It is the supreme Person,
moreover, O Pārtha,
who is attainable
by offering love
to none other,
Within whom beings exist,
by whom all this [world]
is pervaded.[5] 22

Now, under what
circumstances do the yogis
who have passed away
Pass on to the non-repetition
and also the repetition of birth—
I shall speak of those circumstances,
O Best of the Bharatas. 23

5 It is the supreme Person: Here Krishna speaks about his cosmic manifestation in the third person. This objectification of his cosmic personal Self, who is approachable by offering love, implies that he who stands before Arjuna is the highest and most intimate Self with whom souls can relate.

Fire, light, day,
the waxing moon,
the six-month northern
course of the sun—
Those who have passed on
under these circumstances,
such persons, who are
knowers of Brahman,
go to Brahman.[6] 24

Smoke, night, also
the waning moon,
the six-month southern
course of the sun—
Under these circumstances,
after attaining
the light of the moon,
the yogi returns. 25

For these two passages
from the world,
light and dark, are
thought to be perpetual.
By one, the yogi passes on
with no return;
by the other,
the yogi again returns. 26

6 These elements—fire, light, day, etc. —in verses 24 and 25 also refer to the guidance of specific divinities on the two paths out of this world. These are the methods of liberation and departure from life found in the Chāndogya Upanishad 4.5, Bṛhadāraṇyaka Upanishad 5.10, and Muṇḍaka Upanishad 2.11. However, Krishna ultimately expresses that offering one's heart transcends these processes, positive or negative. In bhakti, all the technicalities of these paths are unnecessary and even a higher liberation can be achieved in the practice of loving devotion. In this verse and the following, Krishna is acknowledging these various elements for passing on that correspond to the internal dimensions of the self in its passage beyond this life.

Knowing these two paths,
O Pārtha, the yogi is
not bewildered in any way.
Therefore, at all times,
be absorbed in yoga
by means of yoga, O Arjuna. 27

In the Vedas, in sacrifices,
in austerities, and also
In charitable gifts,
whatever meritorious
fruit is ordained—
One who goes beyond that,
having understood all this,
Such a yogi goes
on to the supreme
and incomparable realm. 28

9

The King of Secrets

The Beloved Lord said:

Now I shall reveal to you
this greatest secret,
for you are without envy.
It is knowledge together
with realized knowledge,
knowing which you shall
be free from inauspiciousness. 1

This is the king of knowledge,
the king of secrets,
the ultimate means
of purification.
Understood by
direct perception,
in harmony with dharma,
it is joyful to perform
and everlasting.[1] 2

Those persons who have
no faith in this dharma,
O Destroyer of the Enemy,
Not achieving me,
again return to the path
of recurring death. 3

---

1 "The king of knowledge" and "the king of secrets" are each taken as a special type of *karmadharya* compound, known as *puruṣavyāgra*. The first of these two phrases can thus be understood as meaning, "There is a knowledge that should rule souls just as a king rules his people."

By me this entire universe
is pervaded, by my
unmanifest form.
All beings rest on me
and I do not
rest upon them. 4

And [yet] beings
do not rest on me—
behold my divine
power of yoga!
Supporting beings
and not resting on beings,
my Self causes beings to be. 5

As the mighty wind
moving everywhere
rests on space,
So all beings
rest on me—
understand this! 6

All beings, O Kaunteya,
enter my
primordial nature
At the end of a life-cycle
of the universe;
again, I send them forth
at the beginning of
[another] cycle.[2] 7

2 A life-cycle of the universe: translates the term *kalpa,* which equals 311 trillion years. A *kalpa* is divided into four sub-periods called *yugas,* during each of which a manifestation of the Divinity descends to the earth.

Being firmly supported by
my own primordial nature,
I send forth again and again
This entire aggregate of beings,
which is powerless under
the power of primordial nature. 8

And these actions
do not bind me,
O Conqueror of Wealth.
Remaining aloof,
I am not attached
to these actions. 9

With my supervision,
primordial nature
brings forth the moving
and the nonmoving.
By this causal force,
O Kaunteya,
the universe
revolves in cycles.[3] 10

The bewildered discount me
for having assumed
the limited form
of a human,
Not knowing
the supreme nature
of my Lordship
over all that exists.[4] 11

---

3 Supervision: Translates *adhyakṣa,* which can also connote "the divine glance," identified as the "causal force." This translation can be justified by the way the word appears in Aitareya Upanishad 1.1.1 and Bṛhadāraṇyaka Upanishad 1.2.5.

4 Limited form: Translates *tanum,* which indicates an insignificant or small form. The sense here is that Krishna possesses an eternal humanlike form that he does not assume at any point in time.

Those who are of vain hopes,
of vain actions,
of vain knowledge;
who are thoughtless,
Demonic, and godless—
they indeed are enslaved
by the bewildering
primordial nature. 12

However, those whose selves
are extraordinary,
O Pārtha, who abide
in the divine nature,
Offer love to me
with their minds
focused on none other,
knowing me as
the everpresent
origin of beings.[5] 13

Constantly praising me
and striving with
intense devotion,
And honoring me
with an offering of love,
always absorbed in yoga,
they worship me. 14

---

5 Divine nature: Translates *daivīṁ prakṛtim*. Both words of this phrase are in the feminine gender, indicating that the divine realm is of a feminine nature, as is *prakṛti* ("primordial nature") and Māyā ("divine illusive power").

And there are also others
who, sacrificing
with the sacrifice
of knowledge,
worship me
In my oneness,
in my separateness,
and in my many forms
facing everywhere. 15

I am the ritual,
I am the sacrifice,
I am the oblation,
I am the healing herb;
I am the sacred mantra,
I am indeed
the clarified butter,
I am the fire, and
I am the offering. 16

I am the father of this universe,
the mother, the creator,
the grandfather;
That which is to be known,
the means of purification,
the sacred sound OM,
and indeed the Rig,
Sāma, and Yajur [Vedas].[6] 17

---

6 Rig, Sāma, and Yajur: These are the major sections of the Vedic literature. The Rig Veda presents hymns of praise and philosophical reflection; the Sāma Veda focuses primarily on the methods of recitation of the verses in the Rig Veda; and the Yajur Veda emphasizes Vedic ritual performance and practice.

I am the goal, the sustainer,
the Lord, the witness,
the dwelling, the shelter,
the innermost heart;
The coming forth into being,
the going forth into
cosmic absorption;
the continuance of existence,
the cosmic receptacle,
and the everpresent seed. 18

I radiate warmth;
I withhold and
send forth the rain.
I am mortality
and indeed immortality,
being and nonbeing,
O Arjuna. 19

Those who know the three Vedas,
the soma drinkers purified of vice
Who worship me with sacrifices,
seek passage
to the celestial realm.
Approaching the pious world
of the lord of celestials,
Such persons partake
of the divine pleasures
of divinities, in the divine realm.[7] 20

---

7 Soma: One of the primary substances utilized as a libation in the Vedic sacrifice. It is a very intoxicating drink derived from a specific plant, still unknown.

Celestial realm: In Hindu cosmology, this is a heavenly realm of celestial beings. The highest abode is beyond even this realm and is the ultimate, divine realm of Krishna.

Those persons,
having enjoyed
that vast celestial world,
Their piety exhausted,
then [again] enter
the mortal world.
Thus following
the dharma of
the three [Vedas],
Desiring certain
objects of desire,
they achieve a state of
going and coming back.[8] 21

Persons who, meditating
on none other,
worship me completely—
For them, who are always
fully absorbed in yoga,
I bring prosperity and security. 22

Even those who
have offered their love
to different deities,
who, filled with faith,
perform sacrifice—
Even they perform
sacrifice for me alone,
O Kaunteya,
though not according
to injunction. 23

8 A state of going and coming back: Expresses the futility of this process: one may go to a higher world but must return to this one, and thus no progress is actually made.

For I am the beloved recipient
and indeed the Lord
of all sacrifices.
But they do not
recognize me in truth;
therefore they fall
[from the celestial realm]. 24

Those who serve divinities
go to the divinities;
those who serve ancestors
go to the ancestors;
Those who sacrifice for spirits
go to the spirits;
those who sacrifice for me
surely come to me. 25

One who, with love,
makes an offering to me
of a leaf, a flower,
fruit, or water—
Such an offering,
presented with love,
I accept from one
whose self is devoted. 26

Whatever you do,
whatever you eat,
whatever you sacrifice,
whatever you bestow,
Whatever austerity
you undertake—
that, enact as
an offering unto me. 27

Thus you shall be freed
from the bondage of action,
which produces
good and bad fruits.
With the self absorbed
in the yoga of renunciation,
completely liberated,
you shall come to me. 28

I am the same
toward all beings;
no one is either hated
or dearly loved by me.
Yet those who,
with an offering of love,
offer their love to me—
they are in me
and I am also in them. 29

Even if one has
behaved very badly,
if one offers one's love
to none other but me,
Indeed, one should be
considered saintly,
for such a person
is rightly absolved. 30

One quickly becomes
a self who embraces dharma
and attains eternal peace;
O Kaunteya,
know this for certain—
one who offers love to me
is never lost. 31

For those taking shelter
 of me, O Pārtha,
 whether they come
 from troubled wombs,
Or whether they be
 women, tradespeople,
 or skilled workers—
 even they reach
 the supreme goal.[9] 32

How much more, then,
 for the virtuous Brahmins,
 as well as the saintly kings
 who have offered their love?
Having come to
 this impermanent
 unhappy world,
 offer your love to me. 33

Be mindful of me
 with love offered to me;
 sacrificing for me,
 act out of reverence for me.
Surely you shall
 come to me,
 thus having absorbed
 your self in yoga with
 me as the supreme goal.[10] 34

---

9 Troubled wombs: Translates *pāpa-yoni.*

10 Be mindful of me . . . come to me: The first half and part of the third quarter of this verse are repeated in BG 18.65.

10

The Sublime Presence of Divinity

The Beloved Lord said:

Once again, indeed,
O Mighty-Armed,
hear my supreme word,
Which I shall speak to you
who are so dearly loved,
with a desire for
your well-being. 1

Neither the multitude
of celestial beings
nor the exalted seers
understand how I have
come forth into being,
For I am the beginning
of the divinities
and exalted seers—
every one of them. 2

One who understands me
as unborn, beginningless,
and as the exalted supreme
Lord of the universe—
That person,
among mortals,
is unbewildered and
free from all misfortune. 3

Discernment, knowledge,
freedom from illusion,
forbearance, truth,
restraint, calmness;
Happiness, suffering,
coming into being
and cessation of being,
fear and indeed fearlessness; 4

Nonviolence, sameness,
contentment, austerity,
charity, fame, and infamy—
In their various forms,
these conditions of beings
arise from me alone. 5

The seven exalted seers,
the four of previous times,
and also the Manus,
Having come into being from me,
are generated from my mind—
those from whom these progeny
of the world have come.[1] 6

This abounding power
and yoga of mine,
one who knows this in truth—
That one is absorbed in yoga
through unwavering yoga practice;
of this there is no doubt. 7

---

1 The seven exalted seers: A group of unnamed sages first mentioned in the Vedas.

The four of previous times: The four Kumāras, whose names are Sanatkumāra, Sananda, Sanaka, and Sanātana.

The Manus: *Manu* means "man," here referring to the primary progenitors of humankind.

"I am, of everything,
the coming forth into being;
from me everything
is set forth into motion."
Mindful [of these words],
they offer their love to me,
the enlightened ones,
being fully immersed
in feelings of love.[2] 8

With their thought on me,
with their life-breath
offered to me,
enlightening one another
And conversing about me
continuously,
they are satiated and
they feel rapturous love.[3] 9

For them, who are constantly
absorbed in yoga,
who offer loving service
with natural affection,
I offer that yoga
of discernment
by which they
come close to me. 10

---

2 The coming forth into being: Translates *prabhavaḥ,* as it is used in a cosmological context. The word is often translated as "source" or "origin."

Is set forth into motion: Translates the verb *pravartate,* often translated as "emanates."

Being . . . feelings of love: Translates *bhāva*.

3 Life-breath: Translates *prāṇa,* a Sanskrit word adopted by the English language.

For them especially,
out of compassion,
dwelling as the Self
within their hearts,
I dispel the darkness
that arises from
the absence of knowledge
with the radiant
lamp of knowledge. 11

Arjuna said:

You are the supreme Brahman,
the supreme dwelling place,
the supreme means of purification;
The eternal divine Person,
the original Divinity,
the unborn, all-pervading one. 12

All the seers describe you,
including the divine seer Nārada;
Also, Asita Devala, Vyāsa,
and now, you yourself tell me.[4] 13

All this that you tell me
I consider to be true,
O Keshava.
Indeed, O Beloved Lord,
neither the divinities
nor the demons
know your personality. 14

---

4 Nārada: The wandering mendicant who carries and plays a long stringed instrument (similar to the Indian sitar), who becomes a catalyst for various divine dramas. His name appears again in BG 10.26 below. The legendary author of the Bhakti Sūtra.

Asita Devala: The compiler of divine hymns, some of which are found in the Rig Veda.

Vyāsa: The great sage who is the compiler of the Vedas and other sacred literature, including the Mahābhārata and the Bhagavad Gītā.

Only you personally
know your Self
by your Self,
O Ultimate Person,
O Source of Beings,
O Lord of Beings,
O Divinity of Divinities,
O Master of the Universe! 15

You are able to fully
describe the divine,
for boundless are
the powers of your Self
By which,
pervading these worlds
with such boundless powers,
you are situated. 16

How may I know you,
O Yogi, while constantly
meditating upon you?
And in what various states
of being am I to meditate
upon you, O Beloved Lord? 17

Elaborating upon the yoga
and abounding power
of your Self,
O Janārdana,
Describe further,
as there is no satiation
for me while hearing
of the immortal. 18

The Beloved Lord said:

Listen! I shall tell you of
the abounding
powers of my Self
That are most prominent,
O Best of the Kurus,
for there is no end
to their extent. 19

I am the Self,
O Gudākesha,
abiding in the hearts
of all beings.
I am also the beginning
and the middle of beings,
as well as their end.[5] 20

Among the Ādityas,
I am Vishnu;
of luminaries,
I am the radiant sun.
Among the Maruts,
I am Marīchi;
of heavenly bodies,
I am the moon.[6] 21

---

5 All beings: Translates the phrase *sarva-bhūta*. The phrase also can be taken as "All Being," an epithet for the first created being, Brahmā, the deity charged with constructing the cosmos.

6 The Ādityas: The twelve celestial beings who preside over the sun.

The Maruts: The lords presiding over the wind.

Of the Vedas,
  I am the Sāma;
  among divinities,
  I am Vāsava.
Of the senses,
  I am the mind;
  and of beings,
  I am consciousness.[7] 22

And among the Rudras,
  I am Shankara [Shiva];
  among Yakshas and Rakshasas,
  I am Kuvera, lord of wealth.
Among the Vasus,
  I am fire;
  and of lofty mountains,
  I am Meru.[8] 23

And among priests,
  know me to be
  the principal one,
  Brihaspati, O Pārtha.
Among military commanders,
  I am Skanda;
  of bodies of water,
  I am the ocean.[9] 24

---

7 Sāma: The section of the Vedas that is sung.

Vāsava: The principal deity, whose name is Indra.

8 The Rudras: The eleven lords who are involved in cosmic destruction; also the celestial beings of roaring thunder.

Shankara: Known by the name of Shiva, the chief of the Rudras; the deity of cosmic dissolution and transformation.

Yakshas: Spirits.

Rakshasas: Horrific beings.

The Vasus: The eight atmospheric lords.

Meru: The golden mountain at the center of the cosmos.

9 Brihaspati: The principal priest of celestial beings.

Skanda: The lord of war, who is also the son of the deity, Shiva.

Among exalted seers,
I am Bhrigu;
of utterances,
I am the one sacred syllable.
Of sacrifices,
I am the sacrifice of
quietly repeated prayer;
of stationary things,
I am the Himalayas;[10] 25

Of all trees,
the sacred Ashwattha;
and among
divine seers, Nārada;
Among the Gandharvas,
Citraratha;
among perfected beings,
the sage Kapila.[11] 26

Of horses, know me
as Ucchaishravas,
who arose from the nectar;
Of princely elephants,
Airāvata;
and among humans,
the ruler who protects the people.[12] 27

---

10 Bhrigu: The mediator between the divinities.

One sacred syllable: This is the syllable OM.

Quietly repeated prayer: Translates *japa;* understood as softly repeated mantra or prayer.

11 The sacred Ashwattha: Often understood as the banyan or fig tree. The image of this tree is used metaphorically to explain the metaphysics of the BG in the beginning of Chapter 15.

Gandharvas: The celestial singers and musicians.

Kapila: There are two personalities with this name who are associated with the Sānkhya philosophical system: one is the founder of the philosophical school, and the other, here referred to by Krishna, is the divine descent of Vishnu presented in the Bhāgavata Purāṇa.

12 Ucchaishravas: This horse arises from the nectar created by the churning of the ocean, and is associated with Indra and the deity of the sun.

Airāvata: The elephant belonging to Indra.

The ruler who protects the people: Translates Narādhipa, the king.

Of weapons,
I am the thunderbolt;
among cows,
I am the one
that fulfills desires.
I am also the procreating force,
Kandarpa;
and of serpents,
I am Vāsuki.[13] 28

Of the Nāgas,
I am Ananta;
of great aquatics,
I am Varuna [their lord].
Among ancestors,
I am Aryaman;
and among subduers,
I am Death.[14] 29

And among the Daityas,
I am Prahlāda;
I am time of all that
moves forward in time.
Of animals,
I am the king of animals;
of winged creatures,
the son of Vinatā, Garuda.[15] 30

---

13 The one that fulfills desires: Translates *kāmadhuk,* the divine cow that grants all one's desires (*kāma*).

Kandarpa: The deity of love, sometimes thought of as India's Cupid.

Vāsuki: The king of serpents.

14 Nāgas: Celestial serpents.

Ananta: "The unlimited one." The serpent on whom the cosmic Vishnu lies to sustain the universe.

Varuna: The lord of the water.

Aryaman: The chief ancestor.

Death: The lord of death, known as Yāma.

15 Daityas: A clan of demons.

Prahlāda: The saintly son of a demon father.

The king of animals: The lion.

The son of Vinatā: Translates *vainateya,* who is Garuda, the divine bird carrier of Lord Vishnu.

Of things that purify,
I am the purifying wind;
among wielders of weapons,
I am Rāma.
Of fish,
I am the shark;
and of flowing waters,
I am the Ganges,
the daughter of Jahnu.[16] 31

Of creations,
I am the beginning,
the end, and indeed
the middle, O Arjuna.
Of knowledge,
I am knowledge of
the 'principle of self';
among those
professing theories,
I am the theorem. 32

16 Rāma: The manifestation of Vishnu known as Paraśurāma, meaning "the wielder of the ax."

The daughter of Jahnu: The sacred river Ganges, which flows from the toe of Vishnu.

Of letters,
  I am the letter A;
  and of compound words,
  the dual form.
Indeed, I am
  imperishable time;
  I am the world-creator,
  with faces in every direction.[17] 33

I am death, which
  takes away everything,
  and the rising into being
  of all that will be.
Of feminine attributes
  [and their presiding goddesses],
  I am fame, beauty, speech,
  remembrance, intelligence,
  constancy, and forbearance. 34

---

17 Compound words: Translates *sāmāsika,* referring to the grammatical construction in Sanskrit that involves the placing together and construal of two or more words to form a compound phrase.

Dual form: Translates *dvandva,* a certain type of compound word phrase in which each of the two members of the compound are given equal significance and are unified by their relationship. This grammatical construction resonates fundamental philosophical and theistic aspects of Vaishnava thought: embedded within this compound is the idea of "difference" between the two members as well as the "non-difference" of form, or the unity provided by the singularity of the compound itself.

The world-creator, with faces in every direction: The cosmic deity, Brahmā. However, it is Krishna who is the ultimate creator and designer of all the universes.

Also, of hymns,
I am the great hymn, Brihatsāma;
of poetic meters,
I am the Gāyatrī,
recited by saintly priests.
Of months,
I am Mārgashīrsha;
of seasons,
I am the season
that abounds in flowers.[18] 35

I am gambling
among cheaters;
I am splendor
of the splendid.
I am victory,
I am firm resolve,
I am courage
among the courageous. 36

Among the descendants of Vrishni,
I am Vāsudeva;
among the Pāndavas,
[you] the Conqueror of Wealth.
Also, among sages,
I am Vyāsa;
among poets,
the poet Ushanā.[19] 37

---

18 Brihatsāma: The "great hymn" for Indra found in the Sāma Veda.

Gāyatrī meter: A meter with eight syllables per quarter verse.

Mārgashīrsha: The span of time that corresponds to the months of November and December.

The season that abounds in flowers: Spring.

19 Vrishni: The dynasty in which Krishna appears.

Vāsudeva: A name for Krishna meaning "the son of Vasudeva." See BG 7.19. This name can also refer to Krishna's older brother, Balarāma.

Ushanā: A famous sage, frequently mentioned in the Vedas, who composed four hymns.

I am the taming rod
among those who tame;
I am moral conduct
among those who seek victory.
And indeed,
I am the silence of secrets;
I am knowledge
among those who have knowledge. 38

And I am also that which is
the seed of all beings,
O Arjuna.
There is nothing that
can exist without me—
no moving or nonmoving being. 39

There is no limit
to my boundless powers,
O Scorcher of the Enemy.
What has been described
by me is merely
an example of the extent
of my boundless power. 40

Whatever form of existence
possesses abounding power,
contains the beautiful,
or is well-endowed
with excellence—
Understand that
every such form
has become fully manifest
from but a part of my splendor. 41

But what is the necessity
of your knowing
so many things,
O Arjuna?
I support
this whole universe
continuously,
with one part [of myself]. 42

11

Vision of the Universal Form

Arjuna said:

Due to your grace upon me,
your supreme secret
known as the 'principle of self',
Which has been spoken
by you in these words,
has dispelled this
bewilderment of mine. 1

For the becoming and
the passing on of beings
has been heard by me
in great detail
From you,
O One with Lotus-like Eyes,
as well as [knowledge]
of your everpresent supreme Self. 2

Thus as you have described
this about your Self,
O Highest Supreme Lord,
I desire to see your
supremely powerful form,
O Ultimate Person. 3

If you think it is possible
for me to see you
in this way, O Lord,
O Supreme Lord of Yoga,
then reveal to me
your everpresent Self.[1] 4

The Beloved Lord said:

Behold my forms,
O Pārtha,
by the hundreds,
or by the thousands—
Divine, of various types,
and of various colors
and appearances. 5

Behold the Ādityas,
the Vasus, the Rudras,
the two Ashvins,
also the Maruts.
Many of these never
have been seen before—
behold these wonders,
O Bhārata.[2] 6

1 Supreme Lord of Yoga: Translates *yogeśvara*. This epithet appears in another instance within this chapter, and in two other instances in the final chapter. It consists of the words *yoga* and *īśvara* (the "Supreme Lord").

2 The Ādityas: Celestial beings related to the sun.

The Vasus: Celestial beings of fire and light.

The Rudras: Celestial beings of roaring thunder.

The two Ashvins: Celestial beings of soothing dawn.

The Maruts: Celestial beings of wind and lightning.

Before you, in one place,
behold now
the entire universe,
with every moving
and nonmoving being
Within my body,
O Gudākesha,
and whatever else
you desire to see. 7

But you are unable to see me
with only this, your own eyes.
I [therefore] give divine eyes to you—
behold my supremely powerful yoga! 8

Sanjaya said:

Thus having spoken,
O King, the exalted
Supreme Lord of Yoga, Hari,
Then revealed to Pārtha
his supremely powerful
majestic form: 9

Of numerous mouths and eyes,
of numerous extraordinary
appearances;
Of numerous divine ornaments,
of numerous upraised
divine weapons; 10

Wearing divine garlands
and garments, with divine
perfumes and ointments;
Consisting of all wonders—
the Divinity, endless,
facing in all directions. 11

If a thousand suns
were to have risen
in the sky at once,
Such brilliance as this
might resemble
the brilliance
of that supreme Self. 12

There, in one place,
the entire universe
was unlimitedly divided.
The Pāndava then
saw this in the body of
the Divinity of divinities. 13

Then struck with amazement,
the hairs of his limbs
standing on end,
the Conqueror of Wealth,
Bowing his head
to the Divinity,
with palms joined
in prayerful gesture, spoke. 14

Arjuna said:

I see the divinities
in your body, O Divinity—
All of this, and also various
assemblages of beings,
Lord Brahmā sitting
on the seat of the lotus,
As well as all the seers
and divine serpents. 15

With many arms, bellies,
   mouths, and eyes,
I see you everywhere
   in your unending form—
No end, nor middle,
   nor even beginning
   of yourself
Do I see, O All-Pervasive
   Supreme Lord,
   of all-pervading form. 16

Wearing a crown,
   bearing a club,
   and holding a disc,
A mass of light
   shining everywhere—
I see you, so difficult
   to perceive all at once,
With the brilliance of
   the sun and blazing fires,
   which is immeasurable! 17

You are the indestructible,
   the supreme object of knowledge.
You are the supreme
   resting place of all.
You are the everpresent
   protector of lasting dharma.
You are the eternal Person—
   so it is understood by me.[3] 18

---

3 Indestructible: Translates *akṣara,* which is the name of the sacred syllable OM, the sonic manifestation of the divinity.

Having no beginning,
middle, or end,
of unlimited prowess,
Of unlimited arms,
with the moon and sun
as your eyes—
I behold you, whose mouths
are of blazing fire,
Burning this entire universe
with your own splendor. 19

Indeed, that which is between
heaven and earth
Is pervaded by you alone
in all directions.
Seeing this wondrous
terrible form of yours,
The three worlds tremble,
O Mighty Self. 20

For over there, multitudes
of celestial beings
enter into you.
Some, daunted,
sing praises to you with
palms prayerfully joined.
Crying out "Glory!"
multitudes of great seers
and perfected beings
Praise you with abundant
prayerful hymns. 21

The Rudras, Ādityas,
Vasus, and Sādhyas;
The Vishva deities,
the two Ashvins, the Maruts,
and the forefathers;
The multitudes of Gandharvas,
Yakshas, Asuras,
and perfected beings—
All behold you
and are truly amazed.[4] 22

Your exalted form of
numerous mouths
and eyes,
O Mighty-Armed,
of numerous arms,
thighs, and feet,
Of numerous bellies,
with numerous
frightful teeth—
Seeing this, the worlds
are trembling,
so also am I. 23

Touching the blazing
sky of many colors,
With mouths opened wide
and expansive blazing eyes—
Truly having seen you,
my inner self trembles,
And I find neither stability
nor tranquility, O Vishnu. 24

---

4. Sādhyas: A class of celestial beings mentioned in Vedic literature.

The Vishva deities: Refers to at least ten minor deities, according to Purānic literature.

Asuras: Within the celestial realm, those "ungodly" beings who oppose the benevolent celestial beings and divinities.

And having seen your mouths
with frightful teeth,
Resembling the fires
of the end of cosmic time,
I know not any sense of direction
and I find no shelter—
Be merciful,
O Lord of Divinities,
dwelling place of the universe! 25

And [rushing] toward you,
over there, are all the sons
of Dhritarāshtra,
Indeed, along with multitudes
of protectors of the earth
Such as Bhīshma, Drona,
and even the son
of the charioteer—
Also along with our
own chief warriors.[5] 26

In haste they enter
your mouths,
Which are terrible
with frightful teeth.
Some, clinging
between your teeth,
Are vividly seen with
their heads crushed. 27

---

5 Bhīshma: The great Kaurava elder and leading warrior.

Drona: The teacher of warfare for both Arjuna and Duryodhana, who fights for the Kauravas.

The son of the charioteer: Karna.

As the rivers' many
currents of water
Rush forward
toward the sea alone,
So, over there,
those heroes
of the world of men
Enter into your
wildly flaming mouths. 28

As moths,
with great velocity,
Enter a blazing fire
unto their destruction,
Similarly,
the worlds also
Enter your mouths
with great velocity,
unto their destruction. 29

Devouring them
from every side,
you lick up
All the worlds with
your flaming mouths.
Filling the entire
universe with splendor,
Your fierce rays burn,
O Vishnu. 30

Tell me, who are you,
  of such terrifying form?
Respects unto you,
  O Best of Divinities—
  be merciful!
I wish to truly know you,
  the Original One,
For I do not fully
  understand what you have
  set forth into motion. 31

The Beloved Lord said:

Time I am,
  acting to destroy the worlds,
  advancing forward
To completely annihilate
  the worlds here,
  ever turning forward.
Even without you [acting],
  they shall all cease to be—
Those who are warriors
  arrayed on the opposing side. 32

Therefore you must rise up,
  aspire to glory;
Conquering your enemies,
  enjoy prosperous kingship!
By me these very men
  have already been slain—
Merely be the instrument,
  O Masterful Archer. 33

Drona and Bhīshma
and Jayadratha,
And also Karna,
as well as other
warrior heroes,
Are already slain by me;
do not hesitate—
you must slay them!
Fight, for you
shall conquer
your rivals in battle! 34

Sanjaya said:

Having heard these
words of Keshava,
With palms joined in
prayerful gesture, trembling,
the diademed one [Arjuna],
Offering obeisance,
spoke yet again to Krishna.
While stuttering,
timid and terrified,
he bowed down. 35

Arjuna said:

It is appropriate, O Hrishīkesha,
that by declaring your fame
The world loudly rejoices
and is overjoyed.
Demons, terrified,
flee in every direction,
And all the multitudes of
perfected beings shall bow down. 36

And why should they not
bow down to you,
O Extraordinary Self?
More venerable even than Brahmā,
you are the original creator.
O Unlimited Lord of Divinities,
dwelling place of the universe,
You are the indestructible,
the existent, the nonexistent,
and that which is beyond. 37

You are the original Divinity,
the ancient cosmic Person.
You are the highest
resting place
of this universe.
You are the knower,
what is to be known,
and the highest domain.
By you this universe is pervaded,
O One of Unlimited Form. 38

You are Vāyu, Yama, Agni,
Varuna, the moon,
Prajāpati, and
the Great-Grandfather.
Obeisance! Obeisance unto you
a thousand times over,
And again, even more—
obeisance, obeisance unto you![6] 39

---

6 Vāyu: A Vedic deity and personification of "the wind."

Yama: A Vedic deity and the personification of "death."

Agni: The powerful Vedic deity of "fire."

Varuna: The Vedic deity of law and order; also identified as the ruler of the universe.

Prajāpati: The "progenitor" of humankind.

The Great-Grandfather: The deity of creation, Brahmā.

Obeisance unto you
from the front
and from behind.
May there also be obeisance
unto you from all sides,
O Everything.
Of immeasurable prowess,
of unlimited might,
You complete everything—
therefore, you are everything. 40

Thus thinking of you as "friend,"
whatever has been spoken
inappropriately by me,
Such as "O Krishna,
O Yādava, O friend,"
Without knowing
this magnificence of yours,
Due to my carelessness
or even out of affection; 41

And if in sporting together
you were treated
disrespectfully by me,
During play or rest,
while sitting or dining,
When alone, O Achyuta,
or even before others' eyes—
For that I beg
your forgiveness,
O Unfathomable One! 42

You are the Father of the world,
of the moving
and the non-moving,
And you are to be honored
as its most worthy guru.
There is no other equal to you—
how could there be
anyone greater,
Even in all the three worlds,
O One of Incomparable Being? 43

Therefore, bowing down,
prostrating my body before you,
I ask you, the worshippable Lord,
to bestow your grace.
As a father is to a son,
as a friend to a friend,
As a dearly loved one
to a dearly beloved—
be pleased to show your
loving kindness, O Divinity. 44

Having seen what never
has been seen before,
I am exceedingly pleased,
Yet my mind is distressed
and filled with fear.
O Divinity, allow me to see
that very [intimate] form.
Bestow upon me your grace,
O Lord of Divinities,
dwelling place of the universe. 45

Adorned by the diadem,
bearing the club,
with disc held in hand,
I desire to see you
just as before.
In that very form
having four arms,
Please become manifest,
O Thousand-Armed One,
O Universal Form! 46

The Beloved Lord said:

Bestowing my grace
upon you, O Arjuna,
This supreme form
has been manifested
from the yoga of my Self.
Consisting of splendor,
it is all-pervasive,
unending, and original—
[This form] which has
not been seen before
by anyone other than you. 47

Not by the Vedas,
sacrifice, or study,
nor by giving [in charity],
Nor even by rites,
nor by severe austerities
Am I able to be seen
in such a form,
within the world of humans,
By anyone other than you,
O Hero of the Kurus. 48

Do not fear
and do not be confused,
Having seen such
a frightful awesome form
as this one of mine.
As one whose fear
has been dispelled,
with mind appeased,
Once again
you may behold
my very [intimate] form.[7] 49

Sanjaya said:

Thus having spoken
this to Arjuna,
Vāsudeva revealed his
own form as before.
And he calmed that
frightened one,
Assuming once again
the gentle appearance
of the exalted Self. 50

Arjuna said:

Seeing this gentle
humanlike form
of yours, O Janārdana,
I am now fulfilled,
with thought restored
to a normal state.[8] 51

---

7 Frightful, awesome: Translates *ghora*, which has both negative and positive senses. I have attempted to include both in this compound phrase.

8 Janārdana: Name for Krishna meaning "one who excites humans."

The Beloved Lord said:

Very rarely seen
is this form of mine
that you have seen.
Even the divinities
are always desiring
a vision of this form. 52

Not by study of the Vedas,
nor by austerity,
nor by giving,
nor by sacrifice
Am I able to be seen
in such a form
as you have seen me. 53

Only by the offering of
one's love to none other,
O Arjuna, am I able,
in such a form,
To be known and
to be truly seen,
and to be attained,
O Fighter of the Enemy. 54

Acting for me
in one's actions,
being devoted to me,
offering love to me,
having no attachments,
Free from enmity
toward all beings—
this is the one
who comes to me,
O Son of Pāndu. 55

12

The Way of Love

Arjuna said:

Those who are thus
constantly absorbed in yoga,
who fully worship you by
offering their love,
And also those who [worship]
the imperishable unmanifest—
which of these is the greatest
among those who know yoga? 1

The Beloved Lord said:

Directing the mind to me,
those who are always
absorbed in yoga
worship me.
Endowed with the highest faith,
they are considered by me
to be the most
absorbed in yoga. 2

But those who worship
the imperishable,
the uncontainable,
the unmanifest;
The all-pervading,
the inconceivable,
the unchanging,
the immovable,
and the constant; 3

Having fully controlled
the aggregate of the senses,
having the same discernment
in all instances—
They also attain me,
delighting in
the welfare of all beings. 4

Difficulty is greater
for those whose thought
is attached
to the unmanifest.
Certainly, the goal of
reaching the unmanifest
is very hard to attain
by the embodied. 5

However, for those who,
having fully renounced
all actions in me,
are devoted to me
Through this yoga
and by no other means;
who, meditating on me,
offer worship; 6

For them, I soon
become the one who
completely lifts them up
from the ocean
of the cycle of death,
O Pārtha,
for their thought
has been drawn
to enter into me. 7

Place your mind on me alone;
let your discernment
enter into me.
You shall dwell
only in me
from now forevermore—
of this there is no doubt. 8

Moreover, if you are
unable to fully absorb
your thought in me
with steadiness,
Then, with the practice of yoga
seek to attain me,
O Conqueror of Wealth. 9

If you also are incapable
of practicing this,
become wholly devoted
to me in action;
For even by
enacting such
actions for my sake,
you shall attain perfection. 10

If even this you
are unable to enact,
then, relying on me
through yoga,
With the relinquishment
of the fruits of all action—
act with restraint,
in possession of the self. 11

For knowledge is better
  than practice;
  meditation
  is preferred
  over knowledge;
From meditation comes
  the relinquishment
  of the fruits of action;
  from relinquishment
  comes peace, immediately. 12

One who has no disdain
  for any being,
  who is amicable
  as well as compassionate;
Who is without
  the sense of 'mine',
  without the notion
  of 'I am acting';
  who is the same in
  suffering and happiness,
  who is patient; 13

The yogi who is
  always fully satisfied,
  whose self is controlled,
  being of firm resolve;
Whose mind and discernment
  are focused on me,
  whose love is offered to me—
  that one is dearly loved by me. 14

One before whom the world
  is not disturbed,
  and who is not disturbed
  by the world;
Who is freed from elation,
  impatience, fear,
  and anxiety—
  that one also
  is dearly loved by me. 15

One who is impartial, pure,
  capable, detached,
  free from anxiety;
Who has completely
  relinquished all undertakings—
  that one, who offers love to me,
  is dearly loved by me. 16

One who neither
  relishes nor loathes,
  who neither
  laments nor desires,
Relinquishing the pleasant
  and the unpleasant—
  that one, who is filled
  with offerings of love,
  is dearly loved by me. 17

The same toward both
  enemy and friend,
  honor and dishonor;
The same in cold and heat,
  happiness and suffering;
  freed from attachment; 18

One for whom blame
and praise are equal,
who is disciplined in speech,
satisfied with whatever
comes of its own accord;
Who is without
[attachment to] home,
who is of steady mind,
replete with offerings of love—
such a person is dearly loved by me. 19

Indeed, this is the immortal
essence of dharma,
which has been declared;
those who participate in
this worship fully,
Who have faith,
who are devoted to me,
who have offered their love—
they are most dearly loved by me. 20

13

Primordial Nature and the Person

Arjuna said:

Primordial nature
  and also the person,
  the field as well as
  the knower of the field,
Knowledge and
  the object of knowledge—
  I desire to learn about these,
  O Keshava.[1]

The Beloved Lord said:

This body,
  O Son of Kuntī,
  is considered "the field."
One who realizes this—
  such a one they call
  "a knower of the field,"
  those who are realized in that. I

---

1 This verse is often not included in editions of the BG. When it is presented, it typically appears unnumbered.

Primordial nature: translates *prakṛti*.

The person: Translates *puruṣa*. It is often translated simply as "spirit" and understood as the antonym of the term *prakṛti,* often taken simply as "matter." However, in the BG, the word *puruṣa* is more fully translated as "person," denoting the "self," an individual spiritual being, a particular center of consciousness. Like the word "self," it can incorporate the sense of the embodied condition of a "person" in this world, or it can refer to the "person" liberated from this world, situated in the highest realm (BG 15.16). The BG also presents the "Person," the divinity personally present in all beings, or "the ultimate Person," the supreme divinity of Krishna, also referred to as "the everpresent supreme Lord" (*avyaya īśvara*) (BG 15.17).

The field: translates *kṣetra*.

The knower of the field: translates *kṣetra-jña*.

Understand me also to be
the knower of the field
in all fields, O Bhārata.
Knowledge of both the field
and the knower of the field—
this is deemed by me to be knowledge. 2

This field—what it is
and what its nature is,
what its transformations are
and from where they [originate];
And who one [the knower] is
and what one's powers are—
hear briefly about these from me. 3

It has been sung
in numerous ways by seers,
in various types of
sacred hymns,
And indeed,
in the aphoristic phrases
concerning Brahman,
which are full of reasoning
and firm resolve.[2] 4

The gross elements,
the notion of 'I am acting',
the faculty of discernment,
and also the unmanifest;
The senses,
which are ten and one,
and the five regions
of the senses; 5

---

2 Various types of sacred hymns: Refers to the Vedas.

The aphoristic phrases concerning Brahman: Translates *brahma-sūtra,* also the name of a famous philosophical text (the Vedānta Sūtra) that presents a vision of the essential philosophy of the Upanishads.

Desire, aversion,
happiness, suffering,
the aggregate whole,
thought, and constancy—
This is described in brief
as the field, along with
its transformations. 6

Absence of pride,
absence of deceit,
nonviolence,
patience, honesty;
Service to the guru,
purity, stability,
control of the self; 7

Dispassion for the objects
of the senses, and also,
absence of the notion
of 'I am acting';
Foreseeing the perils
of birth, death,
old age, disease,
and suffering; 8

Absence of attachment
and excessive affection
for children, spouse,
home, and so on;
Also, constant
same-mindedness in
desirable and undesirable
circumstances;[3] 9

---

3 Children: Translates *pūtra,* literally "a son," taken here as children in general. Spouse: Translates *dāra,* literally "a wife."

And absorbed in me
with no yoga other than
the unwavering
offering of love;
Dwelling in
a secluded place,
having disregard
for crowds of people; 10

Continuity in knowledge of
the 'principle of self',
with a vision of the object
of that knowledge
of the truth—
This is declared
to be knowledge;
the absence of knowledge
is whatever is contrary to this.[4] 11

I shall describe
what is to be known,
knowing which one
attains immortality:
The beginningless
supreme Brahman
is said to be neither
existent nor nonexistent. 12

---

4 Truth: Translates *tattva,* which can also mean "reality."

Having hands and feet everywhere,
with eyes, heads, and faces
everywhere,
Hearing everywhere in the world,
surrounding everything,
it remains constant. 13

Having the appearance
of the 'qualities' of
all the senses,
though devoid
of all the senses;
Unattached yet
supporting everything;
free of the 'qualities'
though the experiencer
of the 'qualities'; 14

Outside and inside of beings,
not moving
and yet moving,
Due to its subtle nature
it is unknowable—
it is both far away and near. 15

And among beings it is
undivided, though
remaining as if divided.
It is to be known
as the sustainer of beings,
and as the one who absorbs them
and sends them forth into being. 16

Also, of luminaries,
it is said to be
the luminary
beyond darkness.
It is knowledge,
what is to be known,
and the purpose of knowledge—
it is seated in the heart of everyone. 17

Thus the field,
as well as knowledge
and the object of knowledge,
have been briefly described.
One whose love
is offered to me,
who realizes this knowledge,
comes forth to my state of being. 18

Primordial nature
and indeed the person—
know for certain that both
are without beginning,
And know that the 'qualities'
and also their transformations
become manifest
from primordial nature. 19

In that which involves
the object of action,
the means of action,
and the cause of action,
primordial nature
is said to be the cause.
[Whereas] the person,
while experiencing the states
of happiness and suffering,
is said to be the cause. 20

For the person situated
in primordial nature
experiences the 'qualities'
born of that primordial nature.
Attachment
to the 'qualities'
is the cause of one's birth
into pure and impure wombs. 21

The observer and consenter,
the supporter,
the beloved recipient,
the exalted supreme Lord,
Or even the "supreme Self"
is declared to be
the highest Person
in this body. 22

Whoever thus knows the Person
and primordial nature,
along with the 'qualities'—
That one, though existing
in any condition whatsoever,
does not take birth again. 23

By means of meditation,
some perceive the Self
within the self, by the self;
Others, by the yoga of Sānkhya,
and even others,
by the yoga of action. 24

Still others,
having no knowledge,
thus only hearing
from others, offer worship.
And indeed they also
cross beyond death,
devoted to what
they have heard. 25

As for any being,
stationary or moving,
it takes birth
Due to the union of the field
with the knower of the field,
O Best of the Bharatas. 26

Situated as the same in
all beings is the highest
supreme Lord,
Who is not perishing
when they are perishing—
one who sees this,
that one [truly] sees. 27

Indeed, seeing the same
supreme Lord fully
established everywhere,
One does not harm
the self by the self—
from there one reaches
the highest goal. 28

By primordial nature alone,
actions are being
completely enacted.
One who sees this,
and thus sees that the self
is not the creator of action—
that one [truly] sees. 29

When one perceives
the various states of being
as abiding in one place,
And from that alone
their emanation,
then one fully
attains Brahman. 30

Due to having no beginning,
free from the effect
of the 'qualities',
that everpresent supreme Self,
Though situated in the body,
O Son of Kuntī,
does not act—
nor is it tainted [by action]. 31

Just as all-pervasive space
  is not tainted
  due to its subtle nature,
Similarly, the Self
  abiding in every body
  is not tainted. 32

As the sun alone
  illuminates
  this entire world,
So the one who
  resides in the field
  illuminates
  the entire field, O Bhārata. 33

Thus the difference
  between the field
  and the knower of the field,
  [seen] with the eye of knowledge,
And the release of beings
  from primordial nature—
  those who know of these,
  it is they who attain the Supreme. 34

14

The Qualities of Nature

The Beloved Lord said:

I shall describe further
  the best of knowledge,
  the ultimate knowledge,
Knowing which, all seers
  have gone from here
  to the highest perfection. 1

Taking refuge in this knowledge,
  having come to a state
  of likeness with me,
Even during creation
  they do not take birth—
  nor do they tremble
  during cosmic absorption. 2

The great Brahman
  is my womb;
  in this I place
  the [cosmic] embryo.
The coming forth
  of all beings becomes
  manifest from that,
  O Bhārata. 3

In all wombs, O Son of Kuntī,
for whatever forms
come into being—
For them, the great Brahman
is the [cosmic] womb;
I am the father
who gives forth the seed. 4

"*Sattva, rajas,* and *tamas,*"
the 'qualities' arising
from primordial nature,
O Mighty-Armed,
bind the everpresent
embodied to the body. 5

Among these, *sattva,*
due to its untainted nature,
is illuminating,
free from contamination.
It binds one by
attachment to happiness,
also by attachment
to knowledge,
O Blameless One. 6

Know that *rajas*
is of the nature of
passion, arising from
thirst and attachment.
It tightly binds
one who is embodied,
O Son of Kuntī,
by attachment to action. 7

Moreover, know
that *tamas* is born of
the absence of knowledge,
bewildering all
who are embodied;
With negligence,
lethargy, and sleep,
it binds tightly,
O Bhārata. 8

Sattva causes attachment
to happiness
and *rajas* to action,
O Bhārata.
Obscuring knowledge,
however, *tamas*
causes attachment
even to negligence.[1] 9

Dominating *rajas* and *tamas*,
sattva becomes
prominent,
O Bhārata;
Likewise *rajas*,
with *sattva* and *tamas*;
and also *tamas*,
with *sattva* and *rajas*. 10

---

1 Negligence: Translates *pramāda,* also meaning "madness" or "intoxication."

When in all
the gates of this body,
illumination gives rise
To knowledge,
then it should be
understood that, indeed,
"*sattva* is dominant." 11

Greed, exertion,
the undertaking of actions,
disquietude, and desire—
These are produced
when *rajas* is dominant,
O Best of the Bharatas. 12

The absence of light,
also inactivity, negligence,
and even bewilderment—
These are produced
when *tamas* is dominant,
O Son of Kuru. 13

Now when, under
the dominance of *sattva,*
the embodied goes
to cosmic absorption,
Then one attains
the pure worlds
of those who
know the highest. 14

Having gone forth
to cosmic absorption
in the state of *rajas,*
one is born among
those attached to action.
Likewise, being absorbed
into the cosmos while
in the state of *tamas,*
one is born into the wombs
of bewildered persons. 15

Of action that is
virtuous when enacted,
they say the fruit is untainted,
having the nature of *sattva.*
The fruit of *rajas,*
however, is suffering;
the absence of knowledge
is the fruit of *tamas.* 16

From *sattva,*
knowledge is born,
and indeed from *rajas,* greed.
Negligence and bewilderment
arise from *tamas,* as well as
the absence of knowledge. 17

Those established in *sattva*
progress upward;
those attached to *rajas*
remain in the middle;
Those established
in the lowest state
progress downward—
those attached to *tamas.* 18

When the observer [self]
perceives no agent of action
other than the 'qualities',
And knows what is
higher than the 'qualities'—
that one attains my state of being. 19

Transcending these
three 'qualities'
emerging from the body,
the embodied one,
Freed from birth,
death, old age,
and suffering,
attains immortality. 20

Arjuna said:

By what characteristics
does one become identified
upon transcending these
three 'qualities',
O Majestic One?
What is one's conduct,
and how does one
transcend these
three 'qualities'? 21

The Beloved Lord said:

Both illumination
and activity, and
even bewilderment,
O Son of Pāndu—
One neither despises
these states when they occur
nor desires them when
they cease to occur.[2] 22

One who is seated
as if seated apart;
who is not disturbed
by the 'qualities',
Thinking only
that "the 'qualities'
[of nature] are at work";
who remains fixed,
who is not shaken; 23

For whom suffering and
happiness are the same,
being in one's natural state;
for whom a lump of earth,
a stone, and gold are the same;
For whom the dearly loved
and the unloved are equal;
who is grave, equal in blame
and praise of one's self; 24

---

2 Illumination: Translates *prakāśam,* describing *sattva.*

Activity: Translates *pravṛttim,* describing *rajas.*

Bewilderment: Translates *moham,* describing *tamas.*

Who is equal in both
honor and dishonor,
equal to friendly
and rival factions,
Completely relinquishing
all undertakings—
that one is said
to have transcended
the 'qualities'. 25

And one who, unfailingly,
with the yoga of
offering love,
serves me—
That one, transcending
these 'qualities',
prepares oneself for
being united with Brahman. 26

Truly, of Brahman,
I am the foundation—
and of the immortal
that is everpresent,
Also, of dharma
that is everlasting,
and of happiness
that is extraordinary. 27

15

The Ultimate Person

The Beloved Lord said:

With its roots upward
and its branches downward,
they speak of the everlasting
Ashwattha tree,
Whose leaves
are the Vedic hymns—
one who knows this
is a knower of the Vedas.[1] 1

Extending downward and upward,
its branches are nourished
By the 'qualities' [of nature],
with its fresh shoots
as the objects of the senses.
Also stretched downward
are its roots,
Promoting action
in the world of humans. 2

1 Ashwattha tree: Understood as a kind of fig tree, first mentioned in BG 10.26. Some commentators understand this name to refer to the banyan tree.

The form of this [tree]
here in the world
cannot be perceived—
Not its end
nor beginning
nor foundation.
Cutting this Ashwattha tree,
whose roots
are fully grown,
With the strong
ax of detachment; 3

Then that place
is to be sought
To which having gone
such persons
never again return,
[Declaring]: And to that,
indeed I offer myself,
to that original Person
From whom cycles
of cosmic activity have
issued forth in former ages. 4

Without pride or bewilderment,
having conquered
the faults of attachment;
Constantly situated
in the 'principle of self'
with desires turned away;
Liberated from
the dualities known
as happiness and suffering—
Those who
are not bewildered
attain that everlasting place. 5

Neither the sun,
nor the moon,
nor fire illuminates
that realm
To which having gone
they do not return—
that is my supreme dwelling. 6

A part of me alone
in the world of the living
is the living being,
which is eternal.
It draws to itself the senses,
the mind being the sixth,
all of which are situated
in primordial nature. 7

When one acquires a body
and also,
when one departs from it,
its master [the self],
Carrying these [senses],
moves on,
as the wind carries
scents from their source. 8

The senses of hearing,
sight, and touch,
as well as taste
and smell—
Presiding over these
and the mind,
one pursues the objects
of the senses. 9

Whether departing from
or remaining in [the body],
or experiencing [sense objects],
affected by the 'qualities',
Those who are very bewildered
do not perceive this [self]—
those with the eye
of knowledge see this. 10

And upon striving,
yogis see that [Self]
which exists
within the self.
But those who are
not self-actualized,
even though striving,
cannot see this,
being unthoughtful. 11

The splendor that comes
forth from the sun,
which illuminates
the entire universe;
That which
is in the moon
and in fire—
know this splendor
as belonging to me. 12

And entering the earth,
I sustain beings
by my potency.
And I nourish all vegetation
by becoming the moon,
which contains
the essence of taste.[2] 13

2 Taste: Translates *rasa,* which also means "juice" or "flavor."

I, becoming the digestive fire
dwelling in the bodies
of breathing beings,
In conjunction
with the incoming
and outgoing breaths,
digest the four types
of foodstuffs.[3] 14

And I have fully entered
into the hearts of all;
From me come remembrance,
knowledge, and forgetfulness.
And by all the Vedas
only I am to be known;
I am the author of Vedānta
and truly the knower of the Vedas.[4] 15

The two types of persons
in the world are these:
the perishable and
also, the imperishable.
The perishable
consists of all beings;
the imperishable is described
as those who are situated
in the highest [state].[5] 16

---

3 Four types of foodstuffs: The four ways in which foods are eaten: licked, chewed, sucked, and swallowed.

4 Forgetfulness: Translates *apohanam,* which can also mean "the removal [of remembrance and knowledge]." For commentators, forgetfulness can be seen as both positive and negative.

Vedānta: Meaning "the end of the Vedas," referring to the Upanishads or to the Vedānta Sūtra, a work composed of a comprehensive interpretation and synthesis of Upanishadic philosophy.

5 The perishable: Translates *kṣara,* which can mean "destructible" or "alterable," referring to the bodies of all beings in this world.

The imperishable: Translates *akṣara,* referring to persons who are not bound to this world, liberated even while in it.

Yet there is another—
an ultimate person
called "the supreme Self,"
Who, entering into
the three worlds,
maintains them
as the everpresent
supreme Lord.[6] 17

Because I am beyond
the perishable
and am even higher
than the imperishable,
Therefore, I am celebrated
in the oldest texts
and in the Vedas
as the Ultimate Person. 18

One who,
unbewildered,
thus knows me
as the Ultimate Person—
That one, who is
a knower of all,
offers love to me with
all of one's being, O Bhārata. 19

---

6 The three worlds: Refers to the upper, lower, and middle worlds of this universe.

Everpresent supreme Lord: Translates *avyaya īśvaraḥ,* presented in the third person. The supreme Lord who enters the worlds and the living beings is a third type of *puruṣa,* or "person," indeed the "ultimate person," a distinctive manifestation of Krishna's supreme divinity. This manifestation is identical with what is described in the following verse, spoken of in the first person, which is Krishna himself as he stands before Arjuna.

Thus the greatest secret
of the revealed scriptures—
this has been disclosed by me,
O Faultless One.
Having discerned this,
one would possess
discernment,
and would have enacted
all that is required
to be enacted, O Bhārata. 20

16

The Divine and Ungodly Natures

The Beloved Lord said:

Fearlessness, complete
purity of existence,
steadfastness in
the yoga of knowledge;
Acts of giving and restraint,
sacrifice, study of scripture,
austerity, and sincerity; 1

Nonviolence, truthfulness,
freedom from anger,
relinquishment, peacefulness,
absence of slander;
Compassion for all beings,
freedom from longing,
gentleness, humility,
absence of agitation; 2

Vitality, patience, tenacity,
purity, freedom from envy,
absence of excessive pride—
These become the attributes
for those of divine birth,
O Bhārata. 3

Deceitfulness, arrogance,
and excessive pride;
wrath, and indeed harshness,
Also absence of knowledge—
these are the attributes,
O Pārtha, for those
of ungodly birth. 4

The divine attributes move one
toward complete freedom;
the ungodly attributes,
it is thought, toward bondage.
Do not worry—
you are wellborn
with divine attributes,
O Son of Pāndu. 5

The creation of beings
in this world is only
of two types: the divine
and the ungodly.
The divine has been
described in detail,
O Pārtha;
now here from me
about the ungodly. 6

Both activity and inactivity
ungodly persons
do not understand.
Neither purity
nor good behavior
nor truth is found in them. 7

Without reality,
without foundation,
the world, they say,
is without the supreme Lord,
That the one is not brought
into being by the other—
then by what?
It is caused by selfish desire. 8

Supporting this view,
persons whose self is lost,
having little discernment,
Whose actions are cruel—
they come forth into being
as enemies of the world
for its destruction. 9

Resorting to insatiable desire,
filled with deceitfulness,
pride, and arrogance;
Due to bewilderment,
holding onto notions
that are held as untrue—
they proceed with impure resolve. 10

And subjected to
immeasurable anxiety,
which continues until
one's final death;
Having gratification
of selfish desires as
one's highest aim,
convinced that
"this is all there is"— 11

Bound by a hundred
chains of hope,
devoted to desire
and wrath,
With the aim of
indulging in desires—
those persons seek
the accumulation of wealth
by unjust means. 12

"Today this has been
acquired by me;
this desire I shall fulfill.
This belongs to me—
even more wealth
shall become mine." 13

"That enemy
has been slain by me,
and I shall also slay others.
I am the supreme lord,
I am the enjoyer;
I am perfect, powerful,
and happy." 14

"I am wealthy,
of high birth;
who else is there
like me?
I shall sacrifice,
I shall offer gifts,
I shall rejoice,"
say those bewildered
by a lack of knowledge. 15

Carried away by many thoughts,
enveloped in a snare
of bewilderment,
Very attached to the enjoyment
of selfish desires—
they fall into an unclean
place of torment. 16

Self-centered, stubborn,
full of pride and conceit
coming from wealth,
They perform sacrifices
in name only, with deceit—
not according to what
previously has been enjoined.[1] 17

The notion of 'I am acting',
also power, arrogance,
selfish desire, wrath—
completely attached to these,
Such envious persons
loathe me
in their own bodies
and in the bodies of others. 18

Those who hate,
who are cruel,
low persons caught in
the cycle [of birth and death]—
I repeatedly hurl
such impure persons
only into the wombs
of the ungodly. 19

---

1 What previously has been enjoined:
Refers to what was stated in the Vedas.

Having come
into an ungodly womb,
those who are bewildered
birth after birth,
Not ever attaining me,
O Son of Kuntī—
they then go
to the lowest place. 20

This is the threefold passage
of a tormented existence,
which destroys the self:
Desire, anger, also greed—
therefore, it is these three
that one should relinquish. 21

Completely freed
from these three
passages of darkness,
O Son of Kuntī,
A human being does
what is best for the self,
then goes to the highest place. 22

One who, abandoning
scriptural injunction,
acts according to one's
own selfish desires—
That person does not
attain perfection,
nor happiness,
nor the highest place. 23

Therefore, let scripture
be your authority
for understanding what
action should be performed
and what action should
not be performed.
Knowing the prescribed
scriptural injunctions,
you are obliged to enact
such action in this world. 24

17

The Three Types of Faith

Arjuna said:

Those who,
having abandoned
scriptural injunctions,
engage in sacrifice,
endowed with faith—
What indeed is
their condition,
O Krishna:
is it *sattva, rajas,* or *tamas*? 1

The Beloved Lord said:

The faith of the embodied
is of three types,
arising from one's
particular state of being:
"That of the nature of *sattva,*
or of the nature of *rajas,*
or even of the nature of *tamas*"—
now hear about this. 2

According to the degree of *sattva,*
the faith of everyone
becomes manifest,
O Bhārata.
A person is made of this faith—
whatever the faith,
that is indeed
what one is.[1] 3

Those of the nature of *sattva*
offer sacrifice to divinities;
those of the nature of *rajas*
offer sacrifice to spirits
and demonic beings.
To ghosts and multitudes
of departed beings,
the others, those humans
of the nature of *tamas,*
offer sacrifice. 4

Those persons
who perform terrible
austerities not enjoined
in the scriptures,
Who are fully united
with deceit and the notion
of 'I am acting',
who are full of selfish
desire, passion, and power; 5

---

1 According to the degree of *sattva:* Translates the phrase, *sattvānurūpāḥ,* meaning the greater the degree of *sattva,* the more pure the faith. Every combination of the essential qualities contains some degree of *sattva.*

Faith: Translates *śraddhā,* which means literally, "where one places one's heart."

A person: Refers to the embodied soul as it is influenced by the essential qualities of nature, and not the soul proper.

Mindless ones,
causing torment
to the aggregate of elements
existing within the body,
And thus to me,
who am also existing
within the body—
know them to be
of ungodly resolve. 6

Indeed, the food
that becomes dear
to each person
is even of three types,
As well as one's sacrifice,
austerity, and also
one's acts of giving—
hear of their differences. 7

Promoting life, energy,
strength, good health,
happiness, and satisfaction;
Flavorful, appealing,
substantial, and hearty—
such foods are dear to those
of the nature of *sattva*. 8

Bitter, sour, salty,
very hot and acidic,
astringent and burning,
Causing misery,
sorrow, and disease—
such foods are desired
by those of the nature of *rajas.* 9

Food that is no longer fresh,
that is tasteless, putrid,
and stale,
That has been rejected
and is also impure—
eating such foods is dear
to those of the nature of *tamas.* 10

Sacrifice offered as observed
in scriptural injunctions
by one who does
not desire its fruits,
Whose mind is completely
absorbed in the thought that,
"only sacrifice is to be made"—
this is of the nature of *sattva.* 11

But that which is offered
with a motive for the fruit,
and indeed, even with
a deceitful purpose,
O Best of the Bharatas—
know that this sacrifice
is of the nature of *rajas*. 12

Sacrifice that is lacking
in scriptural foundation,
with no offering of grains,
with no recitation of mantras,
without monetary donations,
Completely devoid of faith—
this they regard as having
the nature of *tamas*. 13

Respect for the divinities,
the twice-born, the gurus,
and for those who possess
profound knowledge;
purity, sincerity,
Chastity, and
nonviolence—
this is called
austerity of the body.[2] 14

---

2 Twice-born: Translates *dvija*, referring to a Brahmin, a member of the priestly and educated class. The Brahmin is born twice, first through a physical birth, and then through the initiatory rite-of-passage.

Words that do not cause distress,
that are truthful,
endearing, and beneficial;
And further, the practice
of reciting sacred texts—
this is called
austerity of speech. 15

Calmness of mind,
gentleness, silence,
control of the self,
"Complete purity of being"—
this is called austerity
in relation to the mind. 16

That threefold austerity
practiced by humans
who possess the highest faith,
Who do not desire its fruits,
who are absorbed in yoga—
they regard that as having
the nature of *sattva.* 17

That austerity which is enacted
with pretense, and indeed
with the aim of receiving
kind treatment, respect,
and honor—
That is declared
in this world to be
of the nature of *rajas,*
vacillating and unstable. 18

That which is enacted
with bewildered notions,
with self-inflicted pain,
Or with the aim of
destroying another—
that austerity is said to be
of the nature of *tamas*. 19

That gift which is given
with the thought that,
"this should be given,"
to one who may not
act reciprocally,
At an appropriate
time and place,
and to a worthy person—
that gift is to be
remembered as having
the nature of *sattva*. 20

But that gift which is given
with the aim of gaining
a returned favor, or
further, aspiring
for the fruit,
Or which is given
reluctantly—
that gift is to be
remembered as having
the nature of *rajas*. 21

That gift which is given
at an inappropriate
time and place,
to unworthy persons,
Without acting respectfully
or with contempt—
that is declared to be
of the nature of *tamas*. 22

"OM TAT SAT"—
these are the designations
of Brahman, which are
remembered as threefold.
By this, the Brahmins
and the Vedas
and sacrifices were
ordained in ancient times. 23

Therefore, with the sounding
of [the syllable] "OM"—
acts of sacrifice, giving,
and austerity,
Which are prescribed
by scriptural injunction,
are always set into motion
by those who profess Brahman. 24

Uttering "TAT" without
the aim of the fruit—
acts of sacrifice and austerity,
And various acts of giving
are enacted by those
who desire liberation. 25

In the meaning
of 'eternal truth'
and in the meaning
of 'truth-seeking sage'
this word "SAT"
is properly engaged.
When action
is praiseworthy,
O Pārtha,
the word "SAT"
is also engaged. 26

Steadfastness in sacrifice,
in austerity, and in giving
is also called "SAT,"
And any action for
the sake of such purposes
is likewise explained as "SAT." 27

Without faith,
that which is sacrificed,
given, performed as
intense austerity,
or enacted
Is called "*asat*" [not SAT],
O Pārtha, and is not
truly that [as it seems]—
for those having passed on,
or for us remaining here
in this world.[3] 28

3 "*Asat*" [not SAT]: Meaning literally, "not true" or "what is not the supreme truth."

Not truly that: Translates *tat,* the correlative pronoun of *yat* ("which") found in the first half of the verse; "that" refers to that which is "sacrificed, given, etc.," echoing the efficacious TAT presented in BG 17.25.

18

The Supreme Secret of Yoga

Arjuna said:

About renunciation,
O Mighty-Armed,
I desire to know the truth,
And about relinquishment,
O Hrishīkesha;
also the distinctions
between them,
O Slayer of Keshi. 1

The Beloved Lord said:

The renouncing of acts
arising from selfish desire
wise ones understand
to be renunciation.
The relinquishing of
the fruits of all action
seers declare
as relinquishment. 2

"It is to be relinquished
for it is full of fault,"
certain thoughtful persons
declare of action.
"Actions of sacrifice,
giving, and austerity
are not to be relinquished,"
yet others declare. 3

Hear my conclusion
on this subject
of relinquishment,
O Best of the Bharatas.
For relinquishment,
O Tiger Among Men,
is widely proclaimed
to be of three types. 4

Actions of sacrifice,
giving, and austerity
are not to be relinquished;
rather, they are to be enacted.
Sacrifice, giving, and austerity
are certainly sources
of purification for
thoughtful persons. 5

"These actions, however,
only after relinquishing
attachment to them
and their fruits,
Should be enacted,"
O Pārtha—
this, without doubt,
is my highest opinion. 6

So renunciation
of prescribed action
is not appropriate.
Complete relinquishment
of such due to bewilderment
is proclaimed to be
of the nature of *tamas*. 7

Who deems action as "difficult,"
only due to fear
of bodily suffering—
one who should
relinquish in this way,
Enacting relinquishment
of the nature of *rajas,*
certainly would not obtain
the fruits of such relinquishment. 8

"It should be enacted,"
indeed, that action
which is enacted
because it is prescribed,
O Arjuna.
Relinquishing attachment
and certainly the fruit,
such relinquishment
is thought to be
of the nature of *sattva.* 9

One who is not adverse
to disagreeable action
nor attached to that
which is agreeable—
Such a relinquisher
is fully absorbed in *sattva;*
the doubts of that
learned person are severed. 10

For one who bears a body
is not able to relinquish
actions entirely;
Yet one who relinquishes
the fruits of action—
that one is said to be
"one who relinquishes." 11

Undesirable,
desirable, and mixed
are the threefold
fruits of action,
Which continue
to come into being
for those who
do not relinquish,
even after passing on,
but never for those
who are renouncers. 12

The five causes of action,
O Mighty-Armed—
learn from me about these,
Which have been declared
in the enacted conclusions
by the followers of Sānkhya
for success in all actions: 13

[They are] the physical basis,
also the agent of action,
and the various
means of action,
And the different types
of various movements,
and even the divine forces,
the fifth of these. 14

With one's body,
speech, or mind,
whatever action
a human undertakes,
Whether it be normal,
or contrary to the norm—
these are its five causes. 15

This being so,
one who perceives
the self alone as
the agent of action,
Due to one's
inner discernment
not being active—
that one does not
truly perceive things,
being weak-minded. 16

One whose state of being
is free from the notion
of 'I have acted',
whose discernment
is not contaminated—
That one,
even though having
slain these people,
does not slay;
nor is that one bound. 17

Knowledge,
the object of knowledge,
and the knower
are the three factors
that compel one to act.
The means of action,
action itself, and
the agent of action
are the three factors
that constitute action. 18

Knowledge and action
and the agent of action
are [all] of three types,
determined by the divisions
of the 'qualities'.
This is declared
in the Sānkhya theory
of the 'qualities'—
hear also about these,
as they are. 19

That by which one
perceives in all beings
one everpresent being,
Who is undivided
among divided beings—
understand that knowledge
to be of the nature of *sattva*. 20

But with a view of separateness,
that knowledge
which understands
various states of being
As having been separately
formed in all beings—
understand that knowledge
to be of the nature of *rajas*. 21

However, that [knowledge]
wherein one thing
is taken to be the whole—
being attached, without reason,
to the performance of
[a single] activity
Having no true value
or significance—
that is said to be
of the nature of *tamas*. 22

Disciplined,
free from attachment,
acting without
passion or repulsion,
Without desiring to obtain
the fruit of action—
that is said to be
of the nature of *sattva*. 23

But that action which,
with the hope of
fulfilling selfish desires,
or further, with the notion
of 'I am acting',
Is enacted
with great effort—
that is declared to be
of the nature of *rajas*. 24

Disregarding consequences,
loss, harm, and also
personal capacity—
Such action, undertaken
due to bewilderment,
is said to be of
the nature of *tamas*. 25

Freed from attachment,
not speaking of oneself,
fully endowed with
energy and steadfastness,
Unaffected by both success
and lack of success—
such an agent of action
is said to be of
the nature of *sattva*. 26

Passionate, desirous of
gaining the fruits of action,
having an aggressive nature,
greedy, unclean,
Filled with joy and sorrow—
such an agent of action
is proclaimed to be of
the nature of *rajas*. 27

Not absorbed in yoga,
vulgar, stubborn, deceitful,
denouncing others, lethargic,
Despondent, and procrastinating—
such an agent of action is said
to be of the nature of *tamas*. 28

The different types of discernment
and also of determination,
according to the 'qualities'
are divided into three—
now hear of these
Expounded upon separately,
with nothing left out,
O Conqueror of Wealth. 29

Positive engagement
and disengagement,
what is to be enacted
and not to be enacted,
what is to be feared
and not to be feared,
Bondage and freedom—
one who perceives these,
that one's discernment
is of the nature of *sattva*,
O Pārtha. 30

Dharma and what
opposes dharma,
and what is to be enacted,
and also, what is not
to be enacted—
That discernment
which incorrectly
understands these
is of the nature of *rajas,*
O Pārtha. 31

"What opposes dharma
is dharma"—
that which thinks this
is covered by *tamas,*
And that which completely
reverses all meaning;
such discernment is of
the nature of *tamas,* O Pārtha. 32

That determination by which
one is able to hold steady
the activities of the mind,
the breath, and the senses
Through the undisturbed
practice of yoga—
that determination, O Pārtha,
is of the nature of *sattva.* 33

But that by which one
holds steadily to dharma,
desires, and wealth,
with determination,
O Arjuna,
With attachment,
desirous of the fruits—
that determination is
of the nature of *rajas,*
O Pārtha. 34

That by which an ignorant person
does not let go of sleep, fear,
lamentation, depression,
and even madness—
That determination,
O Pārtha, is of
the nature of *tamas.* 35

But now hear from me
about the three
types of happiness,
O Leader of the Bharatas,
In which one experiences
[such happiness]
through repetition,
then finally comes
to the end of suffering. 36

That which in the beginning
  seems like poison
  but in the end
  resembles the immortal—
That is declared
  to be happiness
  of the nature of *sattva,*
  born from the serenity
  of the discerning self. 37

Due to the conjunction
  of the senses with their objects,
  that which in the beginning
  resembles the immortal
But in the end
  seems like poison—
  that happiness is understood
  to be of the nature of *rajas.* 38

Happiness which in the beginning
  and consequently in the end
  is bewildering for the self,
Which arises from sleep,
  lethargy, and confusion—
  that is declared to be
  of the nature of *tamas.* 39

There is nothing
  either on this earth
  or in the divine realm,
  even among the divinities,
With an existence
  that is freed from
  these three 'qualities'
  born of primordial nature. 40

Among Brahmins,
rulers, tradespeople,
and skilled workers,
O Scorcher of the Enemy,
Actions are determined
by the coming forth into being
of their particular natures,
according to the 'qualities'. 41

Calmness, restraint,
austerity, purity, patience,
and also sincerity;
Knowledge, realized knowledge,
and strong faith in the divine
are the active traits of Brahmins,
born of their own nature. 42

Heroism, prowess,
steadfastness, skill, and
also, not fleeing in battle,
Generosity, and lordliness
are the active traits of rulers,
born of their own nature. 43

Cultivating the fields,
protecting cows, and
engaging in commerce
are the actions
of tradespeople,
born of their own nature.
Characterized by performing
all kinds of service for others
are the actions
of skilled workers, also
born of their own nature. 44

Being practiced in one's
own specific activity,
a person attains
full perfection.
How one who is practiced
in such activity
finds perfection—
hear about this. 45

That one from whom the activity
of beings comes forth,
by whom this [universe]
is pervaded—
Worshipping that one
by one's own action,
a human being
finds perfection. 46

Better is one's own dharma
even if imperfect
than another's dharma
followed perfectly.
Performing action
determined by
one's own nature,
one does not incur fault. 47

Action born of one's nature,
  O Son of Kuntī,
  even if faulty,
  should not be relinquished.
For all undertakings
  are covered by faults,
  as fire is by smoke. 48

With one's discernment
  unattached in all circumstances,
  with the self conquered,
  longings having vanished,
One attains
  the supreme perfection
  of actionlessness
  through renunciation.[1] 49

Once having attained perfection,
  how one also attains Brahman,
  learn from me through
Just a brief summary,
  O Son of Kuntī—
  this is the highest
  culmination of knowledge.[2] 50

---

1 Actionlessness: Translates *naiṣkarmya,* which means literally, "action without any binding consequences [for the one who acts]."

2 This verse begins Krishna's summary of the greater secret, which is a transcendent state of being that focuses upon Brahman and Purushottama. From the beginning of this chapter up to the present verse, Krishna's summary of his great secret is presented.

Absorbed in yoga
with pure discernment
and subduing the self
with steadfastness;
Relinquishing
the objects of the senses,
such as sound and so forth,
casting away attraction and repulsion; 51

Dwelling apart from others,
eating lightly,
controlling one's speech,
body, and mental activity;
Constantly devoted
to the yoga of meditation,
taking full refuge
in dispassion; 52

Being completely freed from
the notion of 'I am acting',
from aggressiveness, pride,
selfish desire, anger,
and possessiveness;
Without a sense of
'mine', peaceful—
that one is prepared
to be united with Brahman. 53

Being united with Brahman,
one whose self is tranquil,
who neither laments
nor desires,
Who is the same
toward all beings—
that one attains the highest,
the offering of love to me. 54

By offering love
one recognizes
me fully and
who I am in truth.
Once knowing
me in truth,
one comes to me
immediately.[3] 55

Even though continually
enacting all activities,
fully taking refuge
in me,
By my grace
one attains
the everpresent
eternal dwelling. 56

With one's thought
having renounced
all actions in me,
wholly devoted to me,
Fully taking refuge in
the yoga of discernment—
always be thinking of me. 57

With thought on me,
due to my grace
you shall transcend
all difficulties.
Now, if you shall
not hear because of
the notion of 'I am acting',
then you shall be lost. 58

3 Comes: Translates *viśate*, which can also mean "enters into" or "comes back."

When you think,
having taken shelter
of the notion of 'I am acting',
that "I shall not fight"—
This resolve of yours
is in vain since
primordial nature
shall force you.[4] 59

Being bound by what is
born of your own nature,
O Son of Kuntī,
by your own action—
Whatever way you
desire not to act
due to bewilderment,
that way you shall act,
even against your will. 60

The supreme Lord
of all beings, O Arjuna,
is present within the inner
region of the heart,
Causing all beings
to move about like riders
upon a mystical machine,
by the divine power of Māyā.[5] 61

---

4 "I shall not fight": Translates the phrase, *na yotsya iti*. Note the similar sounding last word of this verse, *niyokṣyati,* which translates the phrase "primordial nature shall force you." This is an example of Krishna's clever play on words.

5 A mystical machine: Translates the word *yantra,* which can refer to "the body" or even to "the complex workings of the whole cosmos."

In him alone take shelter
with your whole being,
O Bhārata.
Through his grace
you shall attain
supreme peace,
the eternal dwelling. 62

Thus for you this knowledge,
which is a greater secret
than the [previous] secret,
is made known by me.
Having fully grasped this,
with nothing overlooked,
then act as you so choose.[6] 63

Hear still further
the greatest secret of all,
my supreme message:
"You are so much loved by me!"
Therefore I shall speak
for your well-being.[7] 64

---

6 A greater secret: Translates *guhyatara*. This "greater" secret, more secret than the [previous] secret, constitutes the transcendent state of realizing Brahman and the development of a vision of the "supreme Self," *puruṣa,* or the "supreme Lord," *īśvara*, within one's own heart and the hearts of all living beings. The "greatest secret" of Krishna is introduced in the following verse and expressed in subsequent verses.

The [previous] secret: The first of three secrets, constituting Krishna's words on acting in the outer world according to one's nature, without being attached to the fruits of one's actions. This first secret is to act out of love, and its summary begins with the first verse of this chapter.

7 The greatest secret of all: Translates *sarva-guhyatama*.

Loved: Translates *iṣṭa,* which literally means "wished" or "desired." "You are so much loved by me" therefore conveys the sense of an impassioned love, a divine yearning.

Well-being: translates *hita,* which can also mean "advantage," "welfare," "benefit," or "good."

Be mindful of me
  with love offered to me;
  sacrificing for me,
  act out of reverence for me.
Truly you shall
  come to me—
  this I promise you
  for you are dearly loved by me. 65

Completely relinquishing
  all forms of dharma,
  come to me
  as your only shelter.
I shall grant you
  freedom from
  all misfortune—
  do not despair![8] 66

This is not to be spoken
  by you at any time
  to one who is
  without discipline,
  nor to one who
  does not offer one's love,
Nor to one who hears
  yet has no desire to follow,
  nor to one who is
  envious of me. 67

8 Forms of dharma: Translates the plural form of dharma.

One who reveals
this supreme secret
to those who have
offered me their love,
Enacting the highest
offering of love for me—
that one shall certainly
come to me, without doubt. 68

And among humans,
there is no one whose acts
are more dearly loved by me
than that one,
Nor shall there be
any other on earth who
is more dearly loved by me
than such a person. 69

Also, whosoever shall study
this sacred dialogue of ours
concerning dharma—
By that person, through
the sacrifice of knowledge,
I shall be lovingly worshipped;
this is my conviction.[9] 70

9 Lovingly worshipped: This phrase translates *iṣṭa,* which, interestingly, is a past participle derived from two different verbal roots, meaning either "sacrificed, worshipped" (*yaj*) or "loved, desired" (*ich*). Though most scholars understand this participle to be the first of these meanings, I have used "lovingly worshipped" to reflect its expressive ambiguity. It is also interesting to note that this participle bears the sense of "loved" or "desired" several verses earlier, in Krishna's impassioned words, "You are so much loved [*iṣṭa*] by me!" (BG 18.64).

Possessing faith
and free from envy,
such a person who
should only hear it—
Even that one,
liberated, would attain
the blissful worlds of
those whose actions are pure. 71

Has this [teaching] been
heard by you, O Pārtha,
with thought focused upon
the single highest point?
Has this profound
bewilderment coming
from the absence of knowledge
been perfectly destroyed in you,
O Conqueror of Wealth? 72

Arjuna said:

With confusion destroyed,
my memory is restored
by your grace,
O Achyuta.
I am firmly resolved
with doubts dispelled—
I shall act according
to your guidance. 73

Sanjaya said:

Thus from Vāsudeva
and Pārtha,
whose self is exalted,
I have heard this
wondrous conversation,
which causes a state
of rapturous bliss.[10] 74

By the grace of Vyāsa
I have heard this
supreme secret of yoga
From Krishna,
the Supreme Lord of Yoga,
appearing directly
before my eyes,
speaking it himself.[11] 75

O King, remembering—
remembering over and over
this wondrous dialogue
Of Keshava and Arjuna,
which is auspicious,
I feel rapturous bliss
moment after moment![12] 76

---

10 Causes a state of rapturous bliss: Translates *romaharshana,* meaning "bodily hairs standing on end" or the "thrilling of bodily hairs."

11 Supreme secret of yoga: Translates *guhyaṁ paraṁ yogam.*

12 O King: Refers to Dhritarāshtra.

And remembering—
remembering over and over
that most wondrous
beautiful form of Hari,
My amazement is great,
O King, and I feel
rapturous bliss
again and again![13] 77

Where there is Krishna,
the Supreme Lord of Yoga,
where there is Pārtha,
Holder of the Bow,
There is fortune,
triumph, well-being,
and lasting righteousness—
that is my conclusion.[14] 78

13 Hari: A name for Krishna meaning "one who takes away," referring either to one's heart or one's troubles.

14 Fortune: Translates *śrī,* which can also mean "light," "splendor," "beauty," "auspiciousness," "success," or "prosperity."

Triumph: Translates *vijaya,* which also means "victory" or "conquest."

Well-being: Translates *bhūti,* which also means "prosperity," "might," "power," "wealth," or "fortune."

Lasting righteousness: Translates *dhruvā nīti*. The word *nīti* means "wise conduct," "political wisdom," or "moral philosophy."

Textual Illuminations

The Yoga of the Bhagavad Gītā

An essential message concerning yoga pervades the text of the Bhagavad Gītā. Yoga, though taking many forms in the Gītā, acts as a unifying force that ties together all the teachings, practices, philosophies, and analyses presented in Krishna's discourse. The various yogas are meant to lead one to the ultimate form of yoga, what the narrator calls "the supreme secret of yoga." Embedded within the text, unifying its diverse themes, this cohesive message of yoga allows the reader to grasp every aspect of the Bhagavad Gītā through its revealing lens.

Many religious traditions and spiritual or yogic practices claim the Bhagavad Gītā as their own. Commentators from these varied traditions frequently interpret verses in ways that support their doctrines, far too often to the exclusion of the evident meaning of the text as a whole. The voice of the Bhagavad Gītā is powerful, and the text tells us how it wants to be understood. There is no need to superimpose anything that is not presented by the text, as is often done, nor is it necessary to privilege aspects of the text that the text itself does not emphasize. Supplementation is thus required only to bring out what is already emphasized by the text. The imposition of a doctrinal or even esoteric vision onto the verses of the Gītā, ungrounded in the text's essential message of yoga, risks an overly free interpretation. Our task here, therefore, is to offer a vision of the text that is generated from the text itself and a translation that is dedicated to this vision, through which sectarian interpretations of this great work may be better understood and assessed. Such a powerful and embracing vision speaks to those both within and outside traditions that revere this text as sacred.

We can begin to grasp the vision of the Bhagavad Gītā by reviewing the many applications of yoga in the text. The term *yoga* denotes a variety of human practices, disciplines, and even experiences to reach the divine, or a state of perfection that is achieved through rigorous meditational or ascetical discipline. The Bhagavad Gītā explains that these many forms of yoga may be practiced to attain a state of transcendent consciousness and ultimately be united with a specific dimension of the divine. Though the word *yoga* is often used to refer to the human achievement of evolving to higher states of consciousness, the Gītā tells us that it is more than that. At the highest level, yoga is a secret state of union within supreme love, bestowed by divinity, who is also subsumed in this union. Indeed, yoga is the power of love that transforms the heart and to which even divinity submits.

Although yoga generally denotes the soul's union with the divine, the term refers more specifically to the numerous paths for attaining several levels of perfection, as well as the perfections themselves. These paths can be perceived in the prefixed words that modify the term *yoga,* for instance in the compound phrase *buddhi-yoga,* "the yoga of discernment" (BG 2.49). Other prefixed words referring to the different forms of yoga are observable in the titles traditionally given to the eighteen chapters of the Gītā. These traditional presentations of the text are most often read independently from its greater epic context. Although there are no titles in the original text (or for that matter, in the whole of the Mahābhārata), over time, in multiple editions, similar or identical titles have been consistently assigned to its chapters. Most significantly, the word *yoga* always appears in each chapter title. The first group of titles below refers to human practices and philosophical visions that enable souls to reach some aspect of the divine; the second to ways that the divinity manifests himself to allow souls to know particular dimensions of the divine:

TITLES INDICATING PRIMARY FORMS OF YOGA FOR SOULS

The Yoga of Action, *karma-yoga* (chapter 3)
The Yoga of Knowledge, *jñāna-yoga* (chapter 4)
The Yoga of Renunciation, *saṁnyāsa-yoga* (chapter 5)
The Yoga of Meditation, *dhyāna-yoga* (chapter 6)
The Yoga of Love, *bhakti-yoga* (chapter 12)

TITLES INDICATING PRIMARY FORMS OF YOGA FOR DIVINITY

The Yoga of Divine Power, *vibhūti-yoga* (chapter 10)
The Yoga of the Universal Form, *viśva-rūpa-yoga* (chapter 11)
The Yoga of the Ultimate Person, *purushottama-yoga* (chapter 15)

Perhaps the most unexpected form of yoga is indicated in the title of the first chapter, "The Yoga of Arjuna's Despair" (*arjuna-viṣāda-yoga*). Indeed, the concept of yoga is so broad that it even can conceive of despondency as a yoga that connects the practitioner with God.

To understand further the depth of yoga as the Bhagavad Gītā presents it, let us examine the term *yoga* itself. Many introductions to yoga explain that it is a Sanskrit word derived from the verbal root *yuj*, meaning to "yoke," "harness," or "connect." Interestingly, the essential elements as well as the ultimate meaning of yoga are revealed in the English definition of the noun *yoke*. The lexical description of *yoke* is a harness or crossbar by which the heads or necks of two farm animals are joined together. The essential elements derived from this definition could be described as: (1) an overarching powerful element, (2) a particular entity, (3) another distinct entity, and (4) an intimate conjunction between the two entities. Thus, the overarching element of power joins one entity with another in order to create an intimate relationship between the two entities. In the simplest of terms, yoga is the intimacy experienced between two entities who are joined together by a special power (see Figure 1 on the following page).

These four elements found in the yoke are clearly present in the yoga of the Bhagavad Gītā: (1) Yoga-Māyā, abbreviated as Māyā, means literally "the power of yoga."[1] This power can be seen as the potency found in all forms of yoga. Broadly, it is the power that both reveals divinity to souls and conceals divinity from souls. More specifically, it is the divine feminine power that either facilitates intimacy between the two entities of yoga or keeps souls who are not interested in this intimacy from discovering it. Yoga-Māyā thus keeps secret all that is divine, and reveals that secret only to those who are ready to receive it. When this divine power of union is not facilitating intimacy between the soul and the divinity, it is arranging a binding connection between the soul and this world of mixed happiness and suffering, in a state of complete forgetfulness of divinity. (2) Yogeshvara is a name applied to Krishna that

---

1 *Yoga-Māyā* appears in BG 7.25; *Māyā* appears in BG 4.6, 7.14, and 18.61.

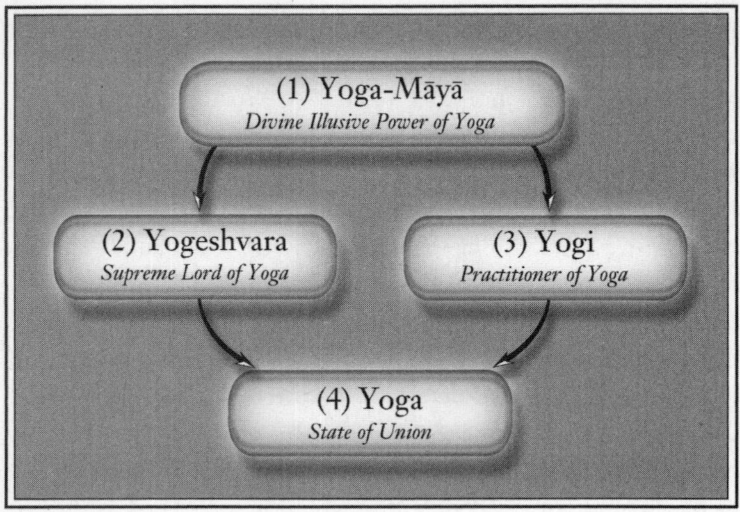

Figure I

means "the Supreme Lord of Yoga."[2] While the name implies that any of Krishna's numerous divine manifestations can be an object of yoga for souls, he himself is the ultimate object. The name also suggests that Krishna is the supreme yogi, that even *he* practices a form of yoga and is himself subsumed by yoga; thus Arjuna addresses Krishna as "O Yogi."[3] When Krishna displays his various manifestations, he is practicing his divine yoga. Arjuna acknowledges this when Krishna reveals his universal form. Moreover, the "ultimate secret," the supreme teaching on yoga, comes from and is sustained by Krishna.[4] (3) A yogi is that soul who practices one of the many forms of yoga presented in the Bhagavad Gītā, of which the primary forms are the yoga of action, the yoga of knowledge, the yoga of meditation, and the yoga of love. Each is a path or discipline that joins the individual self, the yogi, to some dimension of the divine. Thus Krishna tells Arjuna, "Be a yogi!"[5] (4)Yoga here refers to a perfectional union that the soul achieves with a certain level of divinity as the result of yoga practice. In the

---

2 The name Yogeshvara appears in BG 11.4, 11.9, 18.75, and 18.78.
3 The name Yogi for Krishna appears in BG 10.17.
4 The "ultimate secret" is presented in BG 4.3.
5 BG 6.46.

Gītā, this perfectional state of yoga is the supreme love that exists between Yogeshvara and the yogi.

The Bhagavad Gītā demonstrates that, metaphysically, the yoga of divinity has already been achieved, and therefore the divinity is appropriately named Yogeshvara. Krishna expresses his metaphysical achievement of yoga in various ways. He describes the superlatives of this world as his "outer world" manifestations; he presents Brahman, in whom all existences are contained, as his "inner world," or the totality of his spiritual being; and he explains his personal presence as the Purusha in the hearts of living entities, all of which are included within the totality of Brahman, as part of this inner world. Since nothing can exist apart from divinity, and since all living beings are eternally unique and constituent parts of the divine existence, it stands to reason that the only yoga Yogeshvara has yet to achieve is that yoga involving the hearts of humans. In other words, the only thing that God lacks is the personal union with human hearts. Krishna thus beckons souls to come to him in his "innermost" world, the world of his divine heart, where they can offer their love to him freely and fully. The Gītā's ultimate message reflects this choice the human heart makes either to become a part of the intimate world of divinity, or to remain apart from the heart of God in this world of fleeting existence.

The supreme message of the Gītā is revealed gradually in the text, as Krishna discusses the ways in which the hearts of souls can either move toward him, which is the essence of yoga, or away from him, which could be understood as *vi-yoga* ("that which moves one away [*vi-*] from yoga"). The soul that follows the path of *vi-yoga* leads a life of ego-centeredness (*ahaṅkāra*) and selfishness (*mamatva*); whereas the soul that practices some form of yoga focused on divinity leads a life without selfishness and ego-centeredness (*nirmama nirahaṅkāra*). In the former, the self, disconnected from the inner world of the self, becomes entangled in a precarious existence within the outer world of conflict and suffering. In the latter, the self, connected in any number of ways with some dimension of the divine, experiences the inner world of transcendence in which it finds Brahman, "the supreme Spirit," or Purushottama, "the supreme Self." The soul may even see the innermost world of the heart in which it discovers the heart of divinity, as the ultimate human achievement. This concept of the soul moving toward or away from yoga is behind every practice and philosophical discussion presented in the Gītā.

After Krishna has imparted the foundational teaching of the Bhagavad Gītā to Arjuna, and before presenting the ultimate message of his teaching, he boldly declares, "Having fully grasped this, with nothing overlooked, then act as you so choose" (BG 18.63). These words from the final chapter are telling, for they suggest that souls ultimately determine their own destiny. Souls appear to be living in a deterministic universe in which the 'qualities' arising from primordial nature, the *guṇas* (consisting of *sattva, rajas,* and *tamas*), consume them in their daily lives. Souls act according to their unchangeable innate nature, as presented in Krishna's teaching on dharma. No matter what this nature dictates, however, and no matter how forcefully the 'qualities' shape individual lives, when souls have grasped the teachings of the Gītā, they discover that they have a choice—identifying with and serving this temporal world (*vi-yoga*) or identifying with and serving the eternal divine world (*yoga*).

When the soul is bound to this world, it is subject to the powerful conditioning of the 'qualities' of nature. Furthermore, when a soul is reborn, the life of that soul is largely determined by the positive and negative effects arising from the activities of one's previous births. The worldview of the Gītā, however, blends conceptions of free will with this deterministic view. Free will is a necessary ingredient in love; that love cannot be coerced or controlled is axiomatic for the Gītā. This subtle but critical theme shows that souls are given the power of choice, without which there is no possibility of love.

The love call of God, found within his sacred teachings, awakens free will, enabling the soul either to accept the cycle of endless birth and rebirth that binds the soul to this world, or to choose a path leading to the eternal world that frees the soul from the cycle of suffering. This mortal world, the Gītā implies, exists so that souls can exercise choice, without which there is no possibility of love. The implication is that there can be no true love in the divine world without an alternate world. Thus this world, ultimately designed to facilitate love, is brought into being by the divinity to give souls the freedom to love.

The name *Bhagavān* indicates the one from whom love comes and the one who is the most beloved for souls. Wherever Krishna's words are introduced throughout the Gītā, this epithet is utilized. This name also appears as *Bhagavat* (an inflected form of the same word) in the title of the work (in which *t* changes to *d* before the word *Gītā*). The word *Bhagavat* embraces many meanings and connotations, one of which is "the one who possesses (*-vat*) his portions (*bhaga-*)," implying that he is the supreme whole, the totality of all portions. The word also means "one who possesses all superlative attributes" or "one who possesses love." The portions (*bhagas*) of the Bhagavat include all souls, each individual soul constituting a bhakta. The metaphysical meaning of *bhakta,* often translated as "devotee," is literally "an apportioned (soul)," and theologically, it denotes a soul who both loves the divinity and is loved by divinity. *Bhakti,* then, refers to the mutual offerings of love intimately shared between the Bhagavat and the bhakta, and bhakti-yoga is the conjunction of Bhagavat and bhakta, achieved through and perfected in love. In bhakti, Bhagavat sends out his love call to all souls, expressed in the deeper theological meaning of the word *Gītā.*

The Beloved Lord already possesses souls metaphysically and loves souls unconditionally, yet he yearns for our hearts to turn toward him, a desire he expresses through his love song. The highest attainment of yoga is therefore reached when the yogi becomes a bhakta, or one who "offers one's love to God." Such a soul unites with Yogeshvara, who is the Bhagavat, in "the yoga of bhakti" (*bhakti-yoga* in chapter 12). The Gītā defines the relationship of yoga to bhakti at the end of chapter 6, where Krishna conclusively states that among all yogis, the one most absorbed in yoga is the bhakta:[6]

> Even among all yogis,
> one whose inner self
> has come to me,

6 For other examples of how yoga is construed with bhakti, see BG 6.31, 8.10, 9.14, 9.34, 12.1, 12.2, 12.14, 13.10, and 14.26.

Who is full of faith,
who offers love to me—
that one is considered by me
to be the most deeply
absorbed in yoga.

(BG. 6.47)

This verse reveals that the highest form of yoga is the soul's offering of love (*bhajate*) to Krishna. The Yoga Sūtra of Patañjali (YS) also acknowledges the ultimate status of the supreme Lord within the practice of yoga when it states that "the perfection of *samādhi* [which itself is the highest perfectional stage of the eight-limbed yoga system called *aṣṭāṅga*] is dedication to the supreme Lord [*īśvara-praṇidhāna*]" (YS 2.45). Such dedication to the divinity appears most prominently in the Gītā, in which yoga is conceived as a practice that ideally involves the heart:

Among these,
the person of knowledge,
who is constantly absorbed
in yoga that is solely
an offering of love,
is exceptional.
For I am so dearly loved
by the person of knowledge,
and that person
is dearly loved by me.

(BG 7.17)

The supreme divinity is thus the object of love, or the goal of yoga, for all souls; the innumerable souls are the object of love, or the goal of yoga, for the supreme divinity. Because he is unfalteringly receptive to yoga with each and every soul, the divinity is known as the Supreme Lord of Yoga (*yogeshvara*). These two entities, the Lord and the individual soul, are joined, or harnessed as it were, by the yoke, the intimate loving union, which subsumes both the soul and the divinity. We learn from Krishna's teachings that this power of yoga belongs to divinity but is also something to which the divinity himself submits, and upon which even he becomes dependent.

Sanjaya: Minister and Visionary

Sanjaya has a central position in the Bhagavad Gītā. Most obviously he plays the role of minister for King Dhritarāshtra, but it is in his capacity as a visionary that he is extraordinary. Sanjaya also represents the consummate teacher, or guru. He epitomizes the "seer of the truth" (BG 4.34), for he sees and hears what transpires privately between Arjuna and Krishna in a remote location. Sanjaya is privy to the secret vision of the universal form that Krishna insists is only for Arjuna's eyes—the exclusive manifestation reserved for Krishna's dearest friend. Sanjaya, then, appears to be as blessed as Arjuna is by Krishna's presence, teachings, and visions.

This fortunate minister and seer clearly has received the grace of God as a devotee, or bhakta. He transmits his visions directly to the troubled king, indirectly to Vyāsa, the author of the text, and finally, through Vyāsa to all readers of the Bhagavad Gītā. Thus Sanjaya simultaneously functions as a teacher. Krishna could easily be speaking about Sanjaya himself in these concluding verses:

One who reveals
this supreme secret
to those who have
offered me their love,
Enacting the highest
offering of love for me—
that one shall certainly
come to me, without doubt.

And among humans,
there is no one whose acts
are more dearly loved by me
than that one,

Nor shall there be
any other on earth who
is more dearly loved by me
than such a person.
(BG 18.68–18.69)

Clearly, Sanjaya, as an ecstatic devotee and transmitter of Krishna's supreme secret, is loved most dearly by the divinity.

The words of Sanjaya fall into three categories: dialogical, narrative, and rapturous. The text begins with the *dialogical,* when the king, Dhritarāshtra, asks Sanjaya in the first verse what is occurring on the battlefield. Sanjaya responds to the king using *narrative* discourse, as he relates the events at Kurukshetra. In the next nine verses he quotes the king's eldest son, who, from the battlefield, reports on the might of the two armies. Throughout the Gītā, while narrating events, Sanjaya occasionally addresses the king in dialogue. His *narrative* words are his dominant form of expression, however, as he transmits either what is taking place on the battlefield or the interactions between Arjuna and his charioteer. Through his special extrasensory power, Sanjaya functions as the visionary minister for the king and the transmitting teacher for the reader of the Gītā. Not until the final verses of the text do we encounter Sanjaya's third type of expression, that of *rapturous* words, in a suite of verses that begins with the following:

Thus from Vāsudeva
and Pārtha,
whose self is exalted,
I have heard this
wondrous conversation,
which causes a state
of rapturous bliss.
(BG 18.74)

These rapturous expressions, along with those of dialogue and narration, demonstrate Sanjaya's powerful presence as a blissful and compassionate deliverer of souls. Sanjaya thus functions as the archetypal guru, a prominent role in India from ancient times.

Sanjaya's central role in the Bhagavad Gītā is understood in the mystical transmission of this personal dialogue between divinity and devotee, achieved through a complex arrangement. It is Sanjaya alone, far removed from the battle arena, who directly witnesses the dramatic scene:

> By the grace of Vyāsa
> I have heard this
> supreme secret of yoga
> From Krishna,
> the Supreme Lord of Yoga,
> appearing directly
> before my eyes,
> speaking it himself.
>
> (BG 18.75)

The secret dialogue is then received by generations of readers through Vyāsa, the author of the text, from Sanjaya, who is central to its rich delivery (see Figure 2 on the following page).

The Gītā provides us with literary and theological information for understanding the dynamics of the transmission of this sacred dialogue, identified in eight steps: (1) the opening verse of the text, which launches the "outer dialogue," presents Dhritarāshtra, the blind king, who inquires from the enlightened Sanjaya, his minister (BG 1.1); (2) Vyāsa, the famous compiler of the Vedas and other sacred texts, is the renowned sage who grants Sanjaya the power to hear and observe (BG 18.75); (3) what is generally taking place on the battlefield of Kurukshetra (BG 1.2–1.20), specifically the words of Duryodhana (son of Dhritarāshtra) to his teacher, Dronāchārya (BG 1.3–1.11); (4) and, most essentially, the power to transmit the "inner dialogue," those interactions between Arjuna and Krishna (BG 2.11–18.73); (5) Sanjaya narrates what he hears and sees to Dhritarāshtra (BG 18.74–18.78); (6) all of which is then recorded by the author Vyāsa as the complete text of the Bhagavad Gītā (BG 10.13); (7) which is transmitted through teachers of the tradition (BG 4.2); (8) and contemplated by the reader (BG 18.70) either in sacred communities of worshippers (BG 10.9, 18.68-18.69) or intellectual traditions, both keeping the inner and outer dialogues of the Bhagavad Gītā alive.

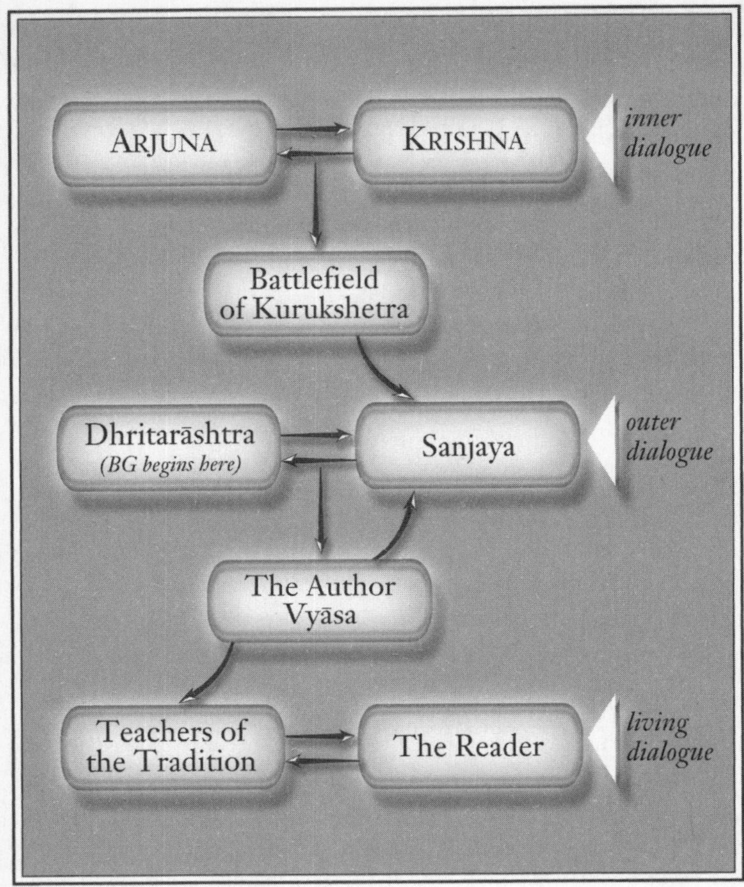

Figure 2

Arjuna: Warrior and Softhearted Soul

Arjuna exhibits a colorful persona. The types of expression exhibited by Arjuna point to the various dimensions of his relationship with Krishna: the chauffeured general, the troubled and softhearted friend, the humble student, and the paradigmatic devotee. We learn that Arjuna is a leading general of his army, who orders his charioteer, Krishna, to place his chariot between the armies in order to assess the challenge before him. Arjuna is overwhelmed when he sees close relatives, friends, and revered gurus on both sides of the battlefield. His heart is naturally torn between his nature as a warrior, which compels him to protect the innocent and establish righteousness, and his deep affection and respect for so many on the opposing side, as well as on his own side. This conflict causes Arjuna to turn to Krishna as a close friend and confidant.

Very quickly, however, their intimate relationship is transformed into that of a humble student with his wise and compassionate teacher. Now Arjuna has become the archetypal spiritual aspirant, the inquiring disciple who is deeply troubled by insurmountable challenges. The shift in his persona, from a warrior to one seeking counsel to a submissive student, occurs over the first chapter and the beginning of the second. Arjuna's role as a disheartened student who receives Krishna's guidance and teachings dominates the remainder of the text.

Later, however, we discover that Krishna also considers Arjuna to be his loving friend, and elsewhere in the Mahābhārata we learn that Arjuna is a cousin to Krishna, whose aunt, Queen Kuntī, is Arjuna's mother. The final aspect of Arjuna's layered relationship with Krishna is that of a devotee whose softheartedness leads him to dedication, strength, and resolve. The reader observes the softhearted Arjuna as he moves along the path of self-realization, all the way to God realization. After exhibiting these distinct dimensions of identity, he returns to his role as a leading general. Finally Arjuna is able to put his heart fully into his duties, even in this treacherous world, having received strength and counsel from his beloved guru, Krishna.

Arjuna's words within the sacred dialogue show struggle, humility, prayer, inquiry, praise, and resolve. These types of expression paint a full portrait of Arjuna as he confronts his dilemma. They are presented in the text as follows: (1) His words of *struggle* are found primarily within the second part of the first chapter, in what we have already described as his "inner conflict." Arjuna's struggle is further expressed by his confusion and despair at the beginning of the second chapter: "My very being is afflicted by a piteous weakness of spirit. My thoughts on dharma are completely bewildered" (BG 2.7). Arjuna also expresses uneasiness while witnessing Krishna's terrific and frightening universal form in chapter 11: "Yet my mind is distressed and filled with fear." (BG 11.45).

(2) Arjuna speaks words of *humility* when approaching Krishna as a disciple, in the words "I am your student—instruct me, for I have offered myself unto you" (BG 2.7). (3) Arjuna's words are *prayerful* in chapter 11: "O Divinity, allow me to see that very [intimate] form. Bestow upon me your grace, O Lord of Divinities, dwelling place of the universe" (BG 11.45). (4) Words of *inquiry* are Arjuna's dominant form of expression throughout the dialogue, such as these found in chapter 6:

Arjuna said:

One who does not strive
  yet possesses faith,
  whose mind has
  deviated from yoga
Without achieving
  full perfection in yoga—
  to what destiny does
  that one go, O Krishna?

(BG 6.37)

Here, Arjuna's questions characterize his relationship with Krishna as a student with his mentor. (5) Arjuna offers words of *praise* or exaltation, as in these worshipful expressions from chapter 10:

You are the supreme Brahman,
  the supreme dwelling place,
  the supreme means of purification;
The eternal divine Person,
  the original Divinity,
  the unborn, all-pervading one.

(BG 10.12)

(6) Words of personal *resolve* are found in the last verse spoken by Arjuna. After receiving Krishna's secret teachings, he is resolved to re-enter the outer world of conflict where he now can act with realization and a full heart:

With confusion destroyed,
my memory is restored
by your grace,
O Achyuta.
I am firmly resolved,
with doubts dispelled—
I shall act according
to your guidance.

(BG 18.73)

These ways in which Arjuna expresses himself are indicative of his various roles in the Bhagavad Gītā, as he evolves in his spiritual quest.

Krishna: Intimate and Infinite Divinity

The portrait of Krishna as the divinity in the Bhagavad Gītā is characterized by intimacy, as well as sublimity and infinite might. Krishna exhibits tender and endearing qualities while serving Arjuna as his charioteer, confidant, teacher, and friend; whereas Krishna's magnificence and sublime power become known when he describes his divine attributes and various forms, and proclaims his cosmological and pantheistic manifestations. He even frightens Arjuna when he displays his terrifying "universal form." Although Krishna's intimate and powerful forms differ dramatically, they share a common element. In each manifestation, Krishna embraces souls through his supreme yoga. He embraces the outer world of souls, those who have not yet discovered his inner worlds of transcendence and divine love, with the yoga of his mighty manifestations, and he embraces the inner world of souls with the yoga of his intimate divine form.

Early on, the Gita reveals Krishna's identity as Arjuna's charioteer. After requesting Krishna to drive his chariot between the two armies (BG 1.21), Arjuna pours his heart out to Krishna, disclosing his torment over the battle that is about to begin. Krishna thus becomes Arjuna's confidant (BG 1.28–2.6). As Arjuna reveals his deep despair to Krishna, who responds with words of wisdom, Arjuna relates to the divinity as his teacher (BG 2.7). Thereafter, Krishna's identity is gradually revealed.

When Krishna begins his philosophical discourse, the narrator identifies him as Bhagavān, which can be taken as simply an honorific for any venerable personage. Moreover, none of Krishna's own words overtly announce his divinity until chapter 4. Krishna's initial role as a charioteer is merely described, but from chapter 2 on he actively plays the part of counselor and teacher. In only a single verse in chapter 2 and one verse in chapter 3 are we given even a hint of Krishna's divinity. These hints take the form of unexpected or even abrupt interjections that express his divine calling, his eternal yearning for souls to come to him. These exhortative expressions give the viewer an underlying powerful message in the form of a communicated subtext. The first hint of Krishna's divinity appears in a verse about yoga:

> Restraining all these [senses],
> one should be seated
> while absorbed in yoga,
> wholly intent on me.
> For one whose senses
> are under control—
> for that one,
> profound knowledge
> is firmly established.
>
> (BG 2.61)

The phrase "wholly intent on me" introduces the idea that Krishna is not only the charioteer, the confidant, and the teacher, but the object of his own teachings. Furthermore, the phrase provides a brief glimpse into Krishna's divine secret. This idea that Krishna is the object of meditation is without precedent in the text.

In these two earlier chapters, Krishna's interjections prepare the reader for what is to come. Krishna's divine identity remains hidden in chapter 3, and yet is suggested:

Renouncing all actions in me,
with one's thought on
the 'principle of self',
Without longings,
without a sense of 'mine'—
fight, with grief cast off.

(BG 3.30)

Here, Krishna refers to himself in the first person, "renouncing all actions in me," and indirectly in the third person, in the phrase "with one's thought on the 'principle of self'," thus cleverly concealing his identity. We learn later in the text that this 'principle of self' is ultimately Krishna as the Purusha, the divinity dwelling within the hearts of all beings, a form to which he will often refer in the third person.

Krishna openly reveals his divine identity for the first time in chapter 4, after which his interjections seem far less abrupt. Through these interjections Krishna communicates that he is the ultimate end of all actions, disciplines, and spiritual attainments, and also explains that everything metaphysical and cosmic is contained within himself. But most significantly, Krishna includes these exhortative bursts in his teachings as an expression of his impassioned love for humans and his desire for humans to love him, to come to him. Krishna first introduces his divine secret through these hints and later, through bold expressions, until it is fully disclosed in the final chapter.

In Krishna's speaking, which dominates the text, the reader encounters eight types of expression: protective, philosophical, edifying, exhortative, declarative, revelational, compassionate, and affectionate. All facilitate the yoga of the divine heart, in which the divinity desires the love of every soul. Thus, collectively, these types of expression constitute the divinity's love call in the Gītā.

Krishna's *protective* words can take the form of encouragement, as found in an earlier chapter: "Relinquishing this poor faintheartedness, stand up, O Scorcher of the Enemy!" (BG 2.3). In his climactic words toward the end of the text Krishna is both protective and reassuring: "I shall grant you freedom from all misfortune—do not despair!" (BG 18.66). Even Krishna's philosophical words can carry an underlying tone of reassurance:

Never, truly,
have I ever not existed—
nor you, nor these kings
who protect the people,
And never
shall any of us
ever cease to be,
now or forevermore.
(BG 2.12)

Again, Krishna's words offer refuge and comfort through his bold declaration of complete protection for souls who never forget him:

One who sees me everywhere
and sees all things in me,
To such a person I am never lost
nor is such a person ever lost to me.
(BG 6.30)

Krishna's *philosophical* words, the second type of expression, are most prominent in the Gītā and can exhibit an objective and even abstract tone:

Of the impermanent
one finds no being;
one finds no nonbeing
of the permanent.
Indeed, the certainty
of both of these
has been perceived
by seers of the truth.
(BG 2.16)

However, these words do not remain abstract for long. As he addresses the practical challenges of life, Krishna's words become more supportive, offered by the divinity to elevate the soul to the highest region within his divine realm. He may even combine philosophical teaching with a rhetorical question:

> One who knows this [self]
> to be indestructible,
> eternal, unborn,
> and everpresent—
> How and whom does
> that person slay, O Pārtha?
> And whom does
> that one cause to slay?
>
> (BG 2.21)

Krishna's *edifying* words, another form of expression, are instructive, often addressed to Arjuna in the second person, "you." Here, a certain directional force leads souls ever closer to the ultimate level of Krishna's divinity. Such edifying speech acts in one of three ways: (1) to prepare the soul for elevation to the divine, (2) to encourage particular practices and disciplines that connect the soul to the divine, or (3) to encourage the perfection of offerings and practices, intensifying the soul's intimate connection with the supreme and personal divinity, Krishna. These three types of edifying speech, found throughout the text, typically direct an individual from the outer world of conflict to the inner world of spirit and transcendence, and finally to the innermost world of the heart, in which a soul finds the perfect love of divinity.

Krishna's edifying preparatory remarks emphasize the importance of performing one's "dharma," the right way of acting in this world determined by one's phase of life (*āshrama*) and one's particular capabilities and talents (*varna*). He stresses the importance of acting *according to one's nature,* thus being true to one's dharma:

Better is one's own dharma
 even if imperfect
 than another's dharma
 followed perfectly.
Performing action
 determined by
 one's own nature,
 one does not incur fault.
(BG 18.47)

Here, Krishna reinforces Arjuna's position as a warrior. He also warns Arjuna that he could not act against his nature even if he were to try to do so (BG 18.60). Krishna teaches in the second type of edifying words that the fruits of action produced from following one's dharma are not to be enjoyed; rather, they are to be renounced, resulting in detachment from the outer world and the lifting of consciousness to the inner world of transcendence, where one becomes freed from the cycle of birth and death:

Indeed, those wise ones
 who are absorbed
 in the yoga of discernment,
 relinquishing the fruits
 born of action,
Who are freed
 from the bondage
 of repeated births,
 go to a place beyond suffering.
(BG 2.51)

These edifying statements of Krishna act as encouraging words that gradually elevate the soul *through practice and discipline* to eternal life, beyond this fleeting world of hardship and impermanence. Finally, when action arising from dharma produces fruits that are offered to the divinity *out of love,* then such a soul reaches the innermost world of the heart, in which the love of divinity is discovered:

For them, who are constantly
absorbed in yoga,
who offer loving service
with natural affection,
I offer that yoga
of discernment
by which they
come close to me.

(BG 10.10)

These words encouraging souls to perfect such offerings of love form the third level of edifying speech. All three types of edifying statements—preparatory, practical, and perfectional—are phases of yoga that connect the soul more and more intimately with the divinity.

The *exhortative* words of Krishna strongly urge souls to know him, act for him, come to him, or love him. This type of expression, through which Krishna draws souls to himself, often contains, overtly or covertly, the objective pronoun *me.* The following verse demonstrates the language of reflexive exhortation:

Place your mind on me alone;
let your discernment
enter into me.
You shall dwell
only in me
from now forevermore—
of this there is no doubt.

(BG 12.8)

This and many other verses exhort souls to take up any of the contemplative or more active practices presented in the Gītā and integrate them as an offering to Krishna. Whatever the path or discipline chosen, Krishna urges souls to tread that path since it ultimately leads to the heart of the divinity. These exhortations express Krishna's passionate yet patient love for souls. He proclaims in a great number of verses his desire that souls know, see, and remember him.[7] Similarly, throughout the text, Krishna encourages souls to "meditate" on him and to remain "wholly intent" on him, "with mind deeply attached" to him and "thought focused" upon him.[8] Furthermore, Krishna implores souls to act only for him when he instructs them to take "full refuge" in him and to "renounce all actions" for him.[9]

Krishna's divine love call is most evident in his exhortations to "love" him and "come to" him. First and foremost, he desires that souls "offer their love" to him, as shown in the numerous words derived from the verbal root *bhaj,* meaning "to offer love to the divine," such as the words *bhakti* or *bhakta.* These derivative words appear thirty-eight times and are present in twelve of the Gītā's eighteen chapters. Krishna also speaks of "worshipping" him, "sacrificing" for him, "praising" and "honoring" him, and "acting out of reverence" for him. Krishna describes souls who have "offered their lives" and who are "devoted" to him. The sheer quantity and pervasiveness of these exhortations convey Krishna's ardent desire for the love of souls. This divine yearning is further expressed in exhortations that invite, even entreat, souls to come to him. Indeed, Krishna explains at least twenty-three times the ways in which souls may "come" to him.[10]

In Krishna's *declarations,* another type of expression, he proclaims his divine identity and the manifestations of his divinity. These statements are most often expressed in the first person as "I am" declarations. In numerous places he identifies himself with the superlative dimensions of this world:

---

7 Some verses exhorting souls to remember Krishna are: 7.30, 8.7, 8.13, 8.14; to know Krishna: 5.29, 7.3, 7.10, 7.12, 7.30, 10.24, 10.27, 15.19, 18.55 (twice); to understand Krishna: 4.14, 7.6, 9.6, 10.2, 10.3; to see Krishna: 4.35, 5.18, 6.29, 6.30, 11.3–8, 11.54.

8 Meditating on Krishna: 9.22, 10.8, 12.6; intent on him: 2.61, 6.14, 12.6, 12.20, 18.57; immersed in him: 4.10, 12.10; with thought focused upon him: 6.14, 10.9, 18.57; with mind on him: 5.13, 7.1, 9.13, 9.34, 12.2, 12.8, 12.14, 18.65; with thought on him: 12.7, 12.9, 18.57, 18.58.

9 Taking refuge in Krishna: 4.10, 7.19, 7.29, 9.18, 9.32, 18.56, 18.66; renouncing actions for Krishna: 3.30, 5.13, 12.6, 18.57.

10 Coming to Krishna: 4.9, 4.10, 6.47, 7.14, 7.15, 7.19, 7.23, 8.7, 8.15, 8.16, 9.11, 9.25, 9.28, 9.34, 10.10, 11.55, 13.18, 14.2, 18.55, 18.65, 18.66, 18.68.

I am the taste in water,
  O Kaunteya;
  I am the radiance
  of the moon and the sun,
The sacred utterance
  in all the Vedas,
  the sound in space,
  the prowess in men.

(BG 7.8)

Krishna finally states that all sublime things in this world are but a reflection of his divine splendor:

Whatever form of existence
  possesses abounding power,
  contains the beautiful,
  or is well-endowed
  with excellence—
Understand that
  every such form
  has become fully manifest
  from but a part of my splendor.

(BG 10.41)

Thus the superlative aspects of creation function as a medium through which divinity embraces souls. This becomes part of Krishna's yoga. The beautiful and the sublime continuously reveal messages from the heart of divinity, directing us toward him.

Krishna's *revelational* words are found mostly in chapter 11. This form of expression, in which Krishna reveals his manifestation of omnipotence as the Vishva Rūpa, and his intimate divinity as the Bhagavat, also dramatizes the relationship between the two. Arjuna asks to see Krishna's mighty and powerful forms, and Krishna tells him that these forms are innumerable:

Behold my forms,
O Pārtha,
by the hundreds,
or by the thousands—
Divine, of various types,
and of various colors
and appearances.

(BG 11.5)

To see these forms would require that Arjuna possess a special kind of vision:

But you are unable to see me
with only this, your own eyes.
I [therefore] give divine eyes to you—
behold my supremely powerful yoga!

(BG 11.8)

This orchestrated vision of the awesome manifestation of Krishna is described not only by the divinity himself, but also by the narrator, Sanjaya, and by Arjuna, as he witnesses the marvelous display of divine grandeur.

The juxtaposition of this majestic form with Krishna's preferred form further reveals the supremacy of the divinity's more intimate form, which has been in dialogue with Arjuna all along. We learn that Krishna's ultimate form is, paradoxically, concealed as the manifestation of divine intimacy with whom Arjuna has interacted but which he has perhaps not fully appreciated until now, after encountering this starkly contrasting and frightful form of might. While attempting to comprehend such a display of overwhelming power, Arjuna implores Krishna to return to the personal affectionate form that he has always cherished:

As a father is to a son,
as a friend to a friend,

As a dearly loved one
to a dearly beloved—
be pleased to show your
loving kindness, O Divinity.
(BG 11.44cd)

Arjuna is careful to express his gratitude for being granted a vision of the divinity's universal form, though he yearns to be reunited with Krishna's intimate form:

Having seen what never
has been seen before,
I am exceedingly pleased,
Yet my mind is distressed
and filled with fear.
O Divinity, allow me to see
that very [intimate] form.
Bestow upon me your grace,
O Lord of Divinities,
dwelling place of the universe.
(BG 11.45)

Many in India, as well as in the West, consider the awesome and terrifying Vishva Rūpa to be the superior form of divinity. In fact, some consider chapter 11 as the climactic chapter of the Bhagavad Gītā because of Krishna's spectacular revelation of the Vishva Rūpa. One might ask, however, why would the climactic portion of an eighteen-chapter work be placed in the eleventh chapter?

Arjuna, in his longing for Krishna's personal form, makes a statement about the superiority of this form. Arjuna's anxious retreat from his vision of the Vishva Rūpa, and his corresponding eagerness to reconnect with Krishna's humanlike form, certainly confirms the Gītā's emphasis on the intimate divinity. Moreover, chapter 12 is solely dedicated to the offering of the heart to this personal form of divinity, leading the reader away from the grandiose form of the eleventh chapter, which further expresses the ultimacy of the intimate deity. Thus the Vishva Rūpa, for Arjuna, functions as an extraordinarily ornate throne that highlights and celebrates Krishna's manifestation as the loving personal deity. And just as Arjuna requires a special vision to see the Vishva Rūpa, he requires a fully devoted heart in order to know the most intimate form of divinity:

Only by the offering of
one's love to none other,
O Arjuna, am I able,
in such a form,
To be known and
to be truly seen,
and to be attained,
O Fighter of the Enemy.

(BG 11.54)

Krishna's words of *compassion,* the next type of expression, demonstrate his loving generosity toward all souls. Krishna clearly is not a jealous God, for out of his infinite compassion he accepts that souls also worship lesser divinities who personify Krishna's divine powers. Krishna even goes so far as to fortify the faith of souls who worship such divinities:

Whoever, with faith,
has offered love
to whatever form that
person desires to worship—
Upon every such person,
I bestow this
immovable faith.

(BG 7.21)

Krishna's openness to the numerous paths by which souls can approach him is an expression of his inclusiveness, as well as his unwavering love:

In the way they offer
themselves to me,
in just that way
I offer my love
to them reciprocally.
Human beings
follow my path
universally,
O Pārtha.

(BG 4.11)

Here, Krishna's words are gentle and accommodating. The divinity's acceptance of all souls is confirmed. Krishna loves souls in whatever ways they are able to love him, directly or indirectly. Moreover, although Krishna states that he is equal toward all souls, he feels especially close to those who offer their hearts directly to him. The following verse demonstrates Krishna's *compassionate* as well as his *affectionate* words:

I am the same
toward all beings;
no one is either hated
or dearly loved by me.
Yet those who,
with an offering of love,
offer their love to me—
they are in me
and I also am in them.

(BG 9.29)

In this verse Krishna declares, perhaps surprisingly, that no one is dearly loved by him. Such impartiality, as expressed in the first half of the verse, is associated with Krishna's manifestation as the Lord within the hearts of beings. Yet in this and several other verses Krishna states that those who have offered their hearts to him are indeed in him and are dearly loved by him. These verses are examples of the final type of expression, Krishna's *affectionate* words:

Indeed, this is the immortal
essence of dharma,
which has been declared;
those who participate in
this worship fully,
Who have faith,
who are devoted to me,
who have offered their love—
they are most dearly loved by me.
(BG 12.20)

This verse is the last one in a grouping of verses found in chapter 12 (BG 12.13–12.20), in which Krishna describes the types of souls who are recipients of his dearest love. As seen above, Krishna emphasizes that there has never been nor will there ever be any soul whom he loves more dearly than the one who reveals his secret of divine love to other souls (BG 18.68–69).

The Secret Love Song

The Bhagavad Gītā is an impassioned expression of divine yearning. Krishna explains that everything is contained in him, that he is the one by whom everything is set forth into motion and sustained, and that he is truly the Bhagavat, the "possessor of all superlatives, existences, and beings." Despite the infinite and absolute fullness of his being, he yearns for one thing that is not within his possession or under his control—the human heart. Thus the divinity experiences some incompleteness within his divine completeness, and longs for what he does not possess. Krishna therefore sends out his secret love call, a song coming from his heart to all hearts, which is the unifying message of the Gītā.

This essential message of divine love, presented in chapter 18 as "the greatest secret of all," is at once revealed and concealed in the

Gītā. It is secret because Krishna desires souls to know about it only when they are ready to receive it, to preserve the purity of the soul's loving response. The secret nature of this divine longing of God's heart is reflected in its subtle presentation in earlier chapters. It is introduced gradually, then more boldly presented in later chapters, not only because it is secret, but also because Krishna wishes to show how everything is related to this message.

Arjuna is informed of Krishna's divine yearning through his teachings on how souls come to him and how all paths, or dharmas, can lead souls to his inner world. Indeed, the penultimate and final verses of many chapters express this. Krishna's acknowledgment and approval of such paths functions in two ways: one is to demonstrate his compassion in accepting the various ways souls desire to move toward him; and the other is to express his intention to keep his ultimate teachings secret from those who are not yet ready to love him, by diverting them to those paths that are themselves preliminary to realizing the divine secret.

The Gītā opens with an irresolvable ethical conflict in Arjuna's outer world. Through this conflict, which acts as a catalyst, Arjuna attains the highest yoga, the yoga of the heart. By hearing Krishna's call to love, by hearing what the divinity most secretly desires, Arjuna's vision of his overwhelming problems is transformed. He learns to see the embrace of divinity behind all the events of this world, even the most dreadful.

The supreme secret is revealed in key places throughout the text. At the beginning of chapter 4, Krishna claims to deliver the ancient secret of yoga, which had been lost from the lineage that once transmitted it. He specifies who may receive such a secret:

> This same ancient yoga
> is now spoken
> by me to you:
> "Having offered your love,
> you have also
> become my friend"—
> truly, this is the ultimate secret.
>
> (BG 4.3)

This verse introduces the reader to divine secrecy, suggested by the words *ultimate secret.* We hear nothing more of divine secrecy until chapter 9, where Krishna states, "Now I shall reveal to you this greatest secret, for you are without envy" (BG 9.1). Krishna himself speaks highly of this secret of secrets: "This is the king of knowledge, the king of secrets" (BG 9.2), then later declares, "I am the silence of secrets" (BG 10.38). In chapter 11, Arjuna speaks of Krishna's "supreme secret" as the 'principle of self' (BG 11.1). Krishna declares "the greatest secret" to be knowledge of his identity as the "Ultimate Person" (BG 15.18–20). The presentation in chapter 18 of "the secret" constitutes the dramatic finale of the entire work. Here, Krishna speaks about the three levels of "the secret" in the climactic point of the chapter (BG 18.63-64), and explains that one who disseminates this "supreme secret" becomes very dear to him (BG 18.68). Furthermore, Sanjaya describes Krishna's complete teachings as "the supreme secret of yoga" in the last words of the text (BG 18.75).

Krishna's supreme message is positioned within the final chapter of the Gītā as its focal point. Chapter 18 can be divided into four sections, each with its own theme:

1. The Secret: Acting According to One's Nature (vss. 1–49)
2. The Greater Secret: Transcendence and the Supreme Self (vss. 50–63)
3. The Greatest Secret of All: Divine Love (vss. 64–66)
4. Concluding Words: Krishna, Arjuna, and Sanjaya (vss. 67–78)

The first section is dedicated to the capacity of the soul to achieve spiritual transcendence through action in the outer world of conflict. It begins with renunciation of selfish actions by relinquishment of the fruits of action (1–12), then addresses the five causes of action (13–19) and how action is affected by the 'qualities' of primordial nature (19–40). Next, it describes the four general classes of society according to their work: the educators or priests, the rulers or warriors, the business- or tradespeople, and the skilled workers (41–48). Finally, the Gītā explains how attainment of transcendence is possible in a state of actionlessness, through renunciation (49). This constitutes the secret.

The second section presents the inner world of transcendence and moves the reader toward the innermost world of the heart in bhakti. It presents disciplines of the self to attain Brahman (50–53), how Brahman leads to bhakti and the nature of bhakti (54–58), as well as how acting according to one's nature in dharma is inevitable (59–60). The text then describes how love is offered to the supreme Self, the indwelling Lord within the heart (61–62). The transitional and pivotal verse (63) reveals the secret in relation to the greater secret, which anticipates the greatest secret of all (64).

The third section, only three verses, focuses exclusively on the innermost world of the heart. In verse 64, Krishna's supreme message is fully disclosed; verse 65 describes the ultimate achievement of offering one's heart to the divinity and a reaffirmation of how such a soul is dearly loved. Verse 66 explains the exclusive attention of the soul for the divinity, a love that goes beyond all forms of dharma. These three verses, beginning with the revelation of the divinity's passion for souls, constitute the ultimate message in Krishna's teachings, the greatest secret of all.

In the fourth section, the voices of Krishna, Arjuna, and Sanjaya are heard. First, the soul who is qualified to receive the supreme secret is presented (67); then comes a declaration that one who reveals this supreme secret to others possesses the highest love for divinity, and is more loved by the divinity than any other soul (68–69). Krishna's words of benediction follow, stating that by contemplating this dialogue, spiritual achievements will be made (70–71). In his final words, Krishna inquires from Arjuna if he has heard "the single highest point" of his teachings, which would dispel his bewildered state (72), and Arjuna responds in the affirmative (73). Sanjaya's ecstatic epilogue then forms the concluding verses of the text (74–78).

Thus divine secrecy is a theme that runs throughout the Gītā, building toward Krishna's full disclosure in the final chapter of all the various forms of secret knowledge that comprise "the supreme secret of yoga." Krishna identifies the first two phases of secrecy explicitly, as the "secret" and the "greater secret":

Thus for you this knowledge,
which is a greater secret
than the [previous] secret,
is made known by me.
Having fully grasped this,
with nothing overlooked,
then act as you so choose.

(BG 18.63)

It is clear from this verse that Krishna gives Arjuna the freedom to either act in accordance with this secret knowledge or not, demonstrating free will within supreme love. Then Krishna discloses the third phase of secrecy, his greatest secret among all secrets:

Hear still further
the greatest secret of all,
my supreme message:
"You are so much loved by me!"
Therefore I shall speak
for your well-being.

(BG 18.64)

This secret of divine secrets is now revealed: "You are so much loved by me!" The simple message here is that the divinity passionately loves souls, as indicated by the use of the Sanskrit word *iṣṭaḥ,* meaning "desired" or "ardently loved," and the use of the adverbial intensive *so much.* These few words constitute the very essence of the song or "Gītā" of the Beloved Lord. Every verse in the Bhagavad Gītā thus revolves around these words. Krishna underscores this declaration of divine love by calling it his "supreme message," and further emphasizes the message with the use of the Sanskrit equivalent of quotation marks. This ultimate statement establishes the tone of the entire text, the inner intention of the author, and the controlling principle for understanding the text. No other statement in the Gītā receives such attention.

Krishna builds up to the revelation of this greatest secret, as we have seen, with a dramatic summary of his teachings in the first sixty-three verses of the chapter, thus positioning the greatest secret of all as the climax of the work. In verse 65, following this greatest secret, Krishna urges souls to love him, and promises that they will come to him since they are "dearly loved" by him:

Be mindful of me
  with love offered to me;
  sacrificing for me,
  act out of reverence for me.
Truly you shall
  come to me—
  this I promise you
  for you are dearly loved by me.
(BG 18.65)

This verse reveals that the best possible response of souls to Krishna's greatest of all secrets is bhakti, the love offered by the soul to the supreme divinity. Bhakti, therefore, is not merely a means to reach the divine, but is itself the perfection of all other means for attaining an intimate connection with the divinity in yoga.

Many commentators, beginning with Rāmānuja of the twelfth century, consider the next verse, BG 18.66, to be the Gītā's ultimate statement. Here, Krishna states his desire that souls give up everything and come to him as their only refuge. He provides divine assurance that such souls will be free from all troubles:

Completely relinquishing
  all forms of dharma,
  come to me
  as your only shelter.
I shall grant you
  freedom from
  all misfortune—
  do not despair!
(BG 18.66)

Krishna presents in this verse a certain irony, even an apparent contradiction, when he directs all forms of dharma to be completely given up, after a significant part of the text has been devoted to establishing the importance of dharma. This request expresses

Krishna's desire for the unmediated love of humans, accentuated by his plea to come to him as one's only shelter. This verse communicates a divine passion for souls, and how such love between the devotee and the divinity is ultimately not limited by dharma. Divine love goes beyond dharma, yet at the same time includes dharma.

Yoga at its highest level is the soul's intimate connection with the divine through the heart. Yoga, for divinity, is the various manifestations of the divine that embrace souls: the all-pervading imperishable Brahman; the presence of divinity in the beautiful and sublime in this world; the powerful and spectacular Vishva Rūpa; the supreme Self dwelling in the hearts of all as the Purusha; and the supreme personal divinity, Krishna, celebrated as Purushottama, the ultimate Person; or Yogeshvara, the supreme Lord of Yoga; or Bhagavān, the Beloved Lord—the most intimate deity for the loving devotee. Through these divine manifestations, the supreme divinity is revealed to souls or concealed from souls according to their desire or lack of desire to come to him, to unite with him.

According to the Gītā, yoga is not a reclusive meditation in some distant mountain hermitage; rather, the hermitage is found within one's heart, and in the hearts of others. The ultimate yoga for souls is to attain a state of full-heartedness — a heart that offers itself in unremitting, unconditional love in response to the divine yearning. This yearning, the greatest secret of all, is pronounced as "You are so much loved by me."

The Bhagavad Gītā is truly the Beloved Lord's "secret love song." This ever-beckoning song urges souls to embrace divinity just as divinity forever embraces souls. The Gītā begins with a question that speaks to every one of us: "How are we to act in this world of conflict and suffering?" The Gītā's answer is simply *to act out of love.* This hidden song of the divinity calls souls to *act out of love* in all that they do, in all that they think, feel, and will. The Gītā insists that human life is meant for hearing this innermost song of the heart. It behooves souls to search for this song, and upon hearing it, to listen to the divine love song as it resonates in everything, everywhere, and at every moment—to hear it through the hearts of all beings and in all of life. Once heard, this secret love song is celebrated as the most blessed gift of divinity to humankind.

Sanskrit Text

On the English Transliteration

The original Sanskrit text is provided here in transliteration. For this I have relied upon the critical edition of the text and its verse divisions presented in the great work of the Bhandarkar Oriental Research Institute (BORI), in Pune, India (see Bibliography). Although popular editions of the BG contain some differences in verse division and numbering in chapters 1 and 13, I have mostly utilized the BORI edition of the text. Readers may find the transliteration helpful in reconciling differences from other translations.

The transliterated text that appears here has been formatted to give nonspecialist readers a visual sense of the versification of the original Sanskrit. The typical eight-syllable quarter-lined metered verses, or *anuṣṭubh,* appear as couplets of Sanskrit text, the quarter lines indicated by commas. For example:

dharma-kṣetre kuru-kṣetre, samavetā yuyutsavaḥ |
māmakāḥ pāṇḍavāś caiva, kim akurvata sañjaya || 1.1 ||

The eleven-syllable quarter-lined verses, or *triṣṭubh,* appear as quatrains, easily distinguishable from the more common two-line *anuṣṭubh* verses by the four lines of embellished metered verses. For example:

gurūn ahatvā hi mahānubhāvān
  śreyo bhoktuṁ bhaikṣyam apīha loke |
hatvārtha-kāmāṁs tu gurūn ihaiva
  bhuñjīya bhogān rudhira-pradigdhān || 2.5 ||

The English translation also imitates this visual distinction between the couplets of the *anuṣṭubh* verses and the quatrains of the longer verse form. This is accomplished in the translated *anuṣṭubh* verses by presenting two "leading lines," nonindented lines of text, followed by one or more indented lines. Likewise, for the more complex *triṣṭubh* verses, I have presented four leading lines, each followed by one or more indented lines.

Recitation of Sanskrit Verse

Sanskrit distinguishes between accent and length of syllables. Syllables within words are spoken in either short or long (held twice the length as short) lengths of time, also called light and heavy respectively, and there are numerous varieties of poetic meters for many types of verse lengths. Following are basic rules to acquaint the reader with the recitation of Sanskrit verse, so important to the language.

Accent

1. The first syllable of two-syllable words: e.g., *bhakti, deva;*
2. The penultimate syllable of all words having more than two syllables if the syllable contains a long vowel, a diphthong, or a short vowel followed by two consonants: e.g., *nirvāna,* Ganeśa, *gṛhastha;*
3. The antepenultimate syllable in most other cases: e.g., Mahābhārata, Himālaya, Rāmāyana, Upaniṣad.

Light and Heavy Syllables in Poetic Meter

1. Light syllables (*laghu*) are those made up of short vowels which are not followed by more than one consonant (*anusvāra* "ṁ" and *avagraha* "ḥ" included), either within a word or between words. Light syllables are short, half the length of heavy or long syllables. For example, *nama oṁ viṣṇupādāya* (underlined vowels indicate light syllables).
2. Heavy syllables (*guru*) are those made up of long vowels or those made of short vowels followed by more than one consonant (*anusvāra* "ṁ" and *avagraha* "ḥ" included), either within a word or between words. For example, *nama oṁ viṣṇupādāya* (underlined vowels indicate heavy syllables).

The Complete Sanskrit Text

I

Dhṛtarāṣṭra uvāca

1 dharma-kṣetre kuru-kṣetre, samavetā yuyutsavaḥ |
mamakāḥ pāṇḍavāś caiva, kim akurvata sañjaya ||

Sañjaya uvāca

2 dṛṣṭvā tu pāṇḍavānīkaṁ, vyūḍhaṁ duryodhanas tadā |
ācāryam upasaṅgamya, rājā vacanam abravīt ||
3 paśyaitāṁ pāṇḍu-putrāṇāṁ, ācārya mahatīṁ camūm |
vyūḍhāṁ drupada-putreṇa, tava śiṣyeṇa dhīmatā ||
4 atra śūrā maheṣv-āsā, bhīmārjuna-samā yudhi |
yuyudhāno virāṭaś ca, drupadaś ca mahā-rathaḥ ||
5 dhṛṣṭaketuś cekitānaḥ, kāśirājaś ca vīryavān |
purujit kuntibhojaś ca, śaibyaś ca nara-puṅgavaḥ ||
6 yudhāmanyuś ca vikrānta, uttamaujāś ca vīryavān |
saubhadro draupadeyāś ca, sarva eva mahā-rathāḥ ||
7 asmākaṁ tu viśiṣṭā ye, tān nibhoda dvijottama |
nāyakā mama sainyasya, saṁjñārthaṁ tān bravīmi te ||
8 bhavān bhīṣmaś ca karṇaś ca, kṛpaś ca samitiṁ-jayaḥ |
aśvatthāmā vikarṇaś ca, saudamattis tathaiva ca ||
9 anye ca bahavaḥ śūrā, mad-arthe tyakta-jīvitāḥ |
nānā-śastra-praharaṇāḥ, sarve yuddha-viśāradāḥ ||
10 aparyāptaṁ tad asmākaṁ, balaṁ bhīṣmābhirakṣitam |
paryāptaṁ tv idam eteṣāṁ, balaṁ bhīmābhirakṣitam ||
11 ayaneṣu ca sarveṣu, yathā-bhāgam avasthitāḥ |
bhīṣmam evābhirakṣantu, bhavantaḥ sarva eva hi ||
12 tasya sañjanayan harṣaṁ, kuru-vṛddhaḥ pitāmahaḥ |
siṁha-nādaṁ vinadyoccaiḥ, śaṅkhaṁ dadhmau pratāpavān ||
13 tataḥ śaṅkhāś ca bheryaś ca, paṇavānaka-gomukhāḥ |
sahasaivābhyahanyanta, sa śabdas tumulo 'bhavat ||
14 tataḥ śvetair hayair yukte, mahati syandane sthitau |
mādhavaḥ pāṇḍavaś caiva, divyau śaṅkhau pradadhmatuḥ ||
15 pāñcajanyaṁ hṛṣīkeśo, devadattaṁ dhanañjayaḥ |
pauṇḍraṁ dadhmau mahā-śaṅkhaṁ, bhīma-karmā vṛkodaraḥ ||
16 anantavijayaṁ rājā, kuntī-putro yudhiṣṭhiraḥ |
nakulaḥ sahadevaś ca, sughoṣa-maṇipuṣpakau ||
17 kāśyaś ca parameṣv-āsaḥ, śikhaṇḍī ca mahā-rathaḥ |
dhṛṣṭadyumno virāṭaś ca, sātyakiś cāparājitaḥ ||

18 drupado draupadeyāś ca, sarvaśaḥ pṛthivī-pate |
saubhadraś ca mahā-bāhuḥ, śaṅkhān dadhmuḥ pṛthak pṛthak ||
19 sa ghoṣo dhārtarāṣṭrāṇāṁ, hṛdayāni vyadārayat |
nabhaś ca pṛthivīṁ caiva, tumulo vyanunādayan ||
20 atha vyavasthitān dṛṣṭvā, dhārtarāṣṭrān kapi-dhvajaḥ |
pravṛtte śastra-sampāte, dhanur udyamya pāṇḍavaḥ ||
21 hṛṣīkeśaṁ tadā vākyam, idam āha mahī-pate |
senayor ubhayor madhye, rathaṁ sthāpaya me 'cyuta ||
22 yāvad etān nirīkṣe 'haṁ, yoddhu-kāmān avasthitān |
kair mayā saha yoddhavyam, asmin raṇa-samudyame ||
23 yotsyamānān avekṣe 'haṁ, ya ete 'tra samāgatāḥ |
dhārtarāṣṭrasya durbuddher, yuddhe priya-cikīrṣavaḥ ||
24 evam ukto hṛṣīkeśo, guḍākeśena bhārata |
senayor ubhayor madhye, sthāpayitvā rathottamam ||
25 bhīṣma-droṇa-pramukhataḥ, sarveṣāṁ ca mahī-kṣitām |
uvāca pārtha paśyaitān, samavetān kurūn iti ||
26 tatrāpaśyat sthitān pārthaḥ, pitṝn atha pitāmahān |
ācāryān mātulān bhrātṝn, putrān pautrān sakhīṁs tathā ||
27 śvaśurān suhṛdaś caiva, senayor ubhayor api |
tān samīkṣya sa kaunteyaḥ, sarvān bandhūn avasthitān ||
28 kṛpayā parayāviṣṭo, viṣīdann idam abravīt |
dṛṣṭvemān sva-janān kṛṣṇa, yuyutsūn samavasthitān ||
29 sīdanti mama gātrāṇi, mukhaṁ ca pariśuṣyati |
vepathuś ca śarīre me, roma-harṣaś ca jāyate ||
30 gāṇḍīvaṁ sraṁsate hastāt, tvak caiva paridahyate |
na ca śaknomy avasthātuṁ, bhramatīva ca me manaḥ ||
31 nimittāni ca paśyāmi, viparītāni keśava |
na ca śreyo 'nupaśyāmi, hatvā sva-janam āhave ||
32 na kāṅkṣe vijayaṁ kṛṣṇa, na ca rājyaṁ sukhāni ca |
kiṁ no rājyena govinda, kiṁ bhogair jīvitena vā ||
33 yeṣām arthe kāṅkṣitaṁ no, rājyaṁ bhogāḥ sukhāni ca |
ta ime 'vasthitā yuddhe, prāṇāṁs tyaktvā dhanāni ca ||
34 ācāryāḥ pitaraḥ putrās, tathaiva ca pitāmahāḥ |
mātulāḥ śvaśurāḥ pautrāḥ, śyālāḥ saṁbandhinas tathā ||
35 etān na hantum icchāmi, ghnato 'pi madhusūdana |
api trailokya-rājyasya, hetoḥ kiṁ nu mahī-kṛte ||
36 nihatya dhārtarāṣṭrān naḥ, kā prītiḥ syāj janārdana |
pāpam evāśrayed asmān, hatvaitān ātatāyinaḥ ||
37 tasmān nārhā vayaṁ hantuṁ, dhārtarāṣṭrān sa-bāndhavān |
sva-janaṁ hi kathaṁ hatvā, sukhinaḥ syāma mādhava ||
38 yady apy ete na paśyanti, lobhopahata-cetasaḥ |
kula-kṣaya-kṛtaṁ doṣaṁ, mitra-drohe ca pātakam ||
39 kathaṁ na jñeyam asmābhiḥ, pāpād asmān nivartitum |
kula-kṣaya-kṛtaṁ doṣaṁ, prapaśyadbhir janārdana ||

40 kula-kṣaye praṇaśyanti, kula-dharmāḥ sanātanāḥ |
dharme naṣṭe kulaṁ kṛtsnam, adharmo 'bhibhavaty uta ||
41 adharmābhibhavāt kṛṣṇa, praduṣyanti kula-striyaḥ |
strīṣu duṣṭāsu vārṣṇeya, jāyate varṇa-saṅkaraḥ ||
42 saṅkaro narakāyaiva, kula-ghnānāṁ kulasya ca |
patanti pitaro hy eṣāṁ, lupta-piṇḍodaka-kriyāḥ ||
43 doṣair etaiḥ kula-ghnānāṁ, varṇa-saṅkara-kārakaiḥ |
utsādyante jāti-dharmāḥ, kula-dharmāś ca śāśvatāḥ ||
44 utsanna-kula-dharmāṇāṁ, manuṣyāṇāṁ janārdana |
narake niyataṁ vāso, bhavatīty anuśuśruma ||
45 aho bata mahat pāpaṁ, kartuṁ vyavasitā vayam |
yad-rājya-sukha-lobhena, hantuṁ sva-janam udyatāḥ ||
46 yadi mām apratīkāram, aśastraṁ śastra-pāṇayaḥ |
dhārtarāṣṭrā raṇe hanyus, tan me kṣemataraṁ bhavet ||
47 evam uktvārjunaḥ saṅkhye, rathopastha upāviśat |
visṛjya sa-śaraṁ cāpaṁ, śoka-saṁvigna-mānasaḥ ||

2

Sañjaya uvāca

1 taṁ tathā kṛpayāviṣṭam, aśru-pūrṇākulekṣaṇam |
viṣīdantam idaṁ vākyam, uvāca madhusūdanaḥ ||

Śrī-Bhagavān uvāca

2 kutas tvā kaśmalam idaṁ, viṣame samupasthitam |
anārya-juṣṭam asvargyam, akīrti-karam arjuna ||
3 klaibyaṁ mā sma gamaḥ pārtha, naitat tvayy upapadyate |
kṣudraṁ hṛdaya-daurbalyaṁ, tyaktvottiṣṭha parantapa ||

Arjuna uvāca

4 kathaṁ bhīṣmam ahaṁ saṅkhye, droṇaṁ ca madhusūdana |
iṣubhiḥ pratiyotsyāmi, pūjārhāv ari-sūdana ||
5 gurūn ahatvā hi mahānubhāvān
śreyo bhoktuṁ bhaikṣyam apīha loke |
hatvārtha-kāmāṁs tu gurūn ihaiva
bhuñjīya bhogān rudhira-pradigdhān ||
6 na caitad vidmaḥ kataran no garīyo
yad vā jayema yadi vā no jayeyuḥ |
yān eva hatvā na jijīviṣāmas
te 'vasthitāḥ pramukhe dhārtarāṣṭrāḥ ||

7 kārpaṇya-doṣopahata-svabhāvaḥ
pṛcchāmi tvāṁ dharma-saṁmūḍha-cetāḥ |
yac chreyaḥ syān niścitaṁ brūhi tan me
śiṣyas te 'ham śādhi māṁ tvāṁ prapannam ||
8 na hi prapaśyāmi mamāpanudyād
yac chokam ucchoṣaṇam indriyāṇām |
avāpya bhūmāv asapatnam ṛddhaṁ
rājyaṁ surāṇām api cādhipatyam ||

Sañjaya uvāca

9 evam uktvā hṛṣīkeśaṁ, guḍākeśaḥ parantapaḥ |
na yotsya iti govindam, uktvā tūṣṇīṁ babhūva ha ||
10 tam uvāca hṛṣīkeśaḥ, prahasann iva bhārata |
senayor ubhayor madhye, viṣīdantam idam vacaḥ ||

Śrī-Bhagavān uvāca

11 aśocyān anvaśocas tvaṁ, prajñā-vādāṁś ca bhāṣase |
gatāsūn agatāsūṁś ca, nānuśocanti paṇḍitāḥ ||
12 na tv evāhaṁ jātu nāsaṁ, na tvaṁ neme janādhipāḥ |
na caiva na bhaviṣyāmaḥ, sarve vayam ataḥ param ||
13 dehino 'smin yathā dehe, kaumāraṁ yauvanaṁ jarā |
tathā dehāntara-prāptir, dhīras tatra na muhyati ||
14 mātrā-sparśās tu kaunteya, śītoṣṇa-sukha-duḥkha-dāḥ |
āgamāpāyino 'nityās, tāṁs titikṣasva bhārata ||
15 yaṁ hi na vyathayanty ete, puruṣaṁ puruṣarṣabha |
sama-duḥkha-sukhaṁ dhīraṁ, so 'mṛtatvāya kalpate ||
16 nāsato vidyate bhāvo, nābhāvo vidyate sataḥ |
ubhayor api dṛṣṭo 'ntas, tv anayos tattva-darśibhiḥ ||
17 avināśi tu tad viddhi, yena sarvam idaṁ tatam |
vināśam avyayasyāsya, na kaścit kartum arhati ||
18 antavanta ime dehā, nityasyoktāḥ śarīriṇaḥ |
anāśino 'prameyasya, tasmād yudhyasva bhārata ||
19 ya enaṁ vetti hantāraṁ, yaś cainaṁ manyate hatam |
ubhau tau na vijānīto, nāyaṁ hanti na hanyate ||
20 na jāyate mriyate vā kadācin
nāyaṁ bhūtvā bhavitā vā na bhūyaḥ |
ajo nityaḥ śāśvato 'yaṁ purāṇo
na hanyate hanyamāne śarīre ||
21 vedāvināśinaṁ nityaṁ, ya enam ajam avyayam |
kathaṁ sa puruṣaḥ pārtha, kaṁ ghātayati hanti kam ||

22 vāsāṁsi jīrṇāni yathā vihāya
navāni gṛhṇāti naro 'parāṇi |
tathā śarīrāṇi vihāya jīrṇāny
anyāni saṁyāti navāni dehī ||
23 nainaṁ chindanti śastrāṇi, nainaṁ dahati pāvakaḥ |
na cainaṁ kledayanty āpo, na śoṣayati mārutaḥ ||
24 acchedyo 'yam adāhyo 'yam, akledyo 'śoṣya eva ca |
nityaḥ sarva-gataḥ sthāṇur, acalo 'yaṁ sanātanaḥ ||
25 avyakto 'yam acintyo 'yam, avikāryo 'yam ucyate |
tasmād evaṁ viditvainaṁ, nānuśocitum arhasi ||
26 atha cainaṁ nitya-jātaṁ, nityaṁ vā manyase mṛtam |
tathāpi tvaṁ mahā-bāho, nainaṁ śocitum arhasi ||
27 jātasya hi dhruvo mṛtyur, dhruvaṁ janma mṛtasya ca |
tasmād aparihārye 'rthe, na tvaṁ śocitum arhasi ||
28 avyaktādīni bhūtāni, vyakta-madhyāni bhārata |
avyakta-nidhanāny eva, tatra kā paridevanā
29 āścarya-vat paśyati kaścid enam
āścarya-vad vadati tathaiva cānyaḥ |
āścarya-vac cainam anyaḥ śṛṇoti
śrutvāpy enaṁ veda na caiva kaścit ||
30 dehī nityam avadhyo 'yaṁ, dehe sarvasya bhārata |
tasmāt sarvāṇi bhūtāni, na tvaṁ śocitum arhasi ||
31 sva-dharmam api cāvekṣya, na vikampitum arhasi |
dharmyād dhi yuddhāc chreyo 'nyat, kṣatriyasya na vidyate ||
32 yadṛcchayā copapannaṁ, svarga-dvāram apāvṛtam |
sukhinaḥ kṣatriyāḥ pārtha, labhante yuddham īdṛśam ||
33 atha cet tvam imaṁ dharmyaṁ, saṅgrāmaṁ na kariṣyasi |
tataḥ sva-dharmaṁ kīrtiṁ ca, hitvā pāpam avāpsyasi ||
34 akīrtiṁ cāpi bhūtāni, kathayiṣyanti te 'vyayām |
sambhāvitasya cākīrtir, maraṇād atiricyate ||
35 bhayād raṇād uparataṁ, maṁsyante tvāṁ mahā-rathāḥ |
yeṣāṁ ca tvaṁ bahu-mato, bhūtvā yāsyasi lāghavam ||
36 avācya-vādāṁś ca bahūn, vadiṣyanti tavāhitāḥ |
nindantas tava sāmarthyaṁ, tato duḥkhataraṁ nu kim ||
37 hato vā prāpsyasi svargaṁ, jitvā vā bhokṣyase mahīm |
tasmād uttiṣṭha kaunteya, yuddhāya kṛta-niścayaḥ ||
38 sukha-duḥkhe same kṛtvā, lābhālābhau jayājayau |
tato yuddhāya yujyasva, naivaṁ pāpam avāpsyasi ||
39 eṣā te 'bhihitā sāṅkhye, buddhir yoge tv imāṁ śṛṇu |
buddhyā yukto yayā pārtha, karma-bandhaṁ prahāsyasi ||
40 nehābhikrama-nāśo 'sti, pratyavāyo na vidyate |
sv-alpam apy asya dharmasya, trāyate mahato bhayāt ||

41 vyavasāyātmikā buddhir, ekeha kuru-nandana |
bahu-śākhā hy anantāś ca, buddhayo 'vyavasāyinām ||
42 yām imāṁ puṣpitāṁ vācaṁ, pravadanty avipaścitaḥ |
veda-vāda-ratāḥ pārtha, nānyad astīti vādinaḥ ||
43 kāmātmānaḥ svarga-parā, janma-karma-phala-pradām |
kriyā-viśeṣa-bahulāṁ, bhogaiśvarya-gatiṁ prati ||
44 bhogaiśvarya-prasaktānāṁ, tayāpahṛta-cetasām |
vyavasāyātmikā buddhiḥ, samādhau na vidhīyate ||
45 trai-guṇya-viṣayā vedā, nistrai-guṇyo bhavārjuna |
nirdvandvo nitya-sattva-stho, niryoga-kṣema ātmavān ||
46 yāvān artha udapāne, sarvataḥ samplutodake |
tāvān sarveṣu vedeṣu, brāhmaṇasya vijānataḥ ||
47 karmaṇy evādhikāras te, mā phaleṣu kadācana |
mā karma-phala-hetur bhūr, mā te saṅgo 'stv akarmaṇi ||
48 yoga-sthaḥ kuru karmāṇi, saṅgaṁ tyaktvā dhanañjaya |
siddhy-asiddhyoḥ samo bhūtvā, samatvaṁ yoga ucyate ||
49 dūreṇa hy avaraṁ karma, buddhi-yogād dhanañjaya |
buddhau śaraṇam anviccha, kṛpaṇāḥ phala-hetavaḥ ||
50 buddhi-yukto jahātīha, ubhe sukṛta-duṣkṛte |
tasmād yogāya yujyasva, yogaḥ karmasu kauśalam ||
51 karma-jaṁ buddhi-yuktā, hi phalaṁ tyaktvā manīṣiṇaḥ |
janma-bandha-vinirmuktāḥ, padaṁ gacchanty anāmayam ||
52 yadā te moha-kalilaṁ, buddhir vyatitariṣyati |
tadā gantāsi nirvedaṁ, śrotavyasya śrutasya ca ||
53 śruti-vipratipannā te, yadā sthāsyati niścalā |
samādhāv acalā buddhis, tadā yogam avāpsyasi ||

Arjuna uvāca

54 sthita-prajñasya kā bhāṣā, samādhi-sthasya keśava |
sthita-dhīḥ kiṁ prabhāṣeta, kim āsīta vrajeta kim ||

Śrī-Bhagavān uvāca

55 prajahāti yadā kāmān, sarvān pārtha mano-gatān |
ātmany evātmanā tuṣṭaḥ, sthita-prajñas tadocyate ||
56 duḥkheṣv anudvigna-manāḥ, sukheṣu vigata-spṛhaḥ |
vīta-rāga-bhaya-krodhaḥ, sthita-dhīr munir ucyate ||
57 yaḥ sarvatrānabhisnehas, tat tat prāpya śubhāśubham |
nābhinandati na dveṣṭi, tasya prajñā pratiṣṭhitā ||
58 yadā saṁharate cāyaṁ, kūrmo 'ṅgānīva sarvaśaḥ |
indriyāṇīndriyārthebhyas, tasya prajñā pratiṣṭhitā ||
59 viṣayā vinivartante, nirāhārasya dehinaḥ |
rasa-varjaṁ raso 'py asya, paraṁ dṛṣṭvā nivartate ||

60 yatato hy api kaunteya, puruṣasya vipaścitaḥ |
indriyāṇi pramāthīni, haranti prasabhaṁ manaḥ ||
61 tāni sarvāṇi saṁyamya, yukta āsīta mat-paraḥ |
vaśe hi yasyendriyāṇi, tasya prajñā pratiṣṭhitā ||
62 dhyāyato viṣayān puṁsaḥ, saṅgas teṣūpajāyate |
saṅgāt sañjāyate kāmaḥ, kāmāt krodho 'bhijāyate ||
63 krodhād bhavati sammohaḥ, sammohāt smṛti-vibhramaḥ |
smṛti-bhraṁśād buddhi-nāśo, buddhi-nāśāt praṇaśyati ||
64 rāga-dveṣa-viyuktais tu, viṣayān indriyaiś caran |
ātma-vaśyair vidheyātmā, prasādam adhigacchati ||
65 prasāde sarva-duḥkhānāṁ, hānir asyopajāyate |
prasanna-cetaso hy āśu, buddhiḥ paryavatiṣṭhate ||
66 nāsti buddhir ayuktasya, na cāyuktasya bhāvanā |
na cābhāvayataḥ śāntir, aśāntasya kutaḥ sukham ||
67 indriyāṇāṁ hi caratāṁ, yan mano 'nuvidhīyate |
tad asya harati prajñāṁ, vāyur nāvam ivāmbhasi ||
68 tasmād yasya mahā-bāho, nigṛhītāni sarvaśaḥ |
indriyāṇīndriyārthebhyas, tasya prajñā pratiṣṭhitā ||
69 yā niśā sarva-bhūtānāṁ, tasyāṁ jāgarti saṁyamī |
yasyāṁ jāgrati bhūtāni, sā niśā paśyato muneḥ ||
70 āpūryamāṇam acala-pratiṣṭhaṁ
samudram āpaḥ praviśanti yadvat |
tadvat kāmā yaṁ praviśanti sarve
sa śāntim āpnoti na kāma-kāmī ||
71 vihāya kāmān yaḥ sarvān, pumāṁś carati niḥspṛhaḥ |
nirmamo nirahaṅkāraḥ, sa śāntim adhigacchati ||
72 eṣā brāhmī sthitiḥ pārtha, naināṁ prāpya vimuhyati |
sthitvāsyām anta-kāle 'pi, brahma-nirvāṇam ṛcchati ||

3

Arjuna uvāca

1 jyāyasī cet karmaṇas te, matā buddhir janārdana |
tat kiṁ karmaṇi ghore māṁ, niyojayasi keśava ||
2 vyāmiśreṇaiva vākyena, buddhiṁ mohayasīva me |
tad ekaṁ vada niścitya, yena śreyo 'ham āpnuyām ||

Śrī-Bhagavān uvāca

3 loke 'smin dvi-vidhā niṣṭhā, purā proktā mayānagha |
jñāna-yogena sāṅkhyānāṁ, karma-yogena yoginām ||
4 na karmaṇām anārambhān, naiṣkarmyaṁ puruṣo 'śnute |
na ca saṁnyasanād eva, siddhiṁ samadhigacchati ||

5 na hi kaścit kṣaṇam api, jātu tiṣṭhaty akarma-kṛt |
kāryate hy avaśaḥ karma, sarvaḥ prakṛti-jair guṇaiḥ ||
6 karmendriyāṇi saṁyamya, ya āste manasā smaran |
indriyārthān vimūḍhātmā, mithyācāraḥ sa ucyate ||
7 yas tv indriyāṇi manasā, niyamyārabhate 'rjuna |
karmendriyaiḥ karma-yogam, asaktaḥ sa viśiṣyate ||
8 niyataṁ kuru karma tvaṁ, karma jyāyo hy akarmaṇaḥ |
śarīra-yātrāpi ca te, na prasiddhyed akarmaṇaḥ ||
9 yajñārthāt karmaṇo 'nyatra, loko 'yam karma-bandhanaḥ |
tad-arthaṁ karma kaunteya, mukta-saṅgaḥ samācara ||
10 saha-yajñāḥ prajāḥ sṛṣṭvā, purovāca prajāpatiḥ |
anena prasaviṣyadhvam, eṣa vo 'stv iṣṭa-kāma-dhuk ||
11 devān bhāvayatānena, te devā bhāvayantu vaḥ |
parasparaṁ bhāvayantaḥ, śreyaḥ param avāpsyatha ||
12 iṣṭān bhogān hi vo devā, dāsyante yajña-bhāvitāḥ |
tair dattān apradāyaibhyo, yo bhuṅkte stena eva saḥ ||
13 yajña-śiṣṭāśinaḥ santo, mucyante sarva-kilbiṣaiḥ |
bhuñjate te tv aghaṁ pāpā, ye pacanty ātma-kāraṇāt ||
14 annād bhavanti bhūtāni, parjanyād anna-sambhavaḥ |
yajñād bhavati parjanyo, yajñaḥ karma-samudbhavaḥ ||
15 karma brahmodbhavaṁ viddhi, brahmākṣara-samudbhavam |
tasmāt sarva-gataṁ brahma, nityaṁ yajñe pratiṣṭhitam ||
16 evaṁ pravartitaṁ cakraṁ, nānuvartayatīha yaḥ |
aghāyur indriyārāmo, moghaṁ pārtha sa jīvati ||
17 yas tv ātma-ratir eva syād, ātma-tṛptaś ca mānavaḥ |
ātmany eva ca santuṣṭas, tasya kāryaṁ na vidyate ||
18 naiva tasya kṛtenārtho, nākṛteneha kaścana |
na cāsya sarva bhūteṣu, kaścid artha-vyapāśrayaḥ ||
19 tasmād asaktaḥ satataṁ, kāryaṁ karma samācara |
asakto hy ācaran karma, param āpnoti pūruṣaḥ ||
20 karmaṇaiva hi saṁsiddhim, āsthitā janakādayaḥ |
loka-saṅgraham evāpi, sampaśyan kartum arhasi ||
21 yad yad ācarati śreṣṭhas, tat tad evetaro janaḥ |
sa yat pramāṇaṁ kurute, lokas tad anuvartate ||
22 na me pārthāsti kartavyaṁ, triṣu lokeṣu kiñcana |
nānavāptam avāptavyaṁ, varta eva ca karmaṇi ||
23 yadi hy ahaṁ na varteyaṁ, jātu karmaṇy atandritaḥ |
mama vartmānuvartante, manuṣyāḥ pārtha sarvaśaḥ ||
24 utsīdeyur ime lokā, na kuryāṁ karma ced aham |
saṅkarasya ca kartā syām, upahanyām imāḥ prajāḥ ||
25 saktāḥ karmaṇy avidvāṁso, yathā kurvanti bhārata |
kuryād vidvāṁs tathāsaktaś, cikīrṣur loka-saṅgraham ||

26 na buddhi-bhedaṁ janayed, ajñānāṁ karma-saṅginām |
joṣayet sarva-karmāṇi, vidvān yuktaḥ samācaran ||
27 parkṛteḥ kriyamāṇāni, guṇaiḥ karmāṇi sarvaśaḥ |
ahaṅkāra-vimūḍhātmā, kartāham iti manyate ||
28 tattva-vit tu mahā-bāho, guṇa-karma-vibhāgayoḥ |
guṇā guṇeṣu vartanta, iti matvā na sajjate ||
29 prakṛter guṇa-sammūḍhāḥ, sajjante guṇa-karmasu |
tān akṛtsna-vido mandān, kṛtsna-vin na vicālayet ||
30 mayi sarvāṇi karmāṇi, saṁnyasyādhyātma-cetasā |
nirāśīr nirmamo bhūtvā, yudhyasva vigata-jvaraḥ ||
31 ye me matam idaṁ nityam, anutiṣṭhanti mānavāḥ |
śraddhāvanto 'nasūyanto, mucyante te 'pi karmabhiḥ ||
32 te tv etad adhyasūyanto, nānutiṣṭhanti me matam |
sarva-jñāna-vimūḍhāṁs tān, viddhi naṣṭān acetasaḥ ||
33 sadṛśaṁ ceṣṭate svasyāḥ, prakṛter jñānavān api |
prakṛtiṁ yānti bhūtāni, nigrahaḥ kiṁ kariṣyati ||
34 indriyasyendriyasyārthe, rāga-dveṣau vyavasthitau |
tayor na vaśam āgachet, tau hy asya paripanthinau ||
35 śreyān sva-dharmo viguṇaḥ, para-dharmāt sv-anuṣṭhitāt |
sva-dharme nidhanaṁ śreyaḥ, para-dharmo bhayāvahaḥ ||

Arjuna uvāca

36 atha kena prayukto 'yaṁ, pāpaṁ carati pūruṣaḥ |
anicchann api vārṣṇeya, balād iva niyojitaḥ ||

Śrī-Bhagavān uvāca

37 kāma eṣa krodha eṣa, rajo-guṇa-samudbhavaḥ |
mahāśano mahā-pāpmā, viddhy enam iha vairiṇam ||
38 dhūmenāvriyate vahnir, yathādarśo malena ca |
yatholbenāvṛto garbhas, tathā tenedam āvṛtam ||
39 āvṛtaṁ jñānam etena, jñānino nitya-vairiṇā |
kāma-rūpeṇa kaunteya, duṣpūreṇānalena ca ||
40 indriyāṇi mano buddhir, asyādhiṣṭhānam ucyate |
etair vimohayaty eṣa, jñānam āvṛtya dehinam ||
41 tasmāt tvam indriyāṇy ādau, niyamya bharatarṣabha |
pāpmānaṁ prajahi hy enaṁ, jñāna-vijñāna-nāśanam ||
42 indriyāṇi parāṇy āhur, indriyebhyaḥ paraṁ manaḥ |
manasas tu parā buddhir, yo buddheḥ paratas tu saḥ ||
43 evaṁ buddheḥ paraṁ buddhvā, saṁstabhyātmānam ātmanā |
jahi śatruṁ mahā-bāho, kāma-rūpaṁ durāsadam ||

4

Śrī-Bhagavān uvāca

1 imaṁ vivasvate yogaṁ, proktavān aham avyayam |
vivasvān manave prāha, manur ikṣvākave 'bravīt ||
2 evaṁ paramparā-prāptam, imaṁ rājarṣayo viduḥ |
sa kāleneha mahatā, yogo naṣṭaḥ parantapa ||
3 sa evāyaṁ mayā te 'dya, yogaḥ proktaḥ purātanaḥ |
bhakto 'si me sakhā ceti, rahasyaṁ hy etad uttamam ||

Arjuna uvāca

4 aparaṁ bhavato janma, paraṁ janma vivasvataḥ |
katham etad vijānīyāṁ, tvam ādau proktavān iti ||

Śrī-Bhagavān uvāca

5 bahūni me vyatītāni, janmāni tava cārjuna |
tāny ahaṁ veda sarvāṇi, na tvaṁ vettha parantapa ||
6 ajo 'pi sann avyayātmā, bhūtānām īśvaro 'pi san |
prakṛtiṁ svām adhiṣṭhāya, sambhavāmy ātma-māyayā ||
7 yadā yadā hi dharmasya, glānir bhavati bhārata |
abhyutthānam adharmasya, tadātmānaṁ sṛjāmy aham ||
8 paritrāṇāya sādhūnāṁ, vināśāya ca duṣkṛtām |
dharma-saṁsthāpanārthāya, sambhavāmi yuge yuge ||
9 janma karma ca me divyam, evaṁ yo vetti tattvataḥ |
tyaktvā dehaṁ punar janma, naiti mām eti so 'rjuna ||
10 vīta-rāga-bhaya-krodhā, man-mayā mām upāśritāḥ |
bahavo jñāna-tapasā, pūtā mad-bhāvam āgatāḥ ||
11 ye yathā māṁ prapadyante, tāṁs tathaiva bhajāmy aham |
mama vartmānuvartante, manuṣyāḥ pārtha sarvaśaḥ ||
12 kāṅkṣantaḥ karmaṇāṁ siddhiṁ, yajanta iha devatāḥ |
kṣipraṁ hi mānuṣe loke, siddhir bhavati karma-jā ||
13 cātur-varṇyaṁ mayā sṛṣṭaṁ, guṇa-karma-vibhāgaśaḥ |
tasya kartāram api māṁ, viddy akartāram avyayam ||
14 na māṁ karmāṇi limpanti, na me karma-phale spṛhā |
iti māṁ yo 'bhijānāti, karmabhir na sa badhyate ||
15 evaṁ jñātvā kṛtaṁ karma, pūrvair api mumukṣubhiḥ |
kuru karmaiva tasmāt tvaṁ, pūrvaiḥ pūrvataraṁ kṛtam ||
16 kiṁ karma kim akarmeti, kavayo 'py atra mohitāḥ |
tat te karma pravakṣyāmi, yaj jñātvā mokṣyase 'śubhāt ||
17 karmaṇo hy api boddhavyaṁ, boddhavyaṁ ca vikarmaṇaḥ |
akarmaṇaś ca boddhavyaṁ, gahanā karmaṇo gatiḥ ||

18 karmaṇy akarma yaḥ paśyed, akarmaṇi ca karma yaḥ |
sa buddhimān manuṣyeṣu, sa yuktaḥ kṛtsna-karma-kṛt ||
19 yasya sarve samārambhāḥ, kāma-saṅkalpa-varjitāḥ |
jñānāgni-dagdha-karmāṇaṁ, tam āhuḥ paṇḍitaṁ budhāḥ ||
20 tyaktvā karma-phalāsaṅgaṁ, nitya-tṛpto nirāśrayaḥ |
karmaṇy abhipravṛtto 'pi, naiva kiñcit karoti saḥ ||
21 nirāśīr yata-cittātmā, tyakta-sarva-parigrahaḥ |
śārīraṁ kevalaṁ karma, kurvan nāpnoti kilbiṣam ||
22 yadṛcchā-lābha-santuṣṭo, dvandvātīto vimatsaraḥ |
samaḥ siddhāv asiddhau ca, kṛtvāpi na nibadhyate ||
23 gata-saṅgasya muktasya, jñānāvasthita-cetasaḥ |
yajñāyācarataḥ karma, samagraṁ pravilīyate ||
24 brahmārpaṇaṁ brahma havir, brahmāgnau brahmaṇā hutam |
brahmaiva tena gantavyaṁ, brahma-karma-samādhinā ||
25 daivam evāpare yajñaṁ, yoginaḥ paryupāsate |
brahmāgnāv apare yajñaṁ, yajñenaivopajuhvati ||
26 śrotrādīnīndriyāṇy anye, saṁyamāgniṣu juhvati |
śabdādīn viṣayān anya, indriyāgniṣu juhvati ||
27 sarvāṇīndriya-karmāṇi, prāṇa-karmāṇi cāpare |
ātma-saṁyama-yogāgnau, juhvati jñāna-dīpite ||
28 dravya-yajñās tapo-yajñā, yoga-yajñās tathāpare |
svādhyāya-jñāna-yajñāś ca, yatayaḥ saṁśita-vratāḥ ||
29 apāne juhvati prāṇaṁ, prāṇe 'pānaṁ tathāpare |
prāṇāpana-gatī ruddhvā, prāṇāyāma-parāyaṇāḥ ||
30 apare niyatāhārāḥ, prāṇān prāṇeṣu juhvati |
sarve 'py ete yajña-vido, yajña-kṣapita-kalmaṣāḥ ||
31 yajña-śiṣṭāmṛta-bhujo, yānti brahma sanātanam |
nāyaṁ loko 'sty ayajñasya, kuto 'nyaḥ kuru-sattama ||
32 evaṁ bahu-vidhā yajñā, vitatā brahmaṇo mukhe |
karma-jān viddhi tān sarvān, evaṁ jñātvā vimokṣase ||
33 śreyān dravya-mayād yajñāj, jñāna-yajñaḥ parantapa |
sarvaṁ karmākhilaṁ pārtha, jñāne parisamāpyate ||
34 tad viddhi praṇipātena, paripraśnena sevayā |
upadekṣyanti te jñānaṁ, jñāninas tattva-darśinaḥ ||
35 yaj jñātvā na punar moham, evaṁ yāsyasi pāṇḍava |
yena bhūtāny āśeṣeṇa, drakṣyasy ātmany atho mayi ||
36 api ced asi pāpebhyaḥ, sarvebhyaḥ pāpa-kṛt-tamaḥ |
sarvaṁ jñāna-plavenaiva, vṛjinaṁ santariṣyasi ||
37 yathaidhāṁsi samiddho 'gnir, bhasma-sāt kurute 'rjuna |
jñānāgniḥ sarva-karmāṇi, bhasma-sāt kurute tathā ||
38 na hi jñānena sadṛśaṁ, pavitram iha vidyate |
tat svayaṁ yoga-saṁsiddhaḥ, kālenātmani vindati ||

39 śraddhāvāṁl labhate jñānaṁ, tat-paraḥ saṁyatendriyaḥ |
jñānaṁ labdhvā parāṁ śāntim, acireṇādhigacchati ||
40 ajñaś cāśraddadhānaś ca, saṁśayātmā vinaśyati |
nāyam loko 'sti na paro, na sukhaṁ saṁśayātmanaḥ ||
41 yoga-saṁnyasta-karmāṇaṁ, jñāna-sañchinna-saṁśayam |
ātmavantaṁ na karmāṇi, nibadhnanti dhanañjaya ||
42 tasmād ajñāna-sambhūtaṁ, hṛt-sthaṁ jñānāsinātmanaḥ |
chittvainaṁ saṁśayaṁ yogam, ātiṣṭhottiṣṭha bhārata ||

5

Arjuna uvāca

1 saṁnyāsaṁ karmaṇāṁ kṛṣṇa, punar yogaṁ ca śaṁsasi |
yac chreya etayor ekaṁ, tan me brūhi su-niścitam ||

Śrī-Bhagavān uvāca

2 saṁnyāsaḥ karma-yogaś ca, niḥśreyasa-karāv ubhau |
tayos tu karma-saṁnyāsāt, karma-yogo viśiṣyate ||
3 jñeyaḥ sa nitya-saṁnyāsī, yo na dveṣṭi na kāṅkṣati |
nirdvando hi mahā-bāho, sukhaṁ bandhāt pramucyate ||
4 sāṅkhya-yogau pṛthag bālāḥ, pravadanti na paṇḍitāḥ |
ekam apy āsthitaḥ samyag, ubhayor vindate phalam ||
5 yat sāṅkhyaiḥ prāpyate sthānaṁ, tad yogair api gamyate |
ekaṁ sāṅkhyaṁ ca yogaṁ ca, yaḥ paśyati sa paśyati ||
6 saṁnyāsas tu mahā-bāho, duḥkham āptum ayogataḥ |
yoga-yukto munir brahma, na cireṇādhigacchati ||
7 yoka-yukto viśuddhātmā, vijitātmā jitendriyaḥ |
sarva-bhūtātma-bhūtātmā, kurvann api na lipyate ||
8 naiva kiñcit karomīti, yukto manyeta tattva-vit |
paśyañ śṛṇvan spṛśañ jighrann, aśnan gacchan svapañ śvasan ||
9 pralapan visṛjan gṛhṇann, unmiṣan nimiṣann api |
indriyāṇīndriyārtheṣu, vartanta iti dhārayan ||
10 brahmaṇy ādhāya karmāṇi, saṅgaṁ tyaktvā karoti yaḥ |
lipyate na sa pāpena, padma-patram ivāmbhasā ||
11 kāyena manasā buddhyā, kevalair indriyair api |
yoginaḥ karma kurvanti, saṅgaṁ tyaktvātma-śuddhaye ||
12 yuktaḥ karma-phalaṁ tyaktvā, śāntim āpnoti naiṣṭhikīm |
ayuktaḥ kāma-kāreṇa, phale sakto nibadhyate ||
13 sarva-karmāṇi manasā, saṁnyasyāste sukhaṁ vaśī |
nava-dvāre pure dehī, naiva kurvan na kārayan ||
14 na kartṛtvaṁ na karmāṇi, lokasya sṛjati prabhuḥ |
na karma-phala saṁyogaṁ, svabhāvas tu pravartate ||

15 nādatte kasyacit pāpaṁ, na caiva sukṛtaṁ vibhuḥ |
ajñānenāvṛtaṁ jñānaṁ, tena muhyanti jantavaḥ ||
16 jñānena tu tad ajñānaṁ, yeṣām nāśitam ātmanaḥ |
teṣām āditya-vaj jñānaṁ, prakāśayati tat param ||
17 tad-buddhayas tad-ātmānas, tan-niṣṭhās tat-parāyaṇāḥ |
gacchanty apunar-āvṛttiṁ, jñāna-nirdhūta-kalmaṣāḥ ||
18 vidyā-vinaya-sampanne, brāhmaṇe gavi hastini |
śuni caiva śva-pāke ca, paṇḍitāḥ sama-darśinaḥ ||
19 ihaiva tair jitaḥ sargo, yeṣāṁ sāmye sthitaṁ manaḥ |
nirdoṣaṁ hi samaṁ brahma, tasmād brahmaṇi te sthitāḥ ||
20 na prahṛṣyet priyaṁ prāpya, nodvijet prāpya cāpriyam |
sthira-buddhir asammūḍho, brahma-vid brahmaṇi sthitaḥ ||
21 bāhya-sparśeṣv asaktātmā, vindaty ātmani yat sukham |
sa brahma-yoga-yuktātmā, sukham akṣayam aśnute ||
22 ye hi saṁsparśa-jā bhogā, duḥkha-yonaya eva te |
ādy-antavantaḥ kaunteya, na teṣu ramate budhaḥ ||
23 śaknotīhaiva yaḥ soḍhuṁ, prāk śarīra-vimokṣaṇāt |
kāma-krodhodbhavaṁ vegaṁ, sa yuktaḥ sa sukhī naraḥ ||
24 yo 'ntaḥ-sukho 'ntar-ārāmas, tathāntar-jyotir eva yaḥ |
sa yogī brahma-nirvāṇaṁ, brahma-bhūto 'dhigacchati ||
25 labhante brahma-nirvāṇam, ṛṣayaḥ kṣīṇa-kalmaṣāḥ |
chinna-dvaidhā yatātmānaḥ, sarva-bhūta-hite ratāḥ ||
26 kāma-krodha-viyuktānāṁ, yatīnāṁ yata-cetasām |
abhito brahma-nirvāṇaṁ, vartate viditātmanām ||
27 sparśān kṛtvā bahir bāhyāṁś, cakṣuś caivāntare bhruvoḥ |
prāṇāpānau samau kṛtvā, nāsābhyantara-cāriṇau ||
28 yatendriya-mano-buddhir, munir mokṣa-parāyaṇaḥ |
vigatecchā-bhaya-krodho, yaḥ sadā mukta eva saḥ ||
29 bhoktāraṁ yajña-tapasāṁ, sarva-loka-maheśvaram |
suhṛdaṁ sarva-bhūtānāṁ, jñātvā māṁ śāntim ṛcchati ||

6

Śrī-Bhagavān uvāca

1 anāśritaḥ karma-phalaṁ, kāryaṁ karma karoti yaḥ |
sa saṁnyāsī ca yogī ca, na niragnir na cākriyaḥ ||
2 yaṁ saṁnyāsam iti prāhur, yogaṁ taṁ viddhi pāṇḍava |
na hy asaṁnyasta-saṅkalpo, yogī bhavati kaścana ||
3 ārurukṣor muner yogaṁ, karma kāraṇam ucyate |
yogārūḍhasya tasyaiva, śamaḥ kāraṇam ucyate ||
4 yadā hi nendriyārtheṣu, na karmasv anuṣajjate |
sarva-saṅkalpa-saṁnyāsī, yogārūḍhas tadocyate ||

5 uddhared ātmanātmānaṁ, nātmānam avasādayet |
ātmaiva hy ātmano bandhur, ātmaiva ripur ātmanaḥ ||
6 bandhur ātmātmanas tasya, yenātmaivātmanā jitaḥ |
anātmanas tu śatrutve, vartetātmaiva śatru-vat ||
7 jitātmanaḥ praśāntasya, paramātmā samāhitaḥ |
śītoṣṇa-sukha-duḥkheṣu, tathā mānāpamānayoḥ ||
8 jñāna-vijñāna-tṛptāmā, kūṭa-stho vijitendriyaḥ |
yukta ity ucyate yogī, sama-loṣṭrāśma-kāñcanaḥ ||
9 suhṛn-mitrāry-udāsīna-, madhyastha-dveṣya-bandhuṣu |
sādhuṣv api ca pāpeṣu, sama-buddhir viśiṣyate ||
10 yogī yuñjīta satatam, ātmānaṁ rahasi sthitaḥ |
ekākī yata-cittātmā, nirāśīr aparigrahaḥ ||
11 śucau deśe pratiṣṭhāpya, sthiram āsanam ātmanaḥ |
nāty-ucchritaṁ nāti-nīcaṁ, cailājina-kuśottaram ||
12 tatraikāgraṁ manaḥ kṛtvā, yata-cittendriya-kriyaḥ |
upaviśyāsane yuñjyād, yogam ātma-viśuddhaye ||
13 samaṁ kāya-śiro-grīvaṁ, dhārayann acalaṁ sthiraḥ |
samprekṣya nāsikāgraṁ svaṁ, diśaś cānavalokayan ||
14 praśāntātmā vigata-bhīr, brahmacāri-vrate sthitaḥ |
manaḥ saṁyamya mac-citto, yukta āsīta mat-paraḥ ||
15 yuñjann evaṁ sadātmānaṁ, yogī niyata-mānasaḥ |
śāntiṁ nirvāṇa-paramāṁ, mat-saṁsthām adhigacchati ||
16 nāty-aśnatas tu yogo 'sti, na caikāntam anaśnataḥ |
na cāti-svapna-śīlasya, jāgrato naiva cārjuna ||
17 yuktāhāra-vihārasya, yukta-ceṣṭasya karmasu |
yukta-svapnāvabodhasya, yogo bhavati duḥkha-hā ||
18 yadā viniyataṁ cittam, ātmany evāvatiṣṭhate |
niḥspṛhaḥ sarva-kāmebhyo, yukta ity ucyate tadā ||
19 yathā dīpo nivāta-stho, neṅgate sopamā smṛtā |
yogino yata-cittasya, yuñjato yogam ātmanaḥ ||
20 yatroparamate cittaṁ, niruddhaṁ yoga-sevayā |
yatra caivātmanātmānaṁ, paśyann ātmani tuṣyati ||
21 sukham ātyantikaṁ yat tad, buddhi-grāhyam atīndriyam |
vetti yatra na caivāyaṁ, sthitaś calati tattvataḥ ||
22 yaṁ labdhvā cāparaṁ lābhaṁ, manyate nādhikaṁ tataḥ |
yasmin sthito na duḥkhena, guruṇāpi vicālyate ||
23 taṁ vidyād duḥkha-saṁyoga-, viyogaṁ yoga-saṁjñitam |
sa niścayena yoktavyo, yogo 'nirviṇṇa-cetasā ||
24 saṅkalpa-prabhavān kāmāṁs, tyaktvā sarvān aśeṣataḥ |
manasaivendriya-grāmaṁ, viniyamya samantataḥ ||
25 śanaiḥ śanair uparamed, buddhyā dhṛti-gṛhītayā |
ātma-saṁsthaṁ manaḥ kṛtvā, na kiñcid api cintayet ||

26 yato yato niścarati, manaś cañcalam asthiram |
tatas tato niyamyaitad, ātmany eva vaśaṁ nayet ||
27 praśānta-manasaṁ hy enaṁ, yoginaṁ sukham uttamam |
upaiti śānta-rajasaṁ, brahma-bhūtam akalmaṣam ||
28 yuñjann evaṁ sadātmānaṁ, yogī vigata-kalmaṣaḥ |
sukhena brahma-saṁsparśam, atyantaṁ sukham aśnute ||
29 sarva-bhūta-stham ātmānaṁ, sarva-bhūtāni cātmani |
īkṣate yoga-yuktātmā, sarvatra sama-darśanaḥ ||
30 yo māṁ paśyati sarvatra, sarvaṁ ca mayi paśyati |
tasyāhaṁ na praṇaśyāmi, sa ca me na praṇaśyati ||
31 sarva-bhūta-sthitaṁ yo māṁ, bhajaty ekatvam āsthitaḥ |
sarvathā vartamāno 'pi, sa yogī mayi vartate ||
32 ātmaupamyena sarvatra, samaṁ paśyati yo 'rjuna |
sukhaṁ vā yadi vā duḥkhaṁ, sa yogī paramo mataḥ ||

Arjuna uvāca

33 yo 'yaṁ yogas tvayā proktaḥ, sāmyena madhusūdana |
etasyāhaṁ na paśyāmi, cañcalatvāt sthitiṁ sthirām ||
34 cañcalaṁ hi manaḥ kṛṣṇa, pramāthi balavad dṛḍham |
tasyāhaṁ nigrahaṁ manye, vāyor iva su-duṣkaram ||

Śrī-Bhagavān uvāca

35 asaṁśayaṁ mahā-bāho, mano durnigrahaṁ calam |
abhyāsena tu kaunteya, vairāgyeṇa ca gṛhyate ||
36 asaṁyatātmanā yogo, duṣprāpa iti me matiḥ |
vaśyātmanā tu yatatā, śakyo 'vāptum upāyataḥ ||

Arjuna uvāca

37 ayatiḥ śraddhayopeto, yogāc calita-mānasaḥ |
aprāpya yoga-saṁsiddhiṁ, kāṁ gatiṁ kṛṣṇa gacchati ||
38 kaccin nobhaya-vibhraṣṭaś, chinnābhram iva naśyati |
apratiṣṭho mahā-bāho, vimūḍho brahmaṇaḥ pathi ||
39 etan me saṁśayaṁ kṛṣṇa, chettum arhasy aśeṣataḥ |
tvad-anyaḥ saṁśayasyāsya, chettā na hy upapadyate ||

Śrī-Bhagavān uvāca

40 pārtha naiveha nāmutra, vināśas tasya vidyate |
na hi kalyāṇa-kṛt kaścid, durgatiṁ tāta gacchati ||
41 prāpya puṇya-kṛtāṁ lokān, uṣitvā śāśvatīḥ samāḥ |
śucīnāṁ śrīmatāṁ gehe, yoga-bhraṣṭo 'bhijāyate ||

42 atha vā yoginām eva, kule bhavati dhīmatām |
etad dhi durlabhataraṁ, loke janma yad īdṛśam ||
43 tatra taṁ buddhi-saṁyogaṁ, labhate paurva-dehikam |
yatate ca tato bhūyaḥ, saṁsiddhau kuru-nandana ||
44 pūrvābhyāsena tenaiva, hriyate hy avaśo 'pi saḥ |
jijñāsur api yogasya, śabda-brahmātivartate ||
45 prayatnād yatamānas tu, yogī saṁśuddha-kilbiṣaḥ |
aneka-janma-saṁsiddhas, tato yāti paraṁ gatim ||
46 tapasvibhyo 'dhiko yogī, jñānibhyo 'pi mato 'dhikaḥ |
karmibhyaś cādhiko yogī, tasmād yogī bhavārjuna ||
47 yoginām api sarveṣāṁ, mad-gatenāntar-ātmanā |
śraddhāvān bhajate yo māṁ, sa me yuktatamo mataḥ ||

7

Śrī-Bhagavān uvāca

1 mayy āsakta-manāḥ pārtha, yogaṁ yuñjan mad-āśrayaḥ |
asaṁśayaṁ samagraṁ māṁ, yathā jñāsyasi tac chṛṇu ||
2 jñānaṁ te 'haṁ sa-vijñānam, idaṁ vakṣyāmy aśeṣataḥ |
yaj jñātvā neha bhūyo 'nyaj, jñātavyam avaśiṣyate ||
3 manuṣyāṇāṁ sahasreṣu, kaścid yatati siddhaye |
yatatām api siddhānāṁ, kaścin māṁ vetti tattvataḥ ||
4 bhūmir āpo 'nalo vāyuḥ, khaṁ mano buddhir eva ca |
ahaṅkāra itīyaṁ me, bhinnā prakṛtir aṣṭadhā ||
5 apareyam itas tv anyāṁ, prakṛtiṁ viddhi me parām |
jīva-bhūtāṁ mahā-bāho, yayedaṁ dhāryate jagat ||
6 etad-yonīni bhūtāni, sarvāṇīty upadhāraya |
ahaṁ kṛtsnasya jagataḥ, prabhavaḥ pralayas tathā ||
7 mattaḥ parataraṁ nānyat, kiñcid asti dhanañjaya |
mayi sarvam idaṁ protaṁ, sūtre maṇi-gaṇā iva ||
8 raso 'ham apsu kaunteya, prabhāsmi śaśi-sūryayoḥ |
praṇavaḥ sarva-vedeṣu, śabdaḥ khe pauruṣaṁ nṛṣu ||
9 puṇyo gandhaḥ pṛthivyāṁ, ca tejaś cāsmi vibhāvasau |
jīvanaṁ sarva-bhūteṣu, tapaś cāsmi tapasviṣu ||
10 bījaṁ māṁ sarva-bhūtānāṁ, viddhi pārtha sanātanam |
buddhir buddhimatām asmi, tejas tejas vinām aham ||
11 balaṁ balavatāṁ cāhaṁ, kāma-rāga-vivarjitam |
dharmāviruddho bhūteṣu, kāmo 'smi bharatarṣabha ||
12 ye caiva sāttvikā bhāvā, rājasās tāmasāś ca ye |
matta eveti tān viddhi, na tv ahaṁ teṣu te mayi ||
13 tribhir guṇa-mayair bhāvair, ebhiḥ sarvam idaṁ jagat |
mohitaṁ nābhijānāti, mām ebhyaḥ param avyayam ||

14 daivī hy eṣā guṇa-mayī, mama māyā duratyayā |
māṁ eva ye prapadyante, māyām etāṁ taranti te ||
15 na māṁ duṣkṛtino mūḍhāḥ, prapadyante narādhamāḥ |
māyayāpahṛta-jñānā, āsuraṁ bhāvam āśritāḥ ||
16 catur-vidhā bhajante māṁ, janāḥ sukṛtino 'rjuna |
ārto jijñāsur arthārthī, jñānī ca bharatarṣabha ||
17 teṣāṁ jñānī nitya-yukta, eka-bhaktir viśiṣyate |
priyo hi jñānino 'tyartham, ahaṁ sa ca mama priyaḥ ||
18 udārāḥ sarva evaite, jñānī tv ātmaiva me matam |
āsthitaḥ sa hi yuktātmā, mām evānuttamāṁ gatim ||
19 bahūnāṁ janmanām ante, jñānavān māṁ prapadyate |
vāsudevaḥ sarvam iti, sa mahātmā su-durlabhaḥ ||
20 kāmais tais tair hṛta-jñānāḥ, prapadyante 'nya-devatāḥ |
taṁ taṁ niyamam āsthāya, prakṛtyā niyatāḥ svayā ||
21 yo yo yāṁ yāṁ tanuṁ bhaktaḥ, śraddhayārcitum icchati |
tasya yasyācalāṁ śraddhāṁ, tām eva vidadhāmy aham ||
22 sa tayā śraddhayā yuktas, tasyārādhanam īhate |
labhate ca tataḥ kāmān, mayaiva vihitān hi tān ||
23 antavat tu phalaṁ teṣāṁ, tad bhavaty alpa-medhasām |
devān deva-yajo yānti, mad-bhaktā yānti mām api ||
24 avyaktaṁ vyaktim āpannaṁ, manyante mām abuddhayaḥ |
paraṁ bhāvam ajānanto, mamāvyayam anuttamam ||
25 nāhaṁ prakāśaḥ sarvasya, yoga-māyā-samāvṛtaḥ |
mūḍho 'yaṁ nābhijānāti, loko mām ajam avyayam ||
26 vedāhaṁ samatītāni, vartamānāni cārjuna |
bhaviṣyāṇi ca bhūtāni, māṁ tu veda na kaścana ||
27 icchā-dveṣa-samutthena, dvandva-mohena bhārata |
sarva-bhūtāni sammohaṁ, sarge yānti parantapa ||
28 yeṣāṁ tv anta-gataṁ pāpaṁ, janānāṁ puṇya-karmaṇām |
te dvandva-moha-nirmuktā, bhajante māṁ dṛḍha-vratāḥ ||
29 jarā-maraṇa-mokṣāya, mām āśritya yatanti ye |
te brahma tad viduḥ kṛtsnam, adhyātmaṁ karma cākhilam ||
30 sādhibhūtādhidaivaṁ māṁ, sādhiyajñaṁ ca ye viduḥ |
prayāṇa-kāle 'pi ca māṁ, te vidur yukta-cetasaḥ ||

8

Arjuna uvāca

1 kiṁ tad brahma kim adhyātmaṁ, kiṁ karma puruṣottama |
adhibhūtaṁ ca kiṁ proktam, adhidaivaṁ kim ucyate ||
2 adhiyajñaḥ kathaṁ ko 'tra, dehe 'smin madhusūdana |
prayāṇa-kāle ca kathaṁ, jñeyo 'si niyatātmabhiḥ ||

Śrī-Bhagavān uvāca

3 akṣaraṁ brahma paramaṁ, svabhāvo 'dhyātmam ucyate |
bhūta-bhāvodbhava-karo, visargaḥ karma-saṁjñitaḥ ||
4 adhibhūtaṁ kṣaro bhāvaḥ, puruṣaś cādhidaivatam |
adhiyajño 'ham evātra, dehe deha-bhṛtāṁ vara ||
5 anta-kāle ca mām eva, smaran muktvā kalevaram |
yaḥ prayāti sa mad-bhāvaṁ, yāti nāsty atra saṁśayaḥ ||
6 yaṁ yaṁ vāpi smaran bhāvaṁ, tyajaty ante kalevaram |
taṁ tam evaiti kaunteya, sadā tad-bhāva-bhāvitaḥ ||
7 tasmāt sarveṣu kāleṣu, mām anusmara yudhya ca |
mayy arpita-mano-buddhir, mām evaiṣyasy asaṁśayaḥ ||
8 abhyāsa-yoga-yuktena, cetasā nānya-gāminā |
paramaṁ puruṣaṁ divyaṁ, yāti pārthānucintayan ||
9 kaviṁ purāṇam anuśāsitāram
anor aṇīyāṁsam anusmared yaḥ |
sarvasya dhātāram acintya-rūpam
āditya-varṇaṁ tamasaḥ parastāt ||
10 prayāṇa-kāle manasācalena
bhaktyā yukto yoga-balena caiva |
bhruvor madhye prāṇam āveśya samyak
sa taṁ paraṁ puruṣam upaiti divyam ||
11 yad akṣaraṁ veda-vido vadanti
viśanti yad yatayo vīta-rāgāḥ |
yad icchanto brahmacaryaṁ caranti
tat te padaṁ saṅgraheṇa pravakṣye ||
12 sarva-dvārāṇi saṁyamya, mano hṛdi nirudhya ca |
mūrdhny ādhāyātmanaḥ prāṇam, āsthito yoga-dhāraṇām ||
13 om ity ekākṣaraṁ brahma, vyāharan mām anusmaran |
yaḥ prayāti tyajan dehaṁ, sa yāti paramāṁ gatim ||
14 ananya-cetāḥ satataṁ, yo māṁ smarati nityaśaḥ |
tasyāhaṁ sulabhaḥ pārtha nitya-yuktasya yoginaḥ ||
15 mām upetya punar janma, duḥkhālayam aśāśvatam |
nāpnuvanti mahātmānaḥ, saṁsiddhiṁ paramāṁ gatāḥ ||
16 ā-brahma-bhuvanāl lokāḥ, punar āvartino 'rjuna |
mām upetya tu kaunteya, punar janma na vidyate ||
17 sahasra-yuga-paryantam, ahar yad brahmaṇo viduḥ |
rātriṁ yuga-sahasrāntāṁ, te 'ho-rātra-vido janāḥ ||
18 avyaktād vyaktayaḥ sarvāḥ, prabhavanty ahar-āgame |
rātry-āgame pralīyante, tatraivāvyakta-saṁjñake ||
19 bhūta-grāmaḥ sa evāyaṁ, bhūtvā bhūtvā pralīyate |
rātry-āgame 'vaśaḥ pārtha, prabhavaty ahar-āgame ||

20 paras tasmāt tu bhāvo 'nyo, 'vyakto 'vyaktāt sanātanaḥ |
yaḥ sa sarveṣu bhūteṣu, naśyatsu na vinaśyati ||
21 avyakto 'kṣara ity uktas, tam āhuḥ paramāṁ gatim |
yaṁ prāpya na nivartante, tad dhāma paramaṁ mama ||
22 puruṣaḥ sa paraḥ pārtha, bhaktyā labhyas tv ananyayā |
yasyāntaḥ-sthāni bhūtāni, yena sarvam idaṁ tatam ||
23 yatra kāle tv anāvṛttim, āvṛttiṁ caiva yoginaḥ |
prayātā yānti taṁ kālaṁ, vakṣyāmi bharatarṣabha ||
24 agnir jyotir ahaḥ śuklaḥ, ṣaṇ-māsā uttarāyaṇam |
tatra prayātā gacchanti, brahma brahma-vido janāḥ ||
25 dhūmo rātris tathā kṛṣṇaḥ, ṣaṇ-māsā dakṣiṇāyanam |
tatra cāndramasaṁ jyotir, yogī prāpya nivartate ||
26 śukla-kṛṣṇe gatī hy ete, jagataḥ śāśvate mate |
ekayā yāty anāvṛttim, anyayāvartate punaḥ ||
27 naite sṛtī pārtha jānan, yogī muhyati kaścana |
tasmāt sarveṣu kāleṣu, yoga-yukto bhavārjuna ||
28 vedeṣu yajñeṣu tapaḥsu caiva
dāneṣu yat puṇya-phalaṁ pradiṣṭam |
atyeti tat sarvam idaṁ viditvā
yogī paraṁ sthānam upaiti cādyam ||

9

Śrī-Bhagavān uvāca

1 idaṁ tu te guhyatamaṁ, pravakṣyāmy anasūyave |
jñānaṁ vijñāna-sahitaṁ, yaj jñātvā mokṣyase 'śubhāt ||
2 rāja-vidyā rāja-guhyaṁ, pavitram idam uttamam |
pratyakṣāvagamaṁ dharmyaṁ, su-sukhaṁ kartum avyayam ||
3 aśraddadhānāḥ puruṣā, dharmasyāsya parantapa |
aprāpya māṁ nivartante, mṛtyu-saṁsāra-vartmani ||
4 mayā tatam idaṁ sarvaṁ, jagad avyakta-mūrtinā |
mat-sthāni sarva-bhūtāni, na cāhaṁ teṣv avasthitaḥ ||
5 na ca mat-sthāni bhūtāni, paśya me yogam aiśvaram |
bhūta-bhṛn na ca bhūta-stho, mamātmā bhūta-bhāvanaḥ ||
6 yathākāśa-sthito nityaṁ, vāyuḥ sarvatra-go mahān |
tathā sarvāṇi bhūtāni, mat-sthānīty upadhāraya ||
7 sarva-bhūtāni kaunteya, prakṛtiṁ yānti māmikām |
kalpa-kṣaye punas tāni, kalpādau visṛjāmy aham ||
8 prakṛtiṁ svām avaṣṭabhya, visṛjāmi punaḥ punaḥ |
bhūta-grāmam imaṁ kṛtsnam, avaśam prakṛter vaśāt ||

9 na ca māṁ tāni karmāṇi, nibadhnanti dhanañjaya |
udāsīna-vad āsīnam, asaktaṁ teṣu karmasu ||
10 mayādhyakṣeṇa prakṛtiḥ, sūyate sa-carācaram |
hetunānena kaunteya, jagad viparivartate ||
11 avajānanti māṁ mūḍhā, mānuṣīṁ tanum āśritam |
paraṁ bhāvam ajānanto, mama bhūta-maheśvaram ||
12 moghāśā mogha-karmāṇo, mogha-jñānā vicetasaḥ |
rākṣasīm āsurīṁ caiva, prakṛtiṁ mohinīṁ śritāḥ ||
13 mahātmānas tu māṁ pārtha, daivīṁ prakṛtim āśritāḥ |
bhajanty ananya-manaso, jñātvā bhūtādim avyayam ||
14 satataṁ kīrtayanto māṁ, yatantaś ca dṛḍha-vratāḥ |
namasyantaś ca māṁ bhaktyā, nitya-yuktā upāsate ||
15 jñāna-yajñena cāpy anye, yajanto mām upāsate |
ekatvena pṛthaktvena, bahudhā viśvato-mukham ||
16 ahaṁ kratur ahaṁ yajñaḥ, svadhāham aham auṣadham |
mantro 'ham aham evājyam, aham agnir ahaṁ hutam ||
17 pitāham asya jagato, mātā dhātā pitāmahaḥ |
vedyaṁ pavitram oṁkāra, ṛk sāma yajur eva ca ||
18 gatir bhartā prabhū sākṣī, nivāsaḥ śaraṇaṁ suhṛt |
prabhavaḥ pralayaḥ sthānaṁ, nidhānaṁ bījam avyayam ||
19 tapāmy aham ahaṁ varṣaṁ, nigṛhṇāmy utsṛjāmi ca |
amṛtaṁ caiva mṛtyuś ca, sad asac cāham arjuna ||
20 trai-vidyā māṁ soma-pāḥ pūta-pāpā
yajñair iṣṭvā svar-gatiṁ prārthayante |
te puṇyam āsādya surendra-lokam
aśnanti divyān divi deva-bhogān ||
21 te taṁ bhuktvā svarga-lokaṁ viśālaṁ
kṣīṇe puṇye martya-lokaṁ viśanti |
evaṁ trayī-dharmam anuprapannā
gatāgataṁ kāma-kāmā labhante ||
22 ananyāś cintayanto māṁ, ye janāḥ paryupāsate |
teṣāṁ nityābhiyuktānāṁ, yoga-kṣemaṁ vahāmy aham ||
23 ye 'py anya-devatā-bhaktā, yajante śraddhayānvitāḥ |
te 'pi mām eva kaunteya, yajanty avidhi-pūrvakam ||
24 ahaṁ hi sarva-yajñānāṁ, bhoktā ca prabhur eva ca |
na tu mām abhijānanti, tattvenātaś cyavanti te ||
25 yānti deva-vratā devān, pitṝn yānti pitṛ-vratāḥ |
bhūtāni yānti bhūtejyā, yānti mad-yājino 'pi mām ||
26 patraṁ puṣpaṁ phalaṁ toyaṁ, yo me bhaktyā prayacchati |
tad ahaṁ bhakty-upahṛtam, aśnāmi prayatātmanaḥ ||
27 yat karoṣi yad aśnāsi, yaj juhoṣi dadāsi yat |
yat tapasyasi kaunteya, tat kuruṣva mad-arpaṇam ||

28 śubhāśubha-phalair evaṁ, mokṣyase karma-bandhanaiḥ |
samnyāsa-yoga-yuktātmā, vimukto mām upaiṣyasi ||
29 samo 'haṁ sarva-bhūteṣu, na me dveṣyo 'sti na priyaḥ |
ye bhajanti tu māṁ bhaktyā, mayi te teṣu cāpy aham ||
30 api cet su-durācāro, bhajate mām ananya-bhāk |
sādhur eva sa mantavyaḥ, samyag vyavasito hi saḥ ||
31 kṣipraṁ bhavati dharmātmā, śaśvac-chāntiṁ nigacchati |
kaunteya pratijānīhi, na me bhaktaḥ praṇaśyati ||
32 māṁ hi pārtha vyapāśritya, ye 'pi syuḥ pāpa-yonayaḥ |
striyo vaiśyās tathā śūdrās, te 'pi yānti parāṁ gatim ||
33 kiṁ punar brāhmaṇāḥ puṇyā, bhaktā rājarṣayas tathā |
anityam asukhaṁ lokam, imaṁ prāpya bhajasva mām ||
34 man-manā bhava mad-bhakto, mad-yājī māṁ namaskuru |
mām evaiṣyasi yuktvaivam, ātmānaṁ mat-parāyaṇaḥ ||

10

Śrī-Bhagavān uvāca

1 bhūya eva mahā-bāho, śṛṇu me paramaṁ vacaḥ |
yat te 'haṁ prīyamāṇāya, vakṣyāmi hita-kāmyayā ||
2 ne me viduḥ sura-gaṇāḥ, prabhavaṁ na maharṣayaḥ |
aham ādir hi devānāṁ, maharṣīṇāṁ ca sarvaśaḥ ||
3 yo mām ajam anādiṁ ca, vetti loka-maheśvaram |
asammūḍhaḥ sa martyeṣu, sarva-pāpaiḥ pramucyate ||
4 buddhir jñānam asammohaḥ, kṣamā satyaṁ damaḥ śamaḥ |
sukhaṁ duḥkhaṁ bhavo 'bhāvo, bhayaṁ cābhayam eva ca ||
5 ahiṁsā samatā tuṣṭis, tapo dānaṁ yaśo 'yaśaḥ |
bhavanti bhāvā bhūtānāṁ, matta eva pṛthag-vidhāḥ ||
6 maharṣayaḥ sapta pūrve, catvāro manavas tathā |
mad-bhāvā mānasā jātā, yeṣāṁ loka imāḥ prajāḥ ||
7 etāṁ vibhūtiṁ yogaṁ ca, mama yo vetti tattvataḥ |
so 'vikampena yogena, yujyate nātra saṁśayaḥ ||
8 ahaṁ sarvasya prabhavo, mattaḥ sarvaṁ pravartate |
iti matvā bhajante māṁ, budhā bhāva-samanvitāḥ ||
9 mac-cittā mad-gata-prāṇā, bodhayantaḥ parasparam |
kathayantaś ca māṁ nityaṁ, tuṣyanti ca ramanti ca ||
10 teṣāṁ satata-yuktānāṁ, bhajatāṁ prīti-pūrvakam |
dadāmi buddhi-yogaṁ taṁ, yena mām upayānti te ||
11 teṣām evānukampārtham, aham ajñāna-jaṁ tamaḥ |
nāśayāmy ātma-bhāva-stho, jñāna-dīpena bhāsvatā ||

Arjuna uvāca

12 paraṁ brahma paraṁ dhāma, pavitraṁ paramaṁ bhavān |
puruṣaṁ śāśvataṁ divyam, ādi-devam ajaṁ vibhum ||
13 āhus tvām ṛṣayaḥ sarve, devarṣir nāradas tathā |
asito devalo vyāsaḥ, svayaṁ caiva bravīṣi me ||
14 sarvam etad ṛtaṁ manye, yan māṁ vadasi keśava |
na hi te bhagavan vyaktiṁ, vidur devā na dānavāḥ ||
15 svayam evātmanātmānaṁ, vettha tvaṁ puruṣottama |
bhūta-bhāvana bhūteśa, deva-deva jagat-pate ||
16 vaktum arhasy aśeṣeṇa, divyā hy ātma-vibhūtayaḥ |
yābhir vibhūtibhir lokān, imāṁs tvaṁ vyāpya tiṣṭhasi ||
17 kathaṁ vidyām ahaṁ yogiṁs, tvāṁ sadā paricintayan |
keṣu keṣu ca bhāveṣu, cintyo 'si bhagavan mayā ||
18 vistareṇātmano yogaṁ, vibhūtiṁ ca janārdana |
bhūyaḥ kathaya tṛptir hi, śṛṇvato nāsti me 'mṛtam ||

Śrī-Bhagavān uvāca

19 hanta te kathayiṣyāmi, divyā hy ātma-vibhūtayaḥ |
prādhānyataḥ kuru-śreṣṭha, nāsty anto vistarasya me ||
20 aham ātmā guḍākeśa, sarva-bhūtāśaya-sthitaḥ |
aham ādiś ca madhyaṁ ca, bhūtānām anta eva ca ||
21 ādityānām ahaṁ viṣṇur, jyotiṣāṁ ravir aṁśumān |
marīcir marutām asmi, nakṣatrāṇām ahaṁ śaśī ||
22 vedānāṁ sāma-vedo 'smi, devānām asmi vāsavaḥ |
indriyāṇāṁ manaś cāsmi, bhūtānām asmi cetanā ||
23 rudrāṇāṁ śaṅkaraś cāsmi, vitteśo yakṣa-rakṣasām |
vasūnāṁ pāvakaś cāsmi, meruḥ śikhariṇām aham ||
24 purodhasāṁ ca mukhyaṁ māṁ, viddhi pārtha bṛhaspatim |
senānīnām ahaṁ skandaḥ, sarasām asmi sāgaraḥ ||
25 maharṣīṇāṁ bhṛgur ahaṁ, girām asmy ekam akṣaram |
yajñānāṁ japa-yajño 'smi, sthāvarāṇāṁ himālayaḥ ||
26 aśvatthaḥ sarva-vṛkṣāṇāṁ, devarṣīṇāṁ ca nāradaḥ |
gandharvāṇāṁ citrarathaḥ, siddhānāṁ kapilo muniḥ ||
27 uccaiḥśravasam aśvānāṁ, viddhi mām amṛtodbhavam |
airāvataṁ gajendrāṇāṁ, narāṇāṁ ca narādhipam ||
28 āyudhānām ahaṁ vajraṁ, dhenūnām asmi kāmadhuk |
prajanaś cāsmi kandarpaḥ, sarpāṇām asmi vāsukiḥ ||
29 anantaś cāsmi nāgānāṁ, varuṇo yādasām aham |
pitṝṇām aryamā cāsmi, yamaḥ saṁyamatām aham ||
30 prahlādaś cāsmi daityānāṁ, kālaḥ kalayatām aham |
mṛgāṇāṁ ca mṛgendro 'haṁ, vainateyaś ca pakṣiṇām ||

31 pavanaḥ pavatām asmi, rāmaḥ śastra-bhṛtām aham |
jhaṣāṇāṁ makaraś cāsmi, srotasām asmi jāhnavī ||
32 sargāṇām ādir antaś ca, madhyaṁ caivāham arjuna |
adhyātma-vidyā vidyānāṁ, vādaḥ pravadatām aham ||
33 akṣarāṇām a-kāro 'smi, dvandvaḥ sāmāsikasya ca |
aham evākṣayaḥ kālo, dhātāhaṁ viśvato-mukhaḥ ||
34 mṛtyuḥ sarva-haraś cāham, udbhavaś ca bhaviṣyatām |
kīrtiḥ śrīr vāk ca nārīṇāṁ, smṛtir medhā dhṛtiḥ kṣamā ||
35 bṛhat-sāma tathā sāmnāṁ, gāyatrī chandasām aham |
māsānāṁ mārga-śīrṣo 'ham, ṛtūnāṁ kusumākaraḥ ||
36 dyūtaṁ chlayatām asmi, tejas tejasvinām aham |
jayo 'smi vyavasāyo 'smi, sattvaṁ sattvavatām aham ||
37 vṛṣṇīnāṁ vāsudevo 'smi, pāṇḍavānāṁ dhanañjayaḥ |
munīnām apy ahaṁ vyāsaḥ, kavīnām uśanā kaviḥ ||
38 daṇḍo damayatām asmi, nītir asmi jigīṣatām |
maunaṁ caivāsmi guhyānāṁ, jñānaṁ jñānavatām aham ||
39 yac cāpi sarva-bhūtānāṁ, bījaṁ tad aham arjuna |
na tad asti vinā yat syān, mayā bhūtaṁ carācaram ||
40 nānto 'sti mama divyānāṁ, vibhūtīnāṁ parantapa |
eṣa tūddeśataḥ prokto, vibhūter vistaro mayā ||
41 yad yad vibhūtimat sattvaṁ, śrīmad ūrjitam eva vā |
tat tad evāvagaccha tvaṁ, mama tejo-'ṁśa-sambhavam ||
42 atha vā bahunaitena, kiṁ jñātena tavārjuna |
viṣṭabhyāham idaṁ kṛtsnam, ekāṁśena sthito jagat ||

11

Arjuna uvāca

1 mad-anugrahāya paramaṁ, guhyam adhyātma-saṁjñitam |
yat tvayoktaṁ vacas tena, moho 'yaṁ vigato mama ||
2 bhavāpyayau hi bhūtānāṁ, śrutau vistaraśo mayā |
tvattaḥ kamala-patrākṣa, māhātmyam api cāvyayam ||
3 evam etad yathāttha tvam, ātmānaṁ parameśvara |
draṣṭum icchāmi te rūpam, aiśvaraṁ puruṣottama ||
4 manyase yadi tac chakyaṁ, mayā draṣṭum iti prabho |
yogeśvara tato me tvaṁ, darśayātmānam avyayam ||

Śrī-Bhagavān uvāca

5 paśya me pārtha rūpāṇi, śataśo 'tha sahasraśaḥ |
nānā-vidhāni divyāni, nānā-varṇākṛtīni ca ||

6 paśyādityān vasūn rudrān, aśvinau marutas tathā |
bahūny adṛṣṭa-pūrvāṇi, paśyāścaryāṇi bhārata ||
7 ihaika-sthaṁ jagat kṛtsnaṁ, paśyādya sa-carācaram |
mama dehe guḍākeśa, yac cānyad draṣṭum icchasi ||
8 na tu māṁ śakyase draṣṭum, anenaiva sva-cakṣuṣā |
divyaṁ dadāmi te cakṣuḥ, paśya me yogam aiśvaram ||

Sañjaya uvāca

9 evam uktvā tato rājan, mahā-yogeśvaro hariḥ |
darśayām āsa pārthāya, paramaṁ rūpam aiśvaram ||
10 aneka-vaktra-nayanam, anekādbhuta-darśanam |
aneka-divyābharaṇaṁ, divyānekodyatāyudham ||
11 divya-mālyāmbara-dharaṁ, divya-gandhānulepanam |
sarvāścarya-mayaṁ devam, anantaṁ viśvato-mukham ||
12 divi sūrya-sahasrasya, bhaved yugapad utthitā |
yadi bhāḥ sadṛśī sā syād, bhāsas tasya mahātmanaḥ ||
13 tatraika-stham jagat kṛtsnaṁ, pravibhaktam anekadhā |
apaśyad deva-devasya, śarīre pāṇḍavas tadā ||
14 tataḥ sa vismayāviṣto, hṛṣṭa-romā dhanañjayaḥ |
praṇamya śirasā devaṁ, kṛtāñjalir abhāṣata ||

Arjuna uvāca

15 paśyāmi devāṁs tava deva dehe
sarvāṁs tathā bhūta-viśeṣa-saṅghān |
brahmāṇam īśaṁ kamalāsana-stham
ṛṣīṁś ca sarvān uragāṁś ca divyān ||
16 aneka-bāhūdara-vaktra-netraṁ
paśyāmi tvā sarvato 'nanta-rūpam |
nāntaṁ na madhyaṁ na punas tavādiṁ
paśyāmi viśveśvara viśva-rūpa ||
17 kirīṭinaṁ gadinaṁ cakriṇaṁ ca
tejo-rāśiṁ sarvato dīptimantam |
paśyāmi tvāṁ durnirīkṣyaṁ samantād
dīptānalārka-dyutim aprameyam ||
18 tvam akṣaraṁ paramaṁ veditavyaṁ
tvam asya viśvasya paraṁ nidhānam |
tvam avyayaḥ śāśvata-dharma-goptā
sanātanas tvaṁ puruṣo mato me ||
19 anādi-madyāntam ananta-vīryam
ananta-bāhuṁ śaśi-sūrya-netram |
paśyāmi tvāṁ dīpta-hutāśa-vaktraṁ
sva-tejasā viśvam idaṁ tapantam ||

20 dyāv ā-pṛthivyor idam antaraṁ hi
vyāptaṁ tvayaikena diśaś ca sarvāḥ |
dṛṣṭvābhutaṁ rūpam idaṁ tavograṁ
loka-trayaṁ pravyathitaṁ mahātman ||
21 amī hi tvā sura-saṅghā viśanti
kecid bhītāḥ prāñjalayo gṛṇanti |
svastīty uktvā maharṣi-siddha-saṅghāḥ
stuvanti tvāṁ stutibhiḥ puṣkalābhiḥ ||
22 rudrādityā vasavo ye ca sādhyā
viśve 'svinau marutaś coṣmapāś ca |
gandharva-yakṣāsura-siddha-saṅghā
vīkṣante tvā vismitāś caiva sarve ||
23 rūpaṁ mahat te bahu-vaktra-netraṁ
mahā-bāho bahu-bāhūru-pādam |
bahūdaraṁ bahu-daṁṣṭrā-karālaṁ
dṛṣṭvā lokāḥ pravyathitās tathāham ||
24 nabhaḥ-spṛśaṁ dīptam aneka-varṇaṁ
vyāttānanaṁ dīpta-viśāla-netram |
dṛṣṭvā hi tvāṁ pravyathitāntar-ātmā
dhṛtiṁ na vindāmi śamaṁ ca viṣṇo ||
25 daṁṣṭrā-karālāni ca te mukhāni
dṛṣṭvaiva kālānala-sannibhāni |
diśo na jāne na labhe ca śarma
prasīda deveśa jagan-nivāsa ||
26 amī ca tvāṁ dhṛtarāṣṭrasya putrāḥ
sarve sahaivāvani-pāla-saṅghaiḥ |
bhīṣmo droṇaḥ sūta-putras tathāsau
sahāsmadīyair api yodha-mukhyaiḥ ||
27 vaktrāṇi te tvaramāṇā viśanti
daṁṣṭrā-karālāni bhayānakāni |
kecid vilagnā daśanāntareṣu
sandṛśyante cūrṇitair uttamāṅgaiḥ ||
28 yathā nadīnāṁ bahavo 'mbu-vegāḥ
samudram evābhimukhā dravanti |
tathā tavāmī nara-loka-vīrā
viśanti vaktrāṇy abhivijvalanti ||
29 yathā pradīptaṁ jvalanaṁ pataṅgā
viśanti nāśāya samṛddha-vegāḥ |
tathaiva nāśāya viśanti lokās
tavāpi vaktrāṇi samṛddha-vegāḥ ||
30 lelihyase grasamānaḥ samantāl
lokān samagrān vadanair jvaladbhiḥ |
tejobhir āpūrya jagat samagraṁ
bhāsas tavogrāḥ pratapanti viṣṇo ||

31 ākhyāhi me ko bhavān ugra-rūpo
namo 'stu te deva-vara prasīda |
vijñātum icchāmi bhavantam ādyaṁ
na hi prajānāmi tava pravṛttim ||

Śrī-Bhagavān uvāca

32 kālo 'smi loka-kṣaya-kṛt pravṛddho
lokān samāhartum iha pravṛttaḥ |
ṛte 'pi tvāṁ na bhaviṣyanti sarve
ye 'vasthitāḥ pratyanīkeṣu yodhāḥ ||
33 tasmāt tvam uttiṣṭha yaśo labhasva
jitvā śatrūn bhuṅkṣva rājyaṁ samṛddham |
mayaivaite nihatāḥ pūrvam eva
nimitta-mātraṁ bhava savya-sācin ||
34 droṇaṁ ca bhīsmaṁ ca jayadrathaṁ ca
karṇaṁ tathānyān api yodha-vīrān |
mayā hatāṁs tvaṁ jahi mā vyathiṣṭhā
yudhyasva jetāsi raṇe sapatnān ||

Sañjaya uvāca

35 etac chrutvā vacanaṁ keśavasya
kṛtāñjalir vepamānaḥ kirīṭī |
namaskṛtvā bhūya evāha kṛṣṇaṁ
sa-gadgadaṁ bhīta-bhītaḥ praṇamya ||

Arjuna uvāca

36 sthāne hṛṣīkeśa tava prakīrtyā
jagat prahṛṣyaty anurajyate ca |
rakṣāmsi bhītāni diśo dravanti
sarve namasyanti ca siddha-saṅghāḥ ||
37 kasmāc ca te na nameran mahātman
garīyase brahmaṇo 'py ādi-kartre |
ananta deveśa jagan-nivāsa
tvam akṣaraṁ sad-asat tat paraṁ yat ||
38 tvam ādi-devaḥ puruṣaḥ purāṇas
tvam asya viśvasya paraṁ nidhānam |
vettāsi vedyaṁ ca paraṁ ca dhāma
tvayā tataṁ viśvam ananta-rūpa ||
39 vāyur yamo 'gnir varuṇaḥ śaśāṅkaḥ
prajāpatis tvaṁ prapitāmahaś ca |
namo namas te 'stu sahasra-kṛtvaḥ
punaś ca bhūyo 'pi namo namas te ||

40 namaḥ purastād atha pṛṣṭhatas te
namo 'stu te sarvata eva sarva |
ananta-vīryāmita-vikramas tvaṁ
sarvaṁ samāpnoṣi tato 'si sarvaḥ ||
41 sakheti matvā prasabhaṁ yad uktaṁ
he kṛṣṇa he yādava he sakheti |
ajānatā mahimānaṁ tavedaṁ
mayā pramādāt praṇayena vāpi ||
42 yac cāvahāsārtham asat-kṛto 'si
vihāra-śayyāsana-bhojaneṣu |
eko 'tha vāpy acyuta tat-samakṣaṁ
tat kṣāmaye tvām aham aprameyam ||
43 pitāsi lokasya carācarasya
tvam asya pūjyaś ca gurur garīyān |
na tvat-samo 'sty abhyadhikaḥ kuto 'nyo
loka-traye 'py apratima-prabhāva ||
44 tasmāt praṇamya praṇidhāya kāyaṁ
prasādaye tvām aham īśam īḍyam |
piteva putrasya sakheva sakhyuḥ
priyaḥ priyāyārhasi deva soḍhum ||
45 adṛṣṭa-pūrvaṁ hṛṣito 'smi dṛṣṭvā
bhayena ca pravyathitaṁ mano me |
tad eva me darśaya deva-rūpaṁ
prasīda deveśa jagan-nivāsa ||
46 kirīṭinaṁ gadinaṁ cakra-hastam
icchāmi tvāṁ draṣṭum ahaṁ tathaiva |
tenaiva rūpeṇa catur-bhujena
sahasra-bāho bhava viśva-mūrte ||

Śrī-Bhagavān uvāca

47 mayā prasannena tavārjunedaṁ
rūpaṁ paraṁ darśitam ātma-yogāt |
tejo-mayaṁ viśvam anantam ādyaṁ
yan me tvad anyena na dṛṣṭa-pūrvam ||
48 na veda-yajñādhyayanair na dānair
na ca kriyābhir na tapobhir ugraiḥ |
evaṁ-rūpaḥ śakya ahaṁ nṛ-loke
draṣṭuṁ tvad anyena kuru-pravīra ||
49 mā te vyathā mā ca vimūḍha-bhāvo
dṛṣṭvā rūpaṁ ghoram īdṛṅ mamedam |
vyapeta-bhīḥ prīta-manāḥ punas tvaṁ
tad eva me rūpam idaṁ prapaśya ||

Sañjaya uvāca

50 ity arjunaṁ vāsudevas tathoktvā
svakaṁ rūpaṁ darśayām āsa bhūyaḥ |
āśvāsayām āsa ca bhītam enaṁ
bhūtvā punaḥ saumya-vapur mahātmā ||

Arjuna uvāca

51 dṛṣṭvedaṁ mānuṣaṁ rūpaṁ, tava saumyaṁ janārdana |
idānīm asmi saṁvṛttaḥ, sa-cetāḥ prakṛtiṁ gataḥ ||

Śrī-Bhagavān uvāca

52 su-durdarśam idaṁ rūpaṁ, dṛṣṭavān asi yan mama |
devā apy asya rūpasya, nityaṁ darśana-kāṅkṣiṇaḥ ||
53 nāhaṁ vedair na tapasā, na dānena na cejyayā |
śakya evaṁ-vidho draṣṭuṁ, dṛṣṭavān asi māṁ yathā ||
54 bhaktyā tv ananyayā śakya, aham evaṁ-vidho 'rjuna |
jñātuṁ draṣṭuṁ ca tattvena, praveṣṭuṁ ca parantapa ||
55 mat-karma-kṛn mat-paramo, mad-bhaktaḥ saṅga-varjitaḥ |
nirvairaḥ sarva-bhūteṣu, yaḥ sa mām eti pāṇḍava ||

12

Arjuna uvāca

1 evaṁ satata-yuktā ye, bhaktās tvāṁ paryupāsate |
ye cāpy akṣaram avyaktaṁ, teṣāṁ ke yoga-vittamāḥ ||

Śrī-Bhagavān uvāca

2 mayy āveśya mano ye māṁ, nitya-yuktā upāsate |
śraddhayā parayopetās, te me yuktatamā matāḥ ||
3 ye tv akṣaram anirdeśyam, avyaktaṁ paryupāsate |
sarvatra-gam acintyaṁ ca, kūṭa-stham acalaṁ dhruvam ||
4 sanniyamyendriya-grāmaṁ, sarvatra sama-buddhayaḥ |
te prāpnuvanti mām eva, sarva-bhūta-hite ratāḥ ||
5 kleśo 'dhikataras teṣām, avyaktāsakta-cetasām |
avyaktā hi gatir duḥkhaṁ, dehavadbhir avāpyate ||
6 ye tu sarvāṇi karmāṇi, mayi saṁnyasya mat-parāḥ |
ananyenaiva yogena, māṁ dhyāyanta upāsate ||
7 teṣām ahaṁ samuddhartā, mṛtyu-saṁsāra-sāgarāt |
bhavāmi na cirāt pārtha, mayy āveśita-cetasām ||
8 mayy eva mana ādhatsva, mayi buddhiṁ niveśaya |
nivasiṣyasi mayy eva, ata ūrdhvaṁ na saṁśayaḥ ||

9 atha cittaṁ samādhātuṁ, na śaknoṣi mayi sthiram |
abhyāsa-yogena tato, mām icchāptuṁ dhanañjaya ||
10 abhyāse 'py asamartho 'si, mat-karma-paramo bhava |
mad-artham api karmāṇi, kurvan siddhim avāpsyasi ||
11 athaitad apy aśakto 'si, kartuṁ mad-yogam āśritaḥ |
sarva-karma-phala-tyāgaṁ, tataḥ kuru yatātmavān ||
12 śreyo hi jñānam abhyāsāj, jñānād dhyānaṁ viśiṣyate |
dhyānāt karma-phala-tyāgas, tyāgāc chāntir anantaram ||
13 adveṣṭā sarva-bhūtānāṁ, maitraḥ karuṇa eva ca |
nirmamo nirahaṅkāraḥ, sama-duḥkha-sukhaḥ kṣamī ||
14 santuṣṭaḥ satataṁ yogī, yatātmā dṛḍha-niścayaḥ |
mayy arpita-mano-budhir, yo mad-bhaktaḥ sa me priyaḥ ||
15 yasmān nodvijate loko, lokān nodvijate ca yaḥ |
harṣāmarṣa-bhayodvegair, mukto yaḥ sa ca me priyaḥ ||
16 anapekṣaḥ śucir dakṣa, udāsīno gata-vyathaḥ |
sarvārambha-parityāgī, yo mad-bhaktaḥ sa me priyaḥ ||
17 yo na hṛṣyati na dveṣṭi, na śocati na kāṅkṣati |
śubhāśubha-parityāgī, bhaktimān yaḥ sa me priyaḥ ||
18 samaḥ śatrau ca mitre ca, tathā mānāpamānayoḥ |
śitoṣṇa-sukha-duḥkheṣu, samaḥ saṅga-vivarjitaḥ ||
19 tulya-nindā-stutir maunī, santuṣṭo yena kenacit |
aniketaḥ sthira-matir, bhaktimān me priyo naraḥ ||
20 ye tu dharmyāmṛtam idaṁ, yathoktaṁ paryupāsate |
śraddadhānā mat-paramā, bhaktās te 'tīva me priyāḥ ||

13

Arjuna uvāca

prakṛtiṁ puruṣaṁ caiva, kṣetraṁ kṣetra-jñam eva ca |
etad veditum icchāmi, jñānaṁ jñeyaṁ ca keśava ||

Śrī-Bhagavān uvāca

1 idaṁ śarīraṁ kaunteya, kṣetram ity abhidhīyate |
etad yo vetti taṁ prāhuḥ, kṣetra-jña iti tad-vidaḥ ||
2 kṣetra-jñaṁ cāpi māṁ viddhi, sarva-kṣetreṣu bhārata |
kṣetra-kṣetrajñayor jñānaṁ, yat taj jñānaṁ mataṁ mama ||
3 tat kṣetraṁ yac ca yādṛk ca, yad-vikāri yataś ca yat |
sa ca yo yat-prabhāvaś ca, tat samāsena me śṛṇu ||
4 ṛṣibhir bahudhā gītaṁ, chandobhir vividhaiḥ pṛthak |
brahma-sūtra-padaiś caiva, hetumadbhir viniścitaiḥ ||
5 mahā-bhūtāny ahaṅkāro, buddhir avyaktam eva ca |
indriyāṇi daśaikaṁ ca, pañca cendriya-gocarāḥ ||

6 icchā dveṣaḥ sukhaṁ duḥkhaṁ, saṅghātaś cetanā dhṛtiḥ |
etat kṣetraṁ samāsena, sa-vikāram udāhṛtam ||
7 amānitvam adambhitvam, ahiṁsā kṣāntir ārjavam |
ācāryopāsanaṁ śaucaṁ, sthairyam ātma-vinigrahaḥ ||
8 indriyārtheṣu vairāgyam, anahaṅkāra eva ca |
janma-mṛtyu-jarā-vyādhi-, duḥkha-doṣānudarśanam ||
9 asaktir anabhiṣvaṅgaḥ, putra-dāra-gṛhādiṣu |
nityaṁ ca sama-cittatvam, iṣṭāniṣṭopapattiṣu ||
10 mayi cānanya-yogena, bhaktir avyabhicāriṇī |
vivikta-deśa-sevitvam, aratir jana-saṁsadi ||
11 adhyātma-jñāna-nityatvaṁ, tattva-jñānārtha-darśanam |
etaj jñānam iti proktam, ajñānaṁ yad ato 'nyathā ||
12 jñeyaṁ yat tat pravakṣyāmi, yaj jñātvāmṛtam āśnute |
anādi mat-paraṁ brahma, na sat tan nāsad ucyate ||
13 sarvataḥ pāṇi-pādaṁ tat, sarvato 'kṣi-śiro-mukham |
sarvataḥ śrutimal loke, sarvam āvṛtya tiṣṭhati ||
14 sarvendriya-guṇābhāsaṁ, sarvendriya-vivarjitam |
asaktaṁ sarva-bhṛc caiva, nirguṇaṁ guṇa-bhoktṛ ca ||
15 bahir antaś ca bhūtānām, acaraṁ caram eva ca |
sūkṣmatvāt tad avijñeyaṁ, dūra-sthaṁ cāntike ca tat ||
16 avibhaktaṁ ca bhūteṣu, vibhaktam iva ca sthitam |
bhūta-bhartṛ ca taj jñeyaṁ, grasiṣṇu prabhaviṣṇu ca ||
17 jyotiṣām api taj jyotis, tamasaḥ param ucyate |
jñānaṁ jñeyaṁ jñāna-gamyaṁ, hṛdi sarvasya viṣṭhitam ||
18 iti kṣetraṁ tathā jñānaṁ, jñeyaṁ coktaṁ samāsataḥ |
mad-bhakta etad vijñāya, mad-bhāvāyopapadyate ||
19 prakṛtiṁ puruṣaṁ caiva, viddhy anādī ubhāv api |
vikārāṁś ca guṇāṁś caiva, viddhi prakṛti-sambhavān ||
20 kārya-kāraṇa-kartṛtve, hetuḥ prakṛtir ucyate |
puruṣaḥ sukha-duḥkhānāṁ, bhoktṛtve hetur ucyate ||
21 puruṣaḥ prakṛti-stho hi, bhuṅkte prakṛti-jān guṇān |
kāraṇaṁ guṇa-saṅgo 'sya, sad-asad-yoni-janmasu ||
22 upadraṣṭānumantā ca, bhartā bhoktā maheśvaraḥ |
paramātmeti cāpy ukto, dehe 'smin puruṣaḥ paraḥ ||
23 ya evaṁ vetti puruṣaṁ, prakṛtiṁ ca guṇaiḥ saha |
sarvathā vartamāno 'pi, na sa bhūyo 'bhijāyate ||
24 dhyānenātmani paśyanti, kecid ātmānam ātmanā |
anye sāṅkhyena yogena, karma-yogena cāpare ||
25 anye tv evam ajānantaḥ, śrutvānyebhya upāsate |
te 'pi cātitaranty eva, mṛtyuṁ śruti-parāyaṇāḥ ||
26 yāvat sañjāyate kiñcit, sattvaṁ sthāvara-jaṅgamam |
kṣetra-kṣetrajña-saṁyogāt, tad viddhi bharatarṣabha ||

27 samaṁ sarveṣu bhūteṣu, tiṣṭhantaṁ parameśvaram |
vinaśyatsv avinaśyantaṁ, yaḥ paśyati sa paśyati ||
28 samaṁ paśyan hi sarvatra, samavasthitam īśvaram |
na hinasty ātmanātmānaṁ, tato yāti parāṁ gatim ||
29 prakṛtyaiva ca karmāṇi, kriyamāṇāni sarvaśaḥ |
yaḥ paśyati tathātmānam, akartāraṁ sa paśyati ||
30 yadā bhūta-pṛthag-bhāvam, eka-stham anupaśyati |
tata eva ca vistāraṁ, brahma sampadyate tadā ||
31 anāditvān nirguṇatvāt, paramātmāyam avyayaḥ |
śarīra-stho 'pi kaunteya, na karoti na lipyate ||
32 yathā sarva-gataṁ saukṣmyād, ākāśaṁ nopalipyate |
sarvatrāvasthito dehe, tathātmā nopalipyate ||
33 yathā prakāśayaty ekaḥ, kṛtsnaṁ lokam imaṁ raviḥ |
kṣetraṁ kṣetrī tathā kṛtsnaṁ, prakāśayati bhārata ||
34 kṣetra-kṣetrajñayor evam, antaraṁ jñāna-cakṣuṣā |
bhūta-prakṛti-mokṣaṁ ca, ye vidur yānti te param ||

14

Śrī-Bhagavān uvāca

1 paraṁ bhūyaḥ pravakṣyāmi, jñānānāṁ jñānam uttamam |
yaj jñātvā munayaḥ sarve, parāṁ siddhim ito gatāḥ ||
2 idaṁ jñānam upāśritya, mama sādharmyam āgatāḥ |
sarge 'pi nopajāyante, pralaye na vyathanti ca ||
3 mama yonir mahad brahma, tasmin garbhaṁ dadhāmy aham |
sambhavaḥ sarva-bhūtānāṁ, tato bhavati bhārata ||
4 sarva-yoniṣu kaunteya, mūrtayaḥ sambhavanti yāḥ |
tāsāṁ brahma mahad yonir, ahaṁ bīja-pradaḥ pitā ||
5 sattvaṁ rajas tama iti, guṇāḥ prakṛti-sambhavāḥ |
nibadhnanti mahā-bāho, dehe dehinam avyayam ||
6 tatra sattvaṁ nirmalatvāt, prakāśakam anāmayam |
sukha-saṅgena badhnāti, jñāna-saṅgena cānagha ||
7 rajo rāgātmakaṁ viddhi, tṛṣṇā-saṅga-samudbhavam |
tan nibadhnāti kaunteya, karma-saṅgena dehinam ||
8 tamas tv ajñāna-jaṁ viddhi, mohanaṁ sarva-dehinām |
pramādālasya-nidrābhis, tan nibadhnāti bhārata ||
9 sattvaṁ sukhe sañjayati, rajaḥ karmaṇi bhārata |
jñānam āvṛtya tu tamaḥ, pramāde sañjayaty uta ||
10 rajas tamaś cābhibhūya, sattvaṁ bhavati bhārata |
rajaḥ sattvaṁ tamaś caiva, tamaḥ sattvaṁ rajas tathā ||
11 sarva-dvāreṣu dehe 'smin, prakāśa upajāyate |
jñānaṁ yadā tadā vidyād, vivṛddhaṁ sattvam ity uta ||

12 lobhaḥ pravṛttir ārambhaḥ, karmaṇām aśamaḥ spṛhā |
rajasy etāni jāyante, vivṛddhe bharatarṣabha ||
13 aprakāśo 'pravṛttiś ca, pramādo moha eva ca |
tamasy etāni jāyante, vivṛddhe kuru-nandana ||
14 yadā sattve pravṛddhe tu, pralayaṁ yāti deha-bhṛt |
tadottama-vidāṁ lokān, amalān pratipadyate ||
15 rajasi pralayaṁ gatvā, karma-saṅgiṣu jāyate |
tathā pralīnas tamasi, mūḍha-yoniṣu jāyate ||
16 karmaṇaḥ sukṛtasyāhuḥ, sāttvikaṁ nirmalaṁ phalam |
rajasas tu phalaṁ duḥkham, ajñānaṁ tamasaḥ phalam ||
17 sattvāt sañjāyate jñānaṁ, rajaso lobha eva ca |
pramāda-mohau tamaso, bhavato 'jñānam eva ca ||
18 ūrdhvaṁ gacchanti sattva-sthā, madhye tiṣṭhanti rājasāḥ |
jaghanya-guṇa-vṛtta-sthā, adho gacchanti tāmasāḥ ||
19 nānyaṁ guṇebhyaḥ kartāraṁ, yadā draṣṭānupaśyati |
guṇebhyaś ca paraṁ vetti, mad-bhāvaṁ so 'dhigacchati ||
20 guṇān etān atītya trīn, dehī deha-samudbhavān |
janma-mṛtyu-jarā-duḥkhair, vimukto 'mṛtam aśnute ||

Arjuna uvāca

21 kair liṅgais trīn guṇān etān, atīto bhavati prabho |
kim ācāraḥ kathaṁ caitāṁs, trīn guṇān ativartate ||

Śrī-Bhagavān uvāca

22 prakāśaṁ ca pravṛttiṁ ca, moham eva ca pāṇḍava |
na dveṣṭi sampravṛttāni, na nivṛttāni kāṅkṣati ||
23 udāsīna-vad āsīno, guṇair yo na vicālyate |
guṇā vartanta ity eva, yo 'vatiṣṭhati neṅgate ||
24 sama-duḥkha-sukhaḥ sva-sthaḥ, sama-loṣṭāśma-kāñcanaḥ |
tulya-priyāpriyo dhīras, tulya-nindātma-saṁstutiḥ ||
25 mānāvamānayos tulyas, tulyo mitrāri-pakṣayoḥ |
sarvārambha-parityāgī, guṇātītaḥ sa ucyate ||
26 māṁ ca yo 'vyabhicāreṇa, bhakti-yogena sevate |
sa guṇān samatītyaitān, brahma-bhūyāya kalpate ||
27 brahmaṇo hi pratiṣṭhāham, amṛtasyāvyayasya ca |
śāśvatasya ca dharmasya, sukhasyaikāntikasya ca ||

15

Śrī-Bhagavān uvāca

1 ūrdhva-mūlam adhaḥ-śākham, aśvatthaṁ prāhur avyayam |
chandāṁsi yasya parṇāni, yas taṁ veda sa veda-vit ||

2 adhaś cordhvaṁ prasṛtās tasya śākhā
guṇa-pravṛddhā viṣaya-pravālāḥ |
adhaś ca mūlāny anusantatāni
karmānubandhīni manuṣya-loke ||
3 na rūpam asyeha tathopalabhyate
nānto na cādir na ca sampratiṣṭhā |
aśvattham enaṁ su-virūḍha-mūlam
asaṅga-śastreṇa dṛḍhena chittvā ||
4 tataḥ padaṁ tat parimārgitavyaṁ
yasmin gatā na nivartanti bhūyaḥ |
tam eva cādyaṁ puruṣaṁ prapadye
yataḥ pravṛttiḥ prasṛtā purāṇī ||
5 nirmāna-mohā jita-saṅga-doṣā
adhyātma-nityā vinivṛtta-kāmāḥ |
dvandvair vimuktāḥ sukha-duḥkha-saṁjñair
gacchanty amūḍhāḥ padam avyayaṁ tat ||
6 na tad bhāsayate sūryo, na śaśāṅko na pāvakaḥ |
yad gatvā na nivartante, tad dhāma paramaṁ mama ||
7 mamaivāṁśo jīva-loke, jīva-bhūtaḥ sanātanaḥ |
manaḥ-ṣaṣṭhānīndriyāṇi, prakṛti-sthāni karṣati ||
8 śarīraṁ yad avāpnoti, yac cāpy utkrāmatīśvaraḥ |
gṛhītvaitāni saṁyāti, vāyur gandhān ivāśayāt ||
9 śrotraṁ cakṣuḥ sparśanaṁ ca, rasanaṁ ghrāṇameva ca |
adhiṣṭhāya manaś cāyaṁ, viṣayān upasevate ||
10 utkrāmantaṁ sthitaṁ vāpi, bhuñjānaṁ vā guṇānvitam |
vimūḍhā nānupaśyanti, paśyanti jñāna-cakṣuṣaḥ ||
11 yatanto yoginaś cainaṁ, paśyanty ātmany avasthitam |
yatanto 'py akṛtātmāno, nainaṁ paśyanty acetasaḥ ||
12 yad āditya-gataṁ tejo, jagad bhāsayate 'khilam |
yac candramasi yac cāgnau, tat tejo viddhi māmakam ||
13 gām āviśya ca bhūtāni, dhārayāmy aham ojasā |
puṣṇāmi cauṣadhīḥ sarvāḥ, somo bhūtvā rasātmakaḥ ||
14 ahaṁ vaiśvānaro bhūtvā, prāṇināṁ deham āśritaḥ |
prāṇāpāna-samāyuktaḥ, pacāmy annaṁ catur-vidham ||
15 sarvasya cāhaṁ hṛdi sanniviṣṭo
mattaḥ smṛtir jñānam apohanaṁ ca |
vedaiś ca sarvair aham eva vedyo
vedānta-kṛd veda-vid eva cāham ||
16 dvāv imau puruṣau loke, kṣaraś cākṣara eva ca |
kṣaraḥ sarvāṇi bhūtāni, kūṭa-stho 'kṣara ucyate ||
17 uttamaḥ puruṣas tv anyaḥ, paramātmety udāhṛtaḥ |
yo loka-trayam āviśya, bibharty avyaya īśvaraḥ ||

18 yasmāt kṣaram atīto 'ham, akṣarād api cottamaḥ |
ato 'smi loke vede ca, prathitaḥ puruṣottamaḥ ||
19 yo mām evam asammūḍho, jānāti puruṣottamam |
sa sarva-vid bhajati māṁ, sarva-bhāvena bhārata ||
20 iti guhyatamaṁ śāstram, idam uktaṁ mayānagha |
etad buddhvā buddhimān syāt, kṛta-kṛtyaś ca bhārata ||

16

Śrī-Bhagavān uvāca

1 abhayaṁ sattva-saṁśuddhir, jñāna-yoga-vyavasthitiḥ |
dānaṁ damaś ca yajñaś ca, svādhyāyas tapa ārjavam ||
2 ahiṁsā satyam akrodhas, tyāgaḥ śāntir apaiśunam |
dayā bhūteṣv aloluptvaṁ, mārdavaṁ hrīr acāpalam ||
3 tejaḥ kṣamā dhṛtiḥ śaucam, adroho nāti-mānitā |
bhavanti sampadaṁ daivīm, abhijātasya bhārata ||
4 dambho darpo 'timānaś ca, krodhaḥ pāruṣyam eva ca |
ajñānaṁ cābhijātasya pārtha sampadam āsurīm ||
5 daivī sampad vimokṣāya, nibandhāyāsurī matā |
mā śucaḥ sampadaṁ daivīm, abhijāto 'si pāṇḍava ||
6 dvau bhūta-sargau loke 'smin, daiva āsura eva ca |
daivo vistaraśaḥ prokta, āsuraṁ pārtha me śṛṇu ||
7 pravṛttiṁ ca nivṛttiṁ ca, janā na vidur āsurāḥ |
na śaucaṁ nāpi cācāro, na satyaṁ teṣu vidyate ||
8 asatyam apratiṣṭhaṁ te, jagad āhur anīśvaram |
aparaspara-sambhūtaṁ, kim anyat kāma-haitukam ||
9 etāṁ dṛṣṭim avaṣṭabhya, naṣṭātmāno 'lpa-buddhayaḥ |
prabhavanty ugra-karmāṇaḥ, kṣayāya jagato 'hitāḥ ||
10 kāmam āśritya duṣpūraṁ, dambha māna-madānvitāḥ |
mohād gṛhītvāsad-grāhān, pravartante 'śuci-vratāḥ ||
11 cintām aparimeyāṁ ca, pralayāntām upāśritāḥ |
kāmopabhoga-paramā, etāvad iti niścitāḥ ||
12 āśā-pāśa-śatair baddhāḥ, kāma-krodha-parāyaṇāḥ |
īhante kāma-bhogārtham, anyāyenārtha-sañcayān ||
13 idam adya mayā labdham, idaṁ prāpsye manoratham |
idam astīdam api me, bhaviṣyati punar dhanam ||
14 asau mayā hataḥ śatrur, haniṣye cāparān api |
īśvaro 'ham ahaṁ bhogī, siddho 'haṁ balavān sukhī ||
15 āḍhyo 'bhijanavān asmi, ko 'nyo 'sti sadṛśo mayā |
yakṣye dāsyāmi modiṣya, ity ajñāna-vimohitāḥ ||
16 aneka-citta-vibhrāntā, moha-jāla-samāvṛtāḥ |
prasaktāḥ kāma-bhogeṣu, patanti narake 'śucau ||

17 ātma-sambhāvitāḥ stadbhā, dhana-māna-madānvitāḥ |
yajante nāma-yajñais te, dambhenāvidhi-pūrvakam ||
18 ahaṅkāraṁ balaṁ darpaṁ, kāmaṁ krodhaṁ ca saṁśritāḥ |
mām ātma-para-deheṣu, pradviṣanto 'bhyasūyakāḥ ||
19 tān ahaṁ dviṣataḥ krūrān, saṁsāreṣu narādhamān |
kṣipāmy ajasram aśubhān, āsurīṣv eva yoniṣu ||
20 āsurīṁ yonim āpannā, mūḍhā janmani janmani |
mām aprāpyaiva kaunteya, tato yānty adhamāṁ gatim ||
21 tri-vidhaṁ narakasyedaṁ, dvāraṁ nāśanam ātmanaḥ |
kāmaḥ krodhas tathā lobhas, tasmād etat trayaṁ tyajet ||
22 etair vimuktaḥ kaunteya, tamo-dvārais tribhir naraḥ |
ācaraty ātmanaḥ śreyas, tato yāti parāṁ gatim ||
23 yaḥ śāstra-vidhim utsṛjya, vartate kāma-kārataḥ |
na sa siddhim avāpnoti, na sukhaṁ na parāṁ gatim ||
24 tasmāc chāstraṁ pramāṇaṁ te, kāryākārya-vyavasthitau |
jñātvā śāstra-vidhānoktaṁ, karma kartum ihārhasi ||

17

Arjuna uvāca

1 ye śāstra-vidhim utsṛjya, yajante śraddhayānvitāḥ |
teṣāṁ niṣṭhā tu kā kṛṣṇa, sattvam āho rajas tamaḥ ||

Śrī-Bhagavān uvāca

2 tri-vidhā bhavati śraddhā, dehināṁ sā svabhāva-jā |
sāttvikī rājasī caiva, tāmasī ceti tāṁ śṛṇu ||
3 sattvānurūpā sarvasya, śraddhā bhavati bhārata |
śraddhā-mayo 'yaṁ puruṣo, yo yac-chraddhaḥ sa eva saḥ ||
4 yajante sāttvikā devān, yakṣa-rakṣāṁsi rājasāḥ |
pretān bhūta-gaṇāṁś cānye, yajante tāmasā janāḥ ||
5 aśāstra-vihitaṁ ghoraṁ, tapyante ye tapo janāḥ |
dambhāhaṅkāra-saṁyuktāḥ, kāma-rāga-balānvitāḥ ||
6 karśayantaḥ śarīra-sthaṁ, bhūta-grāmam acetasaḥ |
māṁ caivāntaḥ śarīra-sthaṁ, tān viddhy āsura-niścayān ||
7 āhāras tv api sarvasya, tri-vidho bhavati priyaḥ |
yajñas tapas tathā dānaṁ, teṣāṁ bhedam imaṁ śṛṇu ||
8 āyuḥ-sattva-balārogya-, sukha-prīti-vivardhanāḥ |
rasyāḥ snigdhāḥ sthirā hṛdyā, āhārāḥ sāttvika-priyāḥ ||
9 kaṭv-amla-lavaṇāty-uṣṇa-, tīkṣṇa-rūkṣa-vidāhinaḥ |
āhārā rājasasyeṣṭā, duḥkha-śokāmaya-pradāḥ ||
10 yāta-yāmaṁ gata-rasaṁ, pūti paryuṣitaṁ ca yat |
ucchiṣṭam api cāmedhyaṁ, bhojanaṁ tāmasa-priyam ||

11 aphalākāṅkṣibhir yajño, vidhi-dṛṣṭo ya ijyate |
yaṣṭavyam eveti manaḥ, samādhāya sa sāttvikaḥ ||
12 abhisandhāya tu phalaṁ, dambhārtham api caiva yat |
ijyate bharata-śreṣṭha, taṁ yajñaṁ viddhi rājasam ||
13 vidhi-hīnam asṛṣṭānnaṁ, mantra-hīnam adakṣiṇam |
śraddhā-virahitaṁ yajñaṁ, tāmasaṁ paricakṣate ||
14 deva-dvija-guru-prājña-, pūjanaṁ śaucam ārjavam |
brahmacaryam ahiṁsā ca, śarīraṁ tapa ucyate ||
15 anudvega-karaṁ vākyaṁ, satyaṁ priya-hitaṁ ca yat |
svādhyāyābhyasanaṁ caiva, vāṅ-mayaṁ tapa ucyate ||
16 manaḥ-prasādaḥ saumyatvaṁ, maunam ātma-vinigrahaḥ |
bhāva-saṁśuddhir ity etat, tapo mānasam ucyate ||
17 śraddhayā parayā taptaṁ, tapas tat tri-vidhaṁ naraiḥ |
aphalākāṅkṣibhir yuktaiḥ, sāttvikaṁ paricakṣate ||
18 satkāra-māna-pūjārthaṁ, tapo dambhena caiva yat |
kriyate tad iha proktaṁ, rājasaṁ calam adhruvam ||
19 mūḍhā-grāheṇātmano yat, pīḍayā kriyate tapaḥ |
parasyotsādanārthaṁ vā, tat tāmasam udāhṛtam ||
20 dātavyam iti yad dānaṁ, dīyate 'nupakāriṇe |
deśe kāle ca pātre ca, tad dānaṁ sāttvikaṁ smṛtam ||
21 yat tu pratyupakārārthaṁ, phalam uddiśya vā punaḥ |
dīyate ca parikliṣṭaṁ, tad dānaṁ rājasaṁ smṛtam ||
22 adeśa-kāle yad dānam, apātrebhyaś ca dīyate |
asat-kṛtam avajñātaṁ, tat tāmasam udāhṛtam ||
23 oṁ tat sad iti nirdeśo, brahmaṇas tri-vidhaḥ smṛtaḥ |
brāhmaṇās tena vedāś ca, yajñāś ca vihitāh purā ||
24 tasmād om ity udāhṛtya, yajña-dāna-tapaḥ-kriyāḥ |
pravartante vidhānoktāḥ, satataṁ brahma-vādinām ||
25 tad ity anabhisandhāya, phalaṁ yajña-tapaḥ-kriyāḥ |
dāna-kriyāś ca vividhāḥ, kriyante mokṣa-kāṅkṣibhiḥ ||
26 sad-bhāve sādhu-bhāve ca, sad ity etat prayujyate |
praśaste karmaṇi tathā, sac-chabdaḥ pārtha yujyate ||
27 yajñe tapasi dāne ca, sthitiḥ sad iti cocyate |
karma caiva tad-arthīyaṁ, sad ity evābhidhīyate ||
28 aśraddhayā hutaṁ dattaṁ, tapas taptaṁ kṛtaṁ ca yat |
asad ity ucyate pārtha, na ca tat pretya no iha ||

18

Arjuna uvāca

1 saṁnyāsasya mahā-bāho, tattvam icchāmi veditum |
tyāgasya ca hṛṣīkeśa, pṛthak keśi-niṣūdana ||

Śrī-Bhagavān uvāca

2 kāmyānāṁ karmaṇāṁ nyāsaṁ, saṁnyāsaṁ kavayo viduḥ |
sarva-karma-phala-tyāgaṁ, prāhus tyāgaṁ vicakṣaṇāḥ ||
3 tyājyaṁ doṣa-vad ity eke, karma prāhur manīṣiṇaḥ |
yajña-dāna-tapaḥ-karma, na tyājyam iti cāpare ||
4 niścayaṁ śṛṇu me tatra, tyāge bharata-sattama |
tyāgo hi puruṣa-vyāghra, tri-vidhaḥ samprakīrtitaḥ ||
5 yajña-dāna-tapaḥ-karma, na tyājyaṁ kāryam eva tat |
yajño dānaṁ tapaś caiva, pāvanāni manīṣiṇām ||
6 etāny api tu karmāṇi, saṅgaṁ tyaktvā phalāni ca |
kartavyānīti me pārtha, niścitaṁ matam uttamam ||
7 niyatasya tu saṁnyāsaḥ, karmaṇo nopapadyate |
mohāt tasya parityāgas, tāmasaḥ parikīrtitaḥ ||
8 duḥkham ity eva yat karma, kāya-kleśa-bhayāt tyajet |
sa kṛtvā rājasaṁ tyāgaṁ, naiva tyāga-phalaṁ labhet ||
9 kāryam ity eva yat karma, niyataṁ kriyate 'rjuna |
saṅgaṁ tyaktvā phalaṁ caiva, sa tyāgaḥ sāttviko mataḥ ||
10 na dveṣṭy akuśalaṁ karma, kuśale nānuṣajjate |
tyāgī sattva-samāviṣṭo, medhāvī chinna-saṁśayaḥ ||
11 na hi deha-bhṛtā śakyaṁ, tyaktuṁ karmāṇy aśeṣataḥ |
yas tu karma-phala-tyāgī, sa tyāgīty abhidhīyate ||
12 amiṣṭam iṣṭaṁ miśraṁ ca, tri-vidhaṁ karmaṇaḥ phalam |
bhavaty atyāgināṁ pretya, na tu saṁnyāsināṁ kvacit ||
13 pañcaitāni mahā-bāho, kāraṇāni nibodha me |
sāṅkhye kṛtānte proktāni, siddhaye sarva-karmaṇām ||
14 adhiṣṭhānaṁ tathā kartā, karaṇaṁ ca pṛthag-vidham |
vividhāś ca pṛthak ceṣṭā, daivaṁ caivātra pañcamam ||
15 śarīra-vāṅ-manobhir yat, karma prārabhate naraḥ |
nyāyyaṁ vā viparītaṁ vā, pañcaite tasya hetavaḥ ||
16 tatraivaṁ sati kartāram, ātmānaṁ kevalaṁ tu yaḥ |
paśyaty akṛta-buddhitvān, na sa paśyati durmatiḥ ||
17 yasya nāhaṅkṛto bhāvo, buddhir yasya na lipyate |
hatvāpi sa imāṅl lokān, na hanti na nibadhyate ||
18 jñānaṁ jñeyaṁ parijñātā, tri-vidhā karma-codanā |
karaṇaṁ karma karteti, tri-vidhaḥ karma-saṅgrahaḥ ||
19 jñānaṁ karma ca kartā ca, tridhaiva guṇa-bhedataḥ |
procyate guṇa-saṅkhyāne, yathāvac chṛṇu tāny api ||
20 sarva-bhūteṣu yenaikaṁ, bhāvam avyayam īkṣate |
avibhaktaṁ vibhakteṣu, taj jñānaṁ viddhi sāttvikam ||
21 pṛthaktvena tu taj jñānaṁ, nānā-bhāvān pṛthag-vidhān |
vetti sarveṣu bhūteṣu, taj jñānaṁ viddhi rājasam ||
22 yat tu kṛtsna-vad ekasmin, kārye saktam ahaitukam |
atattvārtha-vad alpaṁ ca, tat tāmasam udāhṛtam ||

23 niyataṁ saṅga-rahitam, arāga-dveṣataḥ kṛtam |
aphala-prepsunā karma, yat tat sāttvikam ucyate ||
24 yat tu kāmepsunā karma, sāhaṅkāreṇa vā punaḥ |
kriyate bahulāyāsaṁ, tad rājasam udāhṛtam ||
25 anubandhaṁ kṣayaṁ hiṁsām, anapekṣya ca pauruṣam |
mohād ārabhyate karma, yat tat tāmasam ucyate ||
26 mukta-saṅgo 'nahaṁ-vādī, dhṛty-utsāha-samanvitaḥ |
siddhy-asiddhyor nirvikāraḥ, kartā sāttvika ucyate ||
27 rāgī karma-phala-prepsur, lubdho hiṁsātmako 'śuciḥ |
harṣa-śokānvitaḥ kartā, rājasaḥ parikīrtitaḥ ||
28 ayuktaḥ prākṛtaḥ stabdhaḥ, śaṭho naikṛtiko 'lasaḥ |
viṣādī dīrgha-sūtrī ca, kartā tāmasa ucyate ||
29 buddher bhedaṁ dhṛteś caiva, guṇatas tri-vidhaṁ śṛṇu |
procyamānam aśeṣeṇa, pṛthaktvena dhanañjaya ||
30 pravṛttiṁ ca nivṛttiṁ ca, kāryākārye bhayābhaye |
bandhaṁ mokṣaṁ ca yā vetti, buddhiḥ sā pārtha sāttvikī ||
31 yayā dharmam adharmaṁ ca, kāryaṁ cākāryam eva ca |
ayathāvat prajānāti, buddhiḥ sā pārtha rājasī ||
32 adharmaṁ dharmam iti yā, manyate tamasāvṛtā |
sarvārthān viparītāṁś ca, buddhiḥ sā pārtha tāmasī ||
33 dhṛtyā yayā dhārayate, manaḥ-prāṇendriya-kriyāḥ |
yogenāvyabhicāriṇyā, dhṛtiḥ sā pārtha sāttvikī ||
34 yayā tu dharma-kāmārthān, dhṛtyā dhārayate 'rjuna |
prasaṅgena phalākāṅkṣī, dhṛtiḥ sā pārtha rājasī ||
35 yayā svapnaṁ bhayaṁ śokaṁ, viṣādaṁ madam eva ca |
na vimuñcati durmedhā, dhṛtiḥ sā pārtha tāmasī ||
36 sukhaṁ tv idānīṁ tri-vidhaṁ, śṛṇu me bharatarṣabha |
abhyāsād ramate yatra, duḥkhāntaṁ ca nigacchati ||
37 yat tad agre viṣam iva, pariṇāme 'mṛtopamam |
tat sukhaṁ sāttvikaṁ proktam, ātma-buddhi-prasāda-jam ||
38 viṣayendriya-saṁyogād, yat tad agre 'mṛtopamam |
pariṇāme viṣam iva, tat sukhaṁ rājasaṁ smṛtam ||
39 yad agre cānubandhe ca, sukhaṁ mohanam ātmanaḥ |
nidrālasya-pramādotthaṁ, tat tāmasam udāhṛtam ||
40 na tad asti pṛthivyāṁ vā, divi deveṣu vā punaḥ |
sattvaṁ prakṛti-jair muktaṁ, yad ebhiḥ syāt tribhir guṇaiḥ ||
41 brāhmaṇa-kṣtratriya-viśāṁ, śūdrāṇāṁ ca parantapa |
karmāṇi pravibhaktāni, svabhāva-prabhavair guṇaiḥ ||
42 śamo damas tapaḥ śaucaṁ, kṣāntir ārjavam eva ca |
jñānaṁ vijñānam āstikyaṁ, brahma-karma svabhāva-jam ||
43 śauryaṁ tejo dhṛtir dākṣyaṁ, yuddhe cāpy apalāyanam |
dānam īśvara-bhāvaś ca, kṣātra-karma svabhāva-jam ||

44 kṛṣi-go-rakṣya-vāṇijyaṁ, vaiśya-karma svabhāva-jam |
paricaryātmakaṁ karma, śūdrasyāpi svabhāva-jam ||
45 sve sve karmaṇy abhirataḥ, saṁsiddhiṁ labhate naraḥ |
sva-karma-nirataḥ siddhiṁ, yathā vindati tac chṛṇu ||
46 yataḥ pravṛttir bhūtānāṁ, yena sarvam idaṁ tatam |
sva-karmaṇā tam abhyarcya, siddhiṁ vindati mānavaḥ ||
47 śreyān sva-dharmo viguṇaḥ, para-dharmāt sv-anuṣṭhitāt |
svabhāva-niyataṁ karma, kurvan nāpnoti kilbiṣam ||
48 saha-jaṁ karma kaunteya, sa-doṣam api na tyajet |
sarvārambhā hi doṣeṇa, dhūmenāgnir ivāvṛtāḥ ||
49 asakta-buddhiḥ sarvatra, jitātmā vigata-spṛhaḥ |
naiṣkarmya-siddhiṁ paramāṁ, saṁnyāsenādhigacchati ||
50 siddhiṁ prāpto yathā brahma, tathāpnoti nibodha me |
samāsenaiva kaunteya, niṣṭhā jñānasya yā parā ||
51 buddhyā viśuddhayā yukto, dhṛtyātmānaṁ niyamya ca |
śabdādīn viṣayāṁs tyaktvā, rāga-dveṣau vyudasya ca ||
52 vivikta-sevī laghv-āśī, yata-vāk-kāya-mānasaḥ |
dhyāna-yoga-paro nityaṁ, vairāgyaṁ samupāśritaḥ ||
53 ahaṅkāraṁ balaṁ darpaṁ, kāmaṁ krodhaṁ parigraham |
vimucya nirmamaḥ śānto, brahma-bhūyāya kalpate ||
54 brahma-bhūtaḥ prasannātmā, na śocati na kāṅkṣati |
samaḥ sarveṣu bhūteṣu, mad-bhaktiṁ labhate parām ||
55 bhaktyā mām abhijānāti, yāvān yaś cāsmi tattvataḥ |
tato māṁ tattvato jñātvā, viśate tad-anantaram ||
56 sarva-karmāṇy api sadā, kurvāṇo mad-vyapāśrayaḥ |
mat-prasādād avāpnoti, śāśvataṁ padam avyayam ||
57 cetasā sarva-karmāṇi, mayi saṁnyasya mat-paraḥ |
buddhi-yogam upāśritya, mac-cittaḥ satataṁ bhava ||
58 mac-cittaḥ sarva-durgāṇi, mat-prasādāt tariṣyasi |
atha cet tvam ahaṅkārān, na śroṣyasi vinaṅkṣasi ||
59 yad ahaṅkāram āśritya, na yotsya iti manyase |
mithyaiṣa vyavasāyas te, prakṛtis tvāṁ niyokṣyati ||
60 svabhāva-jena kaunteya, nibaddhaḥ svena karmaṇā |
kartuṁ necchasi yan mohāt, kariṣyasy avaśo 'pi tat ||
61 īśvaraḥ sarva-bhūtānāṁ, hṛd-deśe 'rjuna tiṣṭhati |
bhrāmayan sarva-bhūtāni, yantrārūḍhāni māyayā ||
62 tam eva śaraṇaṁ gaccha, sarva-bhāvena bhārata |
tat-prasādāt parāṁ śāntiṁ, sthānaṁ prāpsyasi śāśvatam ||
63 iti te jñānam ākhyātaṁ, guhyād guhyataraṁ mayā |
vimṛśyaitad aśeṣeṇa, yathecchasi tathā kuru ||
64 sarva-guhyatamaṁ bhūyaḥ, śṛṇu me paramaṁ vacaḥ |
iṣṭo 'si me dṛḍham iti, tato vakṣyāmi te hitam ||

65 man-manā bhava mad-bhakto, mad-yājī māṁ namaskuru |
māṁ evaiṣyasi satyaṁ te, pratijāne priyo 'si me ||
66 sarva-dharmān parityajya, mām ekaṁ śaraṇaṁ vraja |
ahaṁ tvā sarva-pāpebhyo, mokṣayiṣyāmi mā śucaḥ ||
67 idaṁ te nātapaskāya, nābhaktāya kadācana |
na cāśuśrūṣave vācyaṁ, na ca māṁ yo 'bhyasūyati ||
68 ya idaṁ paramaṁ guhyaṁ, mad-bhakteṣv abhidhāsyati |
bhaktiṁ mayi parāṁ kṛtvā, mām evaiṣyaty asaṁśayaḥ ||
69 na ca tasmān manuṣyeṣu, kaścin me priya-kṛttamaḥ |
bhavitā na ca me tasmād, anyaḥ priyataro bhuvi ||
70 adhyeṣyate ca ya imaṁ, dharmyaṁ saṁvādam āvayoḥ |
jñāna-yajñena tenāham, iṣṭaḥ syām iti me matiḥ ||
71 śraddhāvān anasūyaś ca, śṛṇuyād api yo naraḥ |
so 'pi muktaḥ śubhāṅl lokān, prāpnuyāt puṇya-karmaṇām ||
72 kaccid etac chrutaṁ pārtha, tvayaikāgreṇa cetasā |
kaccid ajñāna-sammohaḥ, praṇaṣṭas te dhanañjaya ||

Arjuna uvāca

73 naṣṭo mohaḥ smṛtir labdhā, tvat-prasādān mayācyuta |
sthito 'smi gata-sandehaḥ, kariṣye vacanaṁ tava ||

Sañjaya uvāca

74 ity ahaṁ vāsudevasya, pārthasya ca mahātmanaḥ |
saṁvādam imam aśrauṣam, adbhutaṁ roma-harṣaṇam ||
75 vyāsa-prasādāc chrutavān, etad guhyam ahaṁ param |
yogaṁ yogeśvarāt kṛṣṇāt, sākṣāt kathayataḥ svayam ||
76 rājan saṁsmṛtya saṁsmṛtya, saṁvādam imam adbhutam |
keśavārjunayoḥ puṇyaṁ, hṛṣyāmi ca muhur muhuḥ ||
77 tac ca saṁsmṛtya saṁsmṛtya, rūpam aty-adbhutaṁ hareḥ |
vismayo me mahān rājan, hṛṣyāmi ca punaḥ punaḥ ||
78 yatra yogeśvaraḥ kṛṣṇo, yatra pārtho dhanur-dharaḥ |
tatra śrīr vijayo bhūtir, dhruvā nītir matir mama ||

Appendices

Pronunciation of Sanskrit

Sanskrit words and names in the translated verses are given in a phonetic spelling utilizing a macron for alternate pronunciations of the vowels *a, i,* and *u* (see the pronunciation table below for the distinct sounds these six vowels make). The standardized full transliteration system for the Sanskrit alphabet is utilized for Sanskrit words in the notes and other parts of this book. Below are the vowels and consonants that require clarification. Transliterated consonants not listed below are pronounced as in English.

Vowels

a — like *a* in *about*

ā — like *a* in *yacht*

ai — like *ai* in *aisle* (*ai* represents a single transliterated vowel)

au — like *ow* in *cow* (*au* represents a single transliterated vowel)

e — like *e* in *prey*

i — like *i* in *bit*

ī — like *i* in *magazine*

ḷ — like *lree* (this vowel is rarely found; it is pronounced by combining the English *l* and *r* with an *ee* sound following)

o — like *o* in *home*

ṛ — like *ri* in *rich*

ṝ — like *rea* in *reach* (this vowel is rarely found)

u — like *u* in *put*

ū — like *u* in *rude*

Consonants

c — like *ch* in *chart* (never pronounced like the English *k* or *s*)

d — like *d* in *lude*

ḍ — like *d* in *red*

- g like *g* in *gate* (the soft *g* as pronounced in the word *germane* is found only in the Sanskrit letter *j*)
- h like *h* in *hot* (standing alone or followed by a vowel, without following a consonant)
- _+h any consonant followed by *h* is merely aspirated, like the subtle aspirated breath sound naturally occurring in the word *pot* (whereas aspiration is naturally absent from *dot*); thus *ph* sounds like the letter in the word *loophole* (never an *f* sound as in *pharmacy*); and *th* sounds like the *t* in the word *torn* (never the *th* sound as in *thorn*)
- ḥ is the silent consonant often found at the end of words; when the word is at the end of a sentence, the short form of the vowel of the last syllable is duplicated: for example, *rāmaḥ* sounds like *rāmaha,* and *śaktiḥ* sounds like *śaktihee* (underscored letters indicate duplicated syllable)
- j like *j* in *joy*
- ṁ like *n* in the French word *bon*
- n like *n* in *soon*
- ṅ like *n* in *song*
- ñ like *n* in *staunch*
- ṇ like *n* in *sand*
- ph like *p* in *pan* (with aspirated breath; it never makes the sound of *f* as in English, for example, the *ph* in the word *phase*)
- ṛ (is a vowel; see *ṛ* in the section above entitled "Vowels")
- s like *s* in *suit*
- ś like *sh* in *shoot* (this sibilant and the following are commonly pronounced by English speakers without any discernable distinction)
- ṣ like *sh* in *shout*
- t like *t* in *tool* (with tip of tongue near the place where the teeth meet the roof of the mouth)
- ṭ like *t* in *lute* (with tip of tongue toward the middle of the roof of the mouth)

In most compound consonants, each consonant retains its original sound in combination with the others. However, the combination *jñ* as found in the word *jñāna* is often pronounced like the *gy* in the English compound *dog-yard.*

On This Translation

Every verse of the Bhagavad Gītā is a meditation. Each verse is translated so as to bring out its meditative richness, as well as its place within the continuum of verses. I have attempted to make this English translation a "reincarnation" of the mood and feeling of the original Sanskrit verse. My goal is for the reader to receive a powerful experience of the original, to be able to hear something of the poetic form and qualities of the Sanskrit verse in the English rendering.

My approach to translation, aided by the inclusion of supplementary notes, is meant to give the reader an immediate grasp of the ideas of the Gītā. In the notes, readers will find the meanings of untranslated Sanskrit words retained in the translation and further explanation of names and ideas found in the verses. The reader will seldom need to leave the page to consult any other part of the book for better understanding, even during a first reading of the translation, although a comprehensive index has been provided. With the new reader of the text in mind, as well as spiritual aspirants and students or scholars of religion, I have presented the Bhagavad Gītā in a translation that is very faithful to the original text and reflects some of the literary qualities of the original, yet which can be easily read and grasped.

My approach to translating this famous work can be explained in contrast with the two other most common approaches. Other translations often either *free* the original text, in what I call "free prose" style, or *constrict* the original Sanskrit verse, in what I call "constricted quatrain" verse. The result is too often a translation that either ignores the poetic qualities of the original by treating verses as if they were loosely assembled ideas, or one that loses important senses of the original in fitting the translation into a verse form that is necessarily constricting. The free prose approach loosely embodies, at best, only a small sense of the rhythms and ordering of meanings and ideas as they present themselves, giving the text a loose and random form very different from that of the original. On the other hand, the quatrain verse approach attempts to force the English translation to be as concise as the original inflected words of the Sanskrit. This approach proves ineffective precisely because Sanskrit is a highly inflected language that requires more breathing room when reincarnated in English.

The poetics and ideas of each verse demand a unique treatment when translated into English—a very specific type of lineation that is sensitive to the subtleties of phrasing and cadence in the original Sanskrit verse. My approach could be described as "dedicated free verse translation," which preserves as much of the poetic sense as possible, while incorporating the full meaning of the original. This approach seeks to reap the advantages of the other two approaches yet avoid their shortcomings, thus attempting to reincarnate something of the power and spirit of the original verse. Here, "free verse" is not as "free" as we might indicate in the Western poetic sense of the term. Rather, verse lines in the English are strictly and carefully "dedicated," or tied to the verse's original rhythms of meaning and epiphanic qualities. The ordering of ideas and words in the original is retained as much as is possible without sacrificing their meaning in English. This approach gives the English reader a much fuller sense of the actual meaning of the verse. For example, the original Sanskrit in the English transliteration of the first verse of the text appears in the following form:

dhṛtarāṣṭra uvāca
dharma-kṣetre kuru-kṣetre, samavetā yuyutsavaḥ |
māmakāḥ pāṇḍavāś caiva, kim akurvata sañjaya ||

This verse in dedicated free verse translation is presented below, juxtaposed to the corresponding transliterated words of the verse:

Dhritarāshtra said:	*dhṛtarāṣṭra uvāca*
On the field of dharma,	*dharma-kṣetre*
on the field of Kuru,	*kuru-kṣetre*
assembled together	*samavetā*
desiring to fight,	*yuyutsavaḥ*
Were my armies	*māmakāḥ*
and indeed those	*pāṇḍavāś*
of the sons of Pāndu—	*caiva*
how did they act, O Sanjaya?	*kim akurvata sañjaya*

Note that the translation is dedicated to the original ordering of the words in the transliteration. One can also observe that it takes more English words to translate the Sanskrit words. This first verse of the Gītā is the most common verse form found in the work, known as *anuṣṭubh,* with eight syllables per quarter line. The two leading lines mirror the structure of the original. Under the leading lines, indented lines generally present the meanings that appear in the first and second halves of the verses, whenever possible, in the same order in which they appear in the original. The leading lines and respective indented lines are carefully crafted to capture the feeling and phrasing of the Sanskrit verse and to "trans-create" an overall sense of the original poetic form.

Additionally, I have retained a few key Sanskrit words, some of which have made their way into the English lexicon (e.g., *yoga, dharma*), in what is meant to be a literal but poetically sensitive English translation, as these untranslated words carry a certain lexical power and richness all their own that is too difficult to convey in English. Their usage allows me to avoid either protracted or reductive glosses of such significant words within the verses themselves. Note that the word *yoga* is retained in the translation of the word's past participle form of *yukta,* which derives from the verbal root *yuj,* consistently translated as "absorbed in yoga." The word *yoga* is often translated as "discipline" and the verbal form as "disciplined" or "engaged," which loses the sense that yoga is actively experienced. I engage the word *absorbed* to intimate the ultimate act in yoga, which is *samādhi,* a state of total *absorption* in the object of meditation.

In this translation, personal names are either given in the original Sanskrit, with the meaning provided in a note, or are translated within the verse. The various names for Arjuna and Krishna reveal intriguing aspects of their identities, as well as contributing added meaning or even irony to the verses. For example, Arjuna addresses Krishna as Madhusūdana, "slayer of the Madhu demon," when expressing his dismay over the prospect of slaying others: "I do not wish to slay them—even those who are about to slay, O Madhusūdana" (BG I.35). To illuminate the fullness of the original, these special names are not simply replaced with antecedent primary names, as is often done; instead they are preserved.

Pronouns are not replaced by personal names as is often done. I believe the Gītā's poetry and expression are very deliberate, conscious, and erudite, and the ordering and presentation of the original words must be respected and preserved as much as possible. For easier reading, the Sanskrit names as well as all Sanskrit words are spelled phonetically, and only a few diacritics are utilized (see "Pronunciation of Sanskrit"). Furthermore, most of the pronouns in the text, though technically masculine in the original (or, in some verses, unspecified but implied third-person masculine), have been changed to gender-free language. The following verse demonstrates this:

> One who sees me everywhere
>   and sees all things in me,
> To such a person I am never lost
>   nor is such a person ever lost to me.
> (BG 6.30)

Note how I have avoided the gender specificity of *he* by replacing it with words such as *one* and *such a person*. I translate verses in this gender-neutral way in order to preserve the universality that is subtly present in the masculine pronouns of the Sanskrit but lacking in the English.

As a translator, I have not hesitated to repeat words or meanings that are repeated in the original verse. In Sanskrit, repetition is a powerful means of inducing a meditative-like state in the reader. Repetition conveys the depth and pursuit of a vision, but most translations simply avoid this repetitive element. In this translation synonyms are not sought for words that are repeated in the Sanskrit, or even for words that are repeated by virtue of being derivative forms, either from a common verbal root or a noun stem. Instead, I use the same or a similar English word to render the Sanskrit word or its derivative that is repeated in the original:

> One should raise
>   the self by the self;
>   one should not
>   degrade the self.

Indeed, the self alone
is the self's friend;
the self alone
is the self's enemy.

(BG 6.5)

In this verse, the word *self* is used to translate the important Sanskrit word *ātman,* which appears in this verse seven times, more than any other word in any verse. This word is translated throughout as "self." Because in Sanskrit the term can mean "soul," "body," "mind," or "heart," I have selected a word that embraces all these meanings. It has been the tendency of translators to abandon these repetitions so as to reflect specific shades of meaning, make philosophical sense, or avoid repetition. However, one hears and feels the power of the repetition of such a monumental word in the original language. I believe my choice of translation both satisfies the requirements of meaning and retains the power of repetition.

Even in instances in which there is great temptation to translate differently two words with the same noun stem or words related to the same verbal root, Krishna's play on words would be lost if I chose to ignore their close relationship. In the verse quoted above, BG 6.6, the word *shatru,* "enemy," occurs twice. First the abstract form of *shatru-tva* is found, translated in the verse as "enmity," and then the adverbial comparative form of *shatru-vat,* translated as "like an enemy." Again, in BG 4.42, Krishna tells Arjuna to "ascend to yoga," using the verb *ātiṣṭha,* and then immediately tells him to "stand up," using the same verb but with a different prefix, *uttiṣṭha.* Therefore my translation is: "rise in yoga!/Rise up, O Bhārata!" By retaining the word *rise* in both imperative statements, while providing different prepositions to express the force of the different prefixes, we can respect the original effect of the repetition.

Words with a negative prefix in the Sanskrit are not translated into English as if they were a positive form; rather, such words reflect the absence of the word's positive noun stem. For example, the word *sukha* is "happiness," and its negative *a-sukha* is "unhappiness" or "without happiness." This negative form of the word is often translated, however, as "misery" or "suffering," meanings more suitable for the positive word *duḥkha.* Another example would be *a-siddha,* the negation of *siddha,* "success." I translate *asiddha* as "without success," rather than the often used translation of "failure." Again, when a reader hears the word *a-jñāna,* he or she does not hear "ignorance," as it is often translated, but rather "without knowledge." When translators employ antonyms to translate negatives, a very different sense is conveyed.

Wherever possible I have used English cognates for Sanskrit words. Thus the word *sama,* often translated as "equal" or "impartial," I translate as "same." The word's abstract forms, *samatva* and *samatā,* retain the cognate sense of *sama* in the translation of "sameness" rather than the more removed senses of "equanimity" or "equality" so often used.

Because some Sanskrit words are laden with meaning, it often takes several English words to convey their sense. Frequently translators provide a simple translation for such words, which reduces the power of the word's presence or presents a meaning that does not reflect the word's complete sense. For example, the two cosmological words *prabhava* and *pralaya,* antonyms referring to the manifesting and unmanifesting of the universe, are typically translated simply as "origin" and "dissolution," respectively. To convey the richness of the language in the original, and characterize cosmologically the referents for these words, I have translated *prabhava* as "the coming forth into being" and *pralaya* as "the going forth into cosmic absorption," accurately reflecting the purānic cosmology.[1]

With the English word *love,* one finds the opposite challenge. The word *love* incorporates all varieties and intensities of affection, tenderness, endearment, passion, and compassion, and only its context indicates the specific nuance of love, whereas in Sanskrit a great array of words and phrases are used to convey the many nuances of love. Therefore any attempt to translate such words and phrases into English is problematic, since there are no comparable English words that relate the specific experience of love described by such Sanskrit terms. In English, we use the word *love* constantly as the ultimate way to express our hearts, and there is no other word that can be substituted for it; therefore its usage is indispensible in the expression of the human heart.

---

1 See BG 7.6 and 9.18; in BG 10.8, the word *prabhava* is presented without *pralaya,* but is juxtaposed in the next line with the verb *pravartate,* meaning "is set forth into motion," further continuing the cosmological idea of *prabhava*.

This translation resorts to the ultimate English word *love* when translating any of the numerous Sanskrit words that express particular dimensions of love, so that the English translation is not deprived of the absolute sense intended by the more specific Sanskrit words. Therefore, the word *bhakta,* often translated as "devotee" or "the devoted one," is translated here as "one who has offered love" (see the first instance of this word in BG 4.3), utilizing *offered* along with *love.* The word's related verbal form *bhajāmi,* typically translated as "I worship" or "I honor," is translated as "I offer my love" (BG 4.11). The word *priya,* usually translated as "dear," is translated as "dearly loved," and in the Sanskrit carries a sense of the purity of love (BG 7.17). And the word *bhāva,* literally "feeling," is translated as "feelings of love" (BG 10.8). The word *iṣṭa,* often translated as "desired," here appears as "loved" (BG 18.64). The result of this approach is that one discovers that the Bhagavad Gītā says much more about love than what we perhaps have appreciated up until now.

Finally, particle words such as *and, even,* and *but* are never ignored, passed off as mere verse fillers or convenient words to complete the verse rhythm or meter. The assumption here is that each of these verses is a jewel that does not need to be altered in any way; rather, each jewel needs only to be polished until its natural glow is revealed.

Select Bibliography

Source for the Sanskrit Text

The Bhagavadgītā, critically edited by Shripad Krishna Belvalkar et al. Poona: Bhandarkar Oriental Research Institute, 1968.

Works on or Related to the Bhagavad Gītā

Minor, Robert N. *Bhagavad-Gītā: An Exegetical Commentary.* New Delhi: Heritage Publishers, 1991.

_________, ed. *Modern Indian Interpreters of the Bhagavadgita.* Albany: State University of New York, 1986.

Rosen, Steven J., ed. *Holy War: Violence and the Bhagavad Gita.* Hampton, VA: Deepak Heritage Books, 2002.

Schweig, Graham M. *Dance of Divine Love: India's Classic Sacred Love Story: The Rāsa Līlā of Krishna from the Bhāgavata Purāṇa.* Princeton, NJ: Princeton University Press, 2005.

_________. "The Essential Meaning of the Bhagavad-gītā According to Caitanyite Vaishnavism." *Journal of Vaishnava Studies* 9, no. 2 (Spring 2001): 227–39.

Sharma, Arvind. *The Hindu Gita: Ancient and Classical Interpretations of the 'Bhagavadgita.'* La Salle, IL: Open Court Publishing, 1986.

Sharpe, Eric J. *The Universal Gītā: Western Images of the Bhagavad Gītā.* La Salle, IL: Open Court Publishing, 1985.

Translations of the Bhagavad Gītā

Bhaktivedanta Swami Prabhupāda, A. C., trans. and comm. *Bhagavad-gītā As It Is.* 2nd ed. Los Angeles: Bhaktivedanta Book Trust, 1989.

Edgerton, Franklin, trans. *The Bhagavad Gītā.* Cambridge, MA: Harvard University Press, 1944.

Patton, Laurie, trans. *The Bhagavad Gītā.* Harmondsworth, UK: Penguin Press, 2007.

Van Buitenen, J. A. B., trans. and ed. *The Bhagavadgītā in the Mahābhārata, A Bilingual Edition.* Chicago: University of Chicago Press, 1981.

Zaehner, R. C., ed. *The Bhagavad-Gītā.* Oxford: Oxford University Press, 1969.

Word References for the Bhagavad Gītā

Apte, Vaman Shivaram. *The Practical Sanskrit-English Dictionary* (Revised and Enlarged Reprint Edition). Kyoto: Rinsen Book Company, [1957] 1978.

Macdonell, Arthur Anthony. *A Practical Sanskrit Dictionary* (with transliteration, accentuation, and etymological analysis). New Delhi: Munshiram Manoharlal Publishers Pvt. Ltd., 1996.

Monier-Williams, Monier. *A Sanskrit-English Dictionary.* Oxford: Clarendon Press, [1899] 1974.

Schweig, Graham M. *Bhagavad Gītā Concordance: Comprehensive Word Reference with Sanskrit and English Indexes.* New York: Columbia University Press, forthcoming.

Index to Verses and Text

Note: Index items are listed by page (e.g., 4 and 4n) and by chapter and verse numbers (e.g., 18.14). For a comprehensive Sanskrit word reference and English index to this text, readers are invited to consult *Bhagavad Gītā Concordance*, also produced by the author.

Acknowledgments

Teachers, colleagues, students, and friends have significantly contributed to my work. With Daniel H. H. Ingalls, my Sanskrit teacher at Harvard, I studied the Sanskrit text of the Bhagavad Gītā. Under J. A. B. van Buitenen at the University of Chicago, I studied Vedānta philosophy and the Mahābhārata. And it was Bhaktivedanta Swami Prabhupāda, who lived the life of the Bhagavad Gītā, from whom I received the tradition's vision of the text through his own monumental work.

Catherine Ghosh offered profound understandings for the depth interpretation of the text and provided poetic and philosophical suggestions for verses. Hridayananda Das Goswami worked with me on evolving the translation approach and carefully reviewed the translation for accuracy. Phillip Murphy pondered and critiqued the verses, engaging invaluable insights from the Hindu philosophical background. Wilhelm Vandenberg and Gerald Surya offered important critiques and recommendations for the verses in their final stages, while Ken Solomon worked meticulously on the proofreading and refinement of the English transliteration of the Sanskrit text from the critical edition. My heartfelt gratitude goes to my wife, Susan Schweig, for her tireless hours spent editing prose and verses in their various stages of development, and for contributing her poetic sensibilities, sensitivity to language, and organizational skills to the project.

I wish to thank all of my university students, as well as those in various seminars and workshops at yoga centers and traditional Vaishnava Hindu temples, with whom I shared the rich teachings of this text. Also, Provost Richard Summerville, Dean Douglas Gordon, Deborah Campbell, the Department Chair, Kenneth Rose, Director of Religious Studies, and secretary Princess Nilen, all at Christopher Newport University, were very supportive of this work. Many thanks go to the staff at Harper San Francisco, especially Eric Brandt, Senior Editor, who believed in this project from the beginning. His constant support, patience, and vision energized the project at every stage.

About the Author

Graham Schweig received his doctorate in Comparative Religion from Harvard University, and is a specialist in the philosophy and history of yoga, bhakti devotional traditions of India, and love mysticism in world religions. He is currently Associate Professor of Religious Studies and Director of the Indic Studies Program at Christopher Newport University on the Virginia peninsula, and also Visiting Associate Professor of Sanskrit at the University of Virginia. He has taught at Duke University and the University of North Carolina. Schweig recently was a Visiting Fellow at the Oxford Centre of Hindu Studies of Oxford University and has been accepted as a Visiting Fellow at Clare Hall of Cambridge University.

Schweig regularly offers yoga workshops and seminars, and he is a longtime practitioner of various forms of meditational and devotional yoga under the guidance of traditional teachers. He has traveled to India seven times, once residing in India for a year, directing a Smithsonian Institution funded research grant for preserving ancient palm-leaf manuscripts.

Schweig has published numerous articles for professional journals and encyclopedias, and chapters for books in his field, and is Senior Editor of the international periodical *Journal of Vaishnava Studies.* Recently, Princeton University Press published his book *Dance of Divine Love: India's Classic Sacred Love Story: The Rāsa Līlā of Krishna from the Bhāgavata Purāṇa.* He is presently working on other book projects, including *Bhagavad Gītā Concordance: A Comprehensive Word Reference with Sanskrit and English Indexes,* and *The Bhakti Sūtra: Concise Teachings of Nārada on Divine Love,* both to be published by Columbia University Press.